2012

Journeys: An Anthology of Adult Student Writing

Keith Rossberg, Annandale

Mission

The mission of the Minnesota Literacy Council is to share the power of learning through education, community building, and advocacy. Through this mission, the literacy council:

- Helps adults become self-sufficient citizens through improved literacy.
- Helps at-risk children and families gain literacy skills to increase school success.
- Strengthens communities by raising literacy levels and encouraging volunteerism.
- Raises awareness of literacy needs and services throughout the state.

Acknowledgements

The Minnesota Literacy Council extends our heartfelt thanks to Stephen Burgdorf, Joe Conry, Sara Pitcher and Natalie Sosnay who have donated their time and talent to the planning, design, editing, and production of this book. Special thanks also to staff Guy Haglund, Allison Runchey, Tricia Brooks, Melissa Martinson and Cathy Grady for helping make *Journeys* a success. Finally, we are deeply grateful for two very generous donations that have helped to make *Journeys* possible this year:

- $3500 from LeAnn and Bill Linder-Scholer; and
- $500 from Mimi and Todd Burke through the Burke Family Fund in memory of Todd's late mother.

Minnesota Literacy Council
mnliteracy.org
651-645-2277
Hotline: 800-222-1990
700 Raymond Avenue, Suite 180
Saint Paul, Minnesota 55114-1404

Go to mnliteracy.org for Journeys Teaching & Learning Guide.

Table of Contents

Front Cover Art
Tuong Pham, Brooklyn Park

Inside Cover Art
Keith Rossberg, Annandale

Back Cover
Torrie Bulson-Bratton, Bayport

Introduction

Dear Reader,

This fall, the Minnesota Literacy Council will be celebrating its 40th anniversary, and I am truly pleased that *Journeys*—now in its 23rd year—has been part of our work for so much of that time. This book helps us fulfill our mission of sharing the power of learning, and it's dear to our hearts as well. Year after year, these stories never fail to move us.

This book contains original writing and artwork by Minnesota adult literacy students enrolled in reading, English as a Second Language, GED and basic skills classes across the state. With the help of their teachers and volunteer tutors, these students have worked hard to be able to share their experiences with you in English poetry and prose.

Some of these writers are immigrants or refugees writing in their second or third language. Others are sharing their writing for the first time after years of frustration and anxiety due to their low literacy skills. All of them are improving their lives through education, often along with huge work and family responsibilities, and we are grateful that they have taken the time to share their thoughts and experiences with us.

Journeys provides a forum for the creative expression of Minnesota adult learners, a text of authentic learner stories for teachers to use in the classroom and an acknowledgement of the tangible value and contributions of adult education to the larger Minnesota community.

During the past two decades, *Journeys* has grown from a thin stack of pages to a full-blown literary journal with nearly 600 writing and drawing submissions. This couldn't happen without the hard work of our four interns, the generous support of our individual donors, and readers like you who purchase the book.

Thank you for your interest in *Journeys* and happy reading!

Sincerely,

Eric Nesheim
Executive Director

I am

Changes
Lucy Brown, Hugo

The person I am now is so different from the person I was ten years ago. I can tell now that I have changed so much in the last ten years. These are some of the differences between then and now: my appearance, my shyness, and my outlook on life.

The first difference I want to talk about is appearance. When I was eleven years old all I wanted to do was hide. To do that, I would dress in dark colors to blend in. I also would wear black lipstick, nail polish, and eyeliner. My shoes were black biker boots or black sneakers with weird shoelaces. This was the 'Goth stage' of my life. I needed it. Now I dress in bright colors and wear clothes that fit me. My shoes look like normal shoes. I also don't wear make-up. Goth is a part of my past. A part I no longer need.

The second thing I want to talk about is my shyness. When I was younger, I was getting yelled at or around people yelling at each other. I just didn't know how to act around people or communicate. Dad would be at work and Mom would be at home ignoring me or grounding me. My mother didn't try to give me the tools I needed for good communication. I felt alone. Now I'm happy and know that my family is there for me.

The third thing is my outlook. In the past, I felt so defeated with no hope. While others moved on, I just stayed in the same place. When I tried to find help, the people I tried to get help from would treat me like I was stupid. They would tell me, "You should know this." How could I know if no one took the time needed to teach me? I felt that I had no self-worth. Now I'm more outgoing. Where I was shy, I am now comfortable talking with people of all ages. My future looks so bright. I have finally gotten the help I so badly needed. I don't have to hide anymore; I feel that I have worth.

This is how I have changed in the last ten years. Those years were tough, but I know now that my future looks bright because I know I'm not alone anymore.

Lucy Brown moved to Minnesota from her native Texas so that she could live with her grandmother for a while. She had had a difficult childhood and hard times in school. Soon after she arrived, she told her grandmother she wished she could get her GED. That was the beginning of Lucy's transformation, and within a year, she achieved that goal. Now back in Texas, Lucy hopes to go on to school in order to develop her artistic talent and great imagination. With newly found confidence in her abilities, success is within reach.

How Can I Change the World?
Gloria Herrera, Saint Louis Park

I am Mexican, and too many times I have asked myself, how can I change the world? Something inside me tells me that you cannot change the world. But you can change people's life who are near you like sharing a smile and help them when it is chances to you, without expecting anything in return. Nobody is so poor than they cannot give a smile. You also have the option of being indifferent to everything, simple that. A smile is contagious and can be the change that many hope for.

We are destined to live in nature and that means we need each other, so that you can learn to live in the midst of misery or trying to change the world. To me the world is the most valuable thing we have and my thinking tells me that with love, patience, dedication and most important to be close to God. And together can change the world.

Ellen Johnson Sirleaf Government
Anonymous, Crystal

I feel very bad about my home-country every day. The President, Ellen Sirleaf, did not do anything for our country. Liberians made a big mistake in electing her president. She is not helpful to our country. She says smart things but does nothing for the people in our country. Their parents did not provide any good ideas for our country but used the Liberian people's money to spend in America. Liberians do not have safe drinking water and have no lights. She did not know how to be president for our country. She went to school in America. She can do anything better for her own country. There are no companies or businesses in Liberia for people to work. They have no skills and no schools for children to attend. She has not built up the people there is no life for them. But Americans look at her to be a good president. The middle-class Liberians are the people who are always at war with her. Ellen has no connection in the world as president because she is missing ideas. We have many good people who went to school in America there. Ellen does not like to work with them. She did this with the past Doe Government. She is taking everything for herself: gold, cars and money. Everything that my father, mother and sister ever looked for in their lives, she and her family enjoy today.

The Real Me
Erik Lundeen, Saint Michael

I am content with where I am,
Although it is not where I would like to be.
I will sit and forecast the forecast,
And hopefully perpetuated Thee.

I constantly strive for perfection,
And hopefully the Judge will see,
That I am better than what I have been doing
And that this is the real me.

I was sober for four years,
Except for smoking trees,
But that is what got me into this mess,
Meth and alcohol brought me to my knees.

Forgiveness is forgiven,
And soon the world will see:
This time the lock will unlock,
Because I have the proper key.

Different Faces
Michael L. Hult Jr., Elk River

As the steam rises, I see it.
But who are you?
I hear lies spew out of your mouth,
But why?
You're not a liar.

As the steam rises, I see it.
But who are you?
I see things broken and destroyed in your life,

But why?
You're not destructive.

As the steam rises, I see it.
But who are you?
I see the dumb choices you have made in your life.
But why?
You're not an idiot.

As the steam rises, I see it.
But who are you?
I see people hurt all around you.
But why?
You're not angry or mean.

As the steam rises, I see it.
But who are you?
I don't like what I see.
How can I change the mirror
When what I am looking at is me?

As I Am
Desmond Tirrell, Alexandria

As I am by myself, I would say I am weak
Born into a world that is tragically bleak
As the tears of my people wash blood from the streets.
As I am by myself I would say I'm afraid
Our blocks looking like they were hit by grenades
And our kids getting stomped by police during raids
As I am by myself I would say I'm a slave
Chained by oppression and trapped in my rage
As I am by myself I would say I'm alone
Oceans away from our Fathers true home
As I am with Him I would say that I'm strong
He gives me strength to carry along
As I am with Him I would never be scared
He fills me with courage and keeps me prepared
As I am with Him I would say I was free
He gave me salvation and took the chains off of me
As I am with Him I'll not be alone
Says my Lord and Father in heaven placed high on His throne.

My Life
Mee Vue Xiong, Minneapolis

My name is Mee Vue Xiong. I am from Laos. I came to the United States last year.

First time I saw many different things. The USA is broad and beautiful. People have good work. They have money to help themselves with no worries to eat and live. In my country people worry too much. People don't have work or money to help family or oneself. I worry about my family in my country. I love my mom and dad very much. I miss my brother and friends. I live in the north city of Minneapolis. I go to school every day. My school has many students. I like to study with my friends. I like everyone in my school. I have many teachers to help me learn. I am happy so much.

Mee Vue Xiong is originally from Laos.

Michelle
Anonymous, Owatonna

My name means a person who likes God.
In the world all the names mean something.
Care and think about your name.
Honor your name like an idol.
Educate everybody to know what their name means.
Look at your name, and you can know what it means.
Love your name like yourself.
Esteem—one's self-esteem is important. I am proud of my beautiful name.

Good Future
Liban Hussein, Minneapolis

My name is Liban Hussein and I am from Somalia. I left Somalia in 1990.

I lived in Nairobi, Kenya for 10 years. I came to the United States on May 15, 2004.

I like the weather in my country. I like U.S.A. because you help refugees. I like to study English. I like Minnesota.

Liban Hussein is originally from Somalia.

Mohamed
Mohamed Abdirahman, Minneapolis

Mohamed likes school
Others ask Mohamed for help
Happy
A man
My son is a student
Everyday I come to school
Drink coffee
Mohamed

Mohamed Abdirahman is originally from Somalia.

Getting Blamed for Something
William Andrew Spence, Blaine

When I was younger, my father accused me of scratching his records. He came up to my bedroom and dragged me downstairs by my ear. He took me over to the stereo and said, "Did you scratch my records?" I said, "No, I didn't." But he didn't believe me. He said, "Who did?" I said, "I don't know." Then he took one of the records and broke it over my head. My mom was sitting there and she said, "Bill, what are you doing?" My dad replied, "I don't care, he scratched my records." To this day, my father has never figured out who scratched his records, but it wasn't me.

My Life
Muhammed Sugaal, Saint Cloud

My name is Muhammed Sugaal. I want to share a little bit about my life. I was born in Somalia in the city of Mogadishu. In my whole life, I've worked with my family, especially my father and my mother. When I came to America everything was different — the weather, the housing, the people, the city and the streets. I worked for a Minnesota company for eight years. When I found this job I decided to move to Saint Cloud. The company's name is Electrolux. Some people have worked more than forty years at this company. This was the most difficult time in my life and I'm looking forward to my future.

First Time in America
Omar Mohamed, Saint Cloud

The first time I came to America my sister welcomed us in Washington D.C. My sister said, "This is my good place." My brother-in-law helped us out a lot of the time. I started school in Washington D. C. My favorite thing about America is education. My teacher said, "Welcome to America." I was very happy. After that I started work and school. My sister said, "I need you to work hard. I don't like you to be lazy. Omar, be a good man and be nice to everybody." I moved to Minnesota in the millennium because my friends moved to Minnesota. The most difficult thing in Minnesota is the weather. Thank you so much.

Accomplishment
Chong Leng Her, Saint Paul

My name is Chong Leng Her. I am from Laos. I live in America for six years. I accomplished to be a citizen. I learn English and have a house. I got my driver license and a car. I want to accomplish by learning more English, earn money, more freedom, and a small land for myself to farm.

Chong Leng Her is originally from Laos.

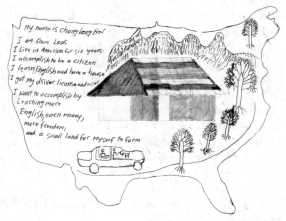

My name is chong Leng Her
I am from Laos
I Live in America for six years.
I accomplish to be a citizen
I learn English and have a house
I got my driver license and a car
I want to accomplish by
Learning more
English, earn money,
more freedom,
and a small land for myself to farm

Chong Leng Her, Saint Paul

My Life
Sagal Muhumed, Saint Cloud

I am from Ogaden (in SE Ethiopia). I have one sister and one brother. My sister and brother still live in Ogaden. I came to the United States in 2002 and I live in Saint Cloud, Minnesota. Now I have a job working in a factory. My favorite thing about the United States is working and helping my family back in my country. I help them by sending money to them. I miss my family, especially my mother and father. I talk to them two or three times a week. It is hard for me to be alone here, but I work and have friends. I hope to keep learning English.

Biak Lian, Saint Paul

Therapy for Me
Karan Frances, Minneapolis

Colored ink running across the pages. The pages soaking up my thoughts like a sponge. Never asking questions, only listening to my heart as it seeps out the tip of the pen. The pen. My pen. My best friend. Creating words that can't be said. In between the lines, who knew that's where my emotions could hide so well from prying eyes. Eyes, attached to faces with worried looks constantly asking me why. Why? I don't know why. Deeper and deeper I sink into the pages. The lines defining how I feel perfectly keeping my heart.

The Nicest Gift I Received
Yer Ha Vue, Coon Rapids

When I was born and until I was a teenager, I didn't receive any presents or gifts. My parents lived in a small village in Laos. They were poor. They didn't know about their children's birthdays or how to celebrate the birthdays. My birthday is in October.

The first year I came to America my husband gave me a present. The present was a little box, and he wrote a letter on the top of the box that said, "Happy Birthday." When I opened that box, the nicest necklace was in there. I was very happy, and I also cried because in my life I had never received a gift. I remember when I was a girl growing up that I had nobody that ever said happy birthday to me. This was the first time I received a gift from my husband, and it was the first time I was excited in my life.

I am thankful for my husband because he loves me, and he is a person who knows my birthday. My husband is the only person I love very much. I think I will be receiving presents or gifts from my husband in the future too.

Yer Ha Vue is originally from Laos

Myself
Amir Albanoun, Minneapolis

I moved from Iraq in 1991 because I had big problems with the government fighting and I didn't like guns. I left my country for Saudi Arabia. I lived in a refugee camp for almost 7 years. I got a big injury from the camp police in July 1993. It was a really bad day for me. I was unconscious for many hours and I don't remember anything, just my friends helping to take care of me. I moved from Saudi Arabia on March 11, 1997 to Fort Worth, Texas in the U.S.A.

Amir Albanoun is originally from Basra, Iraq.

Why I Like Minnesota
Brandon Williams, Minneapolis

I am from Kansas City, Missouri. I came to Minnesota in 1987. I have been back at home a few times. And it was OK, but I could not wait to get back to Minnesota. It's a different way of living in Kansas City compared to Minnesota. There is less crime, better transportation and better schools. So I am glad my parents came to Minnesota when they did so that I could have a better life. That's why I like Minnesota.

Daily Work at Job
Linh Main Hong Dinh, Bloomington

I'm a waitress for a Korean restaurant. Every day I work from 10:30 a.m. to 4:00 p.m. First, I must check every table and place the plates, bowls, spoons, forks and chopsticks. My coworker and I prepare the water, hot tea, coffee and kimchee for the buffet. We start service at 11:00 a.m. After the buffet ends at 2:00 p.m., we quickly clean and have lunch together.

Besides those things, I have other duties at the restaurant. Sometimes I water the trees and flowers inside the restaurant. If we get a special request for a party, such as birthday, we will decorate for that.

About Myself and my Country
Flor Ortiz, Austin

I was born in Cuernavaca, Morelos, Mexico. When I was a child I liked to run, play with my neighbors' kids and I loved to draw. I was good in school.

I came to the United States of America in 1998. We came to this country so that we could have a better life for my children.

I live in Austin, Minnesota. I like my place and my neighbors, because they are nice. Every day I go to school. I love to learn and I believe in education. I learn English because I want to improve my English skills. I have a good job so I can help my family.

My country is beautiful and is a neighbor of the United States. There are too many people. People in my country are friendly and hospitable. The opinion that tourists have of people in Mexico is good. When we have free time we like to know about other countries and having parties is common in my country. The weather in my country depends on the four seasons of the year. The best time to visit my country is summer. It is common for the family to get together. A typical food in my country is tacos. Mexican food is well known all over the world.

In my country it's difficult to find a job; many people in my country are not working. There is a lot of crime and violence. One thing that is better in the United States than in my country is lifestyle. It's possible to find a better job, a house, and a school for children.

What I miss most about my native country is my family, it is very important to me. One interesting thing about my native country is culture. My country has rich history and culture.

I love my country.

My Life in America
Anonymous, Minneapolis

Before 2005, I lived with my family in Somalia. I was also a student. Then, in April 2005, my parents and I went to Nairobi, Kenya. My older sister lived in the United States; she prepared for us to come live with her and she succeeded. In 2006, we arrived in the United States.

After two months, I found a part time job. It finished after two months. Then we moved to Wisconsin and I found a full time job. I started in 2007, and have worked there until 2010. When I had a baby in June, 2010, I quit the job to stay home with my son until he started school.

Life after Dark
Christopher Welch, Bayport

I would like to share exactly what it is that I have been searching for in life. I like to call it, "Life after Dark." To begin, my name is Christopher Kevin Welch. I am 18 years old and was born in the state of Minnesota on the south side of Minneapolis. I have four brothers and two sisters. I have always lived with my mother. My father was never around, so I kind of grew up quickly in a rough neighborhood. At this moment, I am incarcerated for the bad choices I have made in my life. After spending these dark and lonely nights behind these cold walls, a lot has changed about me, including what I would like to do with my future. Being in prison makes you think a lot. Being here has motivated me to get out and do what is best for my family and me. At this point, I am focused on getting my high school diploma before I get released back to the real world.

So, after the darkness has passed and I have received my diploma, I would like to go to college. I realize that I still have a lot to learn and to accomplish in order to get where I want to go in life. In the end, I will have to focus on my education and stay positive until the darkness has passed and my life can begin. That is my story.

My Life Is Ok
Zeinab Noor, Minneapolis

My name is Zeinab Noor. I am from Somalia. I came to America in 2005. I changed my life from Africa to America because my country is hard. America has different weather. It is not an easy life. Right now I work in home care. I am learning English. My life is okay. Thank you.

Zeinab Noor is originally from Somalia.

Rights for Women
Hijazi, Coon Rapids

I think the law before was unfair for women because they couldn't own property. I think the law now allows women and men to own property equally. Now women can vote for who becomes president or who works in the government. Women now can work, teach, run a business, and do other jobs outside of the home. Women now can own land, houses, money, and can open an account in a bank. Because I'm a woman, it's good for me that women can work, own property and be equal to men.

Hijazi is originally from Lebanon.

About Me
Agnele Wilson, Minneapolis

My name is Agnele Lucie and I am from Togo. I came to the U.S. in 2005. I live with my husband and we have two children; one boy and one girl. I have problems speaking in public, because I am afraid to speak English incorrectly. I hope my teacher will help me to do this. I enjoy living in the U.S., but I miss my country, too.

Agnele Wilson is originally from Togo.

My Dream
Aman Alemo, Minneapolis

My name is Aman Alemo and I am from Oromiya. I was born on November 15, 1986. I came to the U.S.A. on March 21, 2007. My dreams are very important for human beings. All people have equal rights to work, to shop, to drive, to vote in the election, for everything. Sometimes, though we are not right. For every right there is a responsibility and rules. My dreams are to help everybody to change their life and to work.

I think my dreams will change the Oromo people. For a long time they haven't had any freedom. Oromo is the biggest region in Ethiopia with more than 14 states. There are so many people there but there are no good opportunities. I have decided to fight for their freedom after my education, especially to fight for the human rights of the people. I would support my dreams for our opportunity to change so many things for every country.

Living in America
Genet Moges, Fridley

My name is Genet Moges. I am from Ethiopia and I was born in Nazareth City. I am married and I have two kids: a girl and a boy. My brother and sister live in Ethiopia.

I went to school in Nazareth. I came to United States of America by Diversity Visa Lottery ticket. When I came to America, everything was different. The winter was cold and the summer was hot. When I saw snow, I was surprised because I have never seen snow before. I like America. I have a job and go to English class in the morning. I have started a new life in America.

Genet Moges is originally from Ethiopia.

My Dream
Laetitia Malungu, Saint Louis Park

My name is Laeticia Malungu. I'm from Congo in the African Continent. I am twenty one years old, and I have lived in the United States for three months.

When I was young, my dream was to become a lawyer in my country to defend many kinds of people and banish injustice. Now, I don't live in my country. However, lawyers need a lot of schooling and need to be able to speak English fluently and correctly. Speaking English is my biggest problem because it is not my first language.

If it is not possible for me to become a lawyer, I want to become a nurse in the United States. First, I am going to learn English and go to training schools for mathematics and computers. Then I can go to college in order to become a nurse.

I want to be a respectable woman anywhere I shall be: in my country, in the United States, in Europe, anywhere!

Life in a New Country
Hasaballah Salman Saloumi, Minneapolis

I came to the U.S.A. on December 1, 2009. The weather was snowing and very cold. The land was white because of the snow. At the start, I was afraid because the change of country and the weather. Then I couldn't speak English and I didn't understand anything. The first weeks, until two months, were very hard for me. The weather was very cold, snowing, raining and storming. I stayed in. Next, I didn't get the license for driving. Finally, I didn't get a job up until two years ago and my family had it hard first, but now it is very good in the school.

Hasaballah is originally from Baghdad, Iraq.

Just a Thought
Camilo, Minneapolis

I went through all the pages of the last edition of this book. For some reason I was looking for someone from Chile. I don't know why exactly, maybe I was looking and thinking that I could find a story similar to mine.

It is hard to think about Chile and everything I left there. It is hard to think that I'm not going to see all those friends anymore, and that I'm not going to be able to spend the same time with my family. It becomes very hard to think about the blessed life that I had in Chile. Now I appreciate the good people there even more.

I regret many things. I would love to go back in time and be a better person with all the ones that I hurt in the past someday, somehow. I still have dreams of some of the people from my country, people that I really loved and wasn't able to see how much I loved them or to say how much I appreciate them. Finally, in my present I have found very nice people, and now my teacher says, "When you are not with the people you love, love the people you are with."

Best wishes!

Camilo is 27 years old and is originally from Chile.

Yes, That's Me
A.H.O., Minneapolis

Yes, that's me
Look and you'll see
My hair is black and long
My eyes are black
My arms are for carrying my kids
My hands are for making food
My heart is for giving love to my family
I have lived in Minneapolis for three years
I hope my kids are healthy
I dream about being in my country
It's all as clear as can be
That's positively, absolutely me

Who I Am
Pamela Marks, Fridley

My name is Pamela and I am a Native American Sioux. I grew up on a reservation in South Dakota. I can remember growing up and getting together with other Native kids every day during the summertime. We would go walking alongside the gravel road, and we would pick gooseberries, chokecherries and plums. This is what we would eat throughout the day. And when we would get thirsty, we would drink cold spring water coming from the ground.

We never understood the meaning of the reservation, why we were placed there, and the many questions behind it all. We just enjoyed having fun together. As an adult, you see things in a different perspective and the understanding behind it all. It had its good side and bad side, but all in all, I will always cherish the memories I have. I will always be proud of who I am, my heritage, and my culture.

A Story About My Life
Farhiyo, Minneapolis

My name is Farhiyo. I was born in Somalia in 1987. When I was three years old, my home country had a civil war. I don't remember it because during the civil war I was too young. I came to the United Sates in September 2005.

The first place I came was Minnesota. When I came to the United States, I couldn't understand English, how to read, write and speak. I couldn't drive a car, but my friends were helping me. After four months, I found a job. Two years later I left my work. When I came to the United States, I was single, but now I am married. I have two children. I have a successful family. Now I am learning English. I know it is very important.

Farhiyo is originally from Somalia.

About Beautiful Story
Asha Amir, Minneapolis

I am from Somalia. I moved to Kenya in 1992 with my family. I have a big family—14 people. I have six sisters and six brothers—all were born in Mogadishu, Somalia.

I was raised in Nairobi, Kenya. I have studied Somali and other languages in Kenya. I am proud of my country, Somalia, because it is my home, but I am sad because my memory is that of a child. My mother tells me always about Somalia. My family had a very good life. My mom in Somalia was a successful woman. She had her own business.

Accomplishment
Vang Lee, Saint Paul

My name is Vang Lee. I was born in Laos and came to America in 2005. I am now in Saint Paul. I had to learn English at Hmong Cultural Center. Back in my country, I never had much. I want a good life and to reach my accomplishments. Coming to America, I finally got what I want. Now, I know how to speak a little English. In America, you have everything, such as freedom and a lot of food to eat. I have clothes to wear, and I have a house to live. I think in America it is better for me. Thank you so much.

Vang Lee is originally from Laos.

Accomplishment
So Yang, Saint Paul

My name is So Yang. I am 21 years old. I live in Saint Paul, Minnesota. I am happy because I got my permit. I know English better now. When I lived in Laos, I wanted to come to America and to be in an airplane. I am happy. I got to be in an airplane. Later, I got married. My husband goes to work every day and my husband gives me money.

So Yang is 21 years old and is originally from Laos.

My Story
Lemane Gutema, Minneapolis

My name is Lemane Gutema and I am from Ethiopia. I like Ethiopia very much because the weather is very nice. In Ethiopia we enjoy winter because there is only rain—no snow, storms or tornados. In the winter season there are a lot of things to eat. The food I like most is corn and fruit. During the wintertime the school is closed and everybody comes home from different places to spend time together. When I was a kid we ran in the rain and we thought we grew up fast. In Ethiopia, children sing, "Please God raise me and put big clothes on me."

America is different from Ethiopia with a lot of things, especially the weather. It was the first thing for me. I came to America on September 14, 2007, when the weather was good, but in November it was a different story. It was the first time I saw this kind of weather in my life. I stayed home for six months. I did not go school or work because I got sick when I went outside. It was very difficult time for me. After eight months, I found a job and started school at Lehmann Center for a short time. Now I thank God everything is going good.

Finally, after working four years in this country, I decided to go college to get my degree because if I get more education I am very sure I can get more opportunities in my work place. So I am here to prepare myself for college.

My Story
Rabi Ibrahim, Brooklyn Park

My name is Rabi. I am from East Africa and I came to America in 1994. I came here with my family. I lived In San Jose, California for 3 months, and after that I moved to Minnesota. The only reason I came here was because my brother and sister and all my family lives here. I liked Minnesota when I came here. I went looking for a job and I got a job right away. After a while I started taking English classes and my English has become a lot better and I like to learn the English language. I hope one day my English becomes more improved and it's easier for people to understand when I talk.

My Self
Rimay Htoo, Saint Paul

My name is Rimay Htoo. My country is Burma. I am a Karen person. I have three brothers and one sister. I lived in the mountain village. My village name is Ye Mu Plaw. When I lived in Burma my parents were farmers. We had many animals; they were pigs, one cat, goats, dogs, ducks, chickens, and buffalo. But always we ran to the forest because of Burmese soldiers' oppression. I love my village, but because of the Burmese soldier's oppression I went to Thailand with my aunt's family. I am the only one who went with them.

I came to the U.S. on July 13, 2011. Now my family lives in America. We live in Saint Paul, Minnesota. I have two children. But now my parents live in my village in Burma with my brothers and sister. They ran to the forest often because of Burmese soldiers' oppression.

Thank you so much. May god bless you always. Bye.

Rimay Htoo is originally from Karen State, Burma.

My Story
Black Stone, Saint Paul

My name is Ler Thoo. I lived in Burma. My country is Burma and my state is Karen State. I was born on December 25, 1962. I have nine sisters and brothers; six sisters and three brothers. I'm the fourth oldest child in my family. I was a farmer in Burma.

I started school in 1972 when I was ten years old. When I was 16, I was a farmer. When I was 23, I started to work in my community. I moved to Thailand in 1991, 19 years ago. I lived in Mae La Camp and then Mae La Oo Camp. I trained to be a pastor there.

I am married. My wife's name is Mu Mu. We have 10 children; five daughters and five sons. My family came to the United States six months ago on July 5,

2011. We came to Saint Paul, Minnesota. Saint Paul is a very big and beautiful city. We live in a home. It is small, but it is OK for now.

Black Stone is 49 years old and is originally from Karen State and Papun State, Burma.

Minnesota
Rahel Adenew, Minneapolis

I like Minnesota because it is very nice and quiet. Many of my friends are from different countries. I study English as second language because I want a better job and go to a technical college to study something. I like it in Minnesota.

Accomplishment
Mao Xiong, Saint Paul

My name is Mao Xiong and I am from Laos. I live 6 years in America. What I like about America is freedom. I already got my permit and I want to get my license. I accomplish so far by getting my citizen, and I have a silver car. I know how to make pizza, bake cookies, and other stuff in America. Not only that but I also learn a little English.

My Thoughts
Ricardo Delgado, Zimmerman

Hello my name is Ricardo Delgado. I come from of El Salvador. I lived in the U.S. (Minnesota) for six months. I feel fortunate to live in a place where most people are very kind and friendly and helped me a lot. One of the reasons why I love living in the United States is that I feel safe and free. It is a country with a great history and a culture. Many of the things most important in world history have happened in this country.

I think the hardest part for me and every stranger is the language, but I hope with time to overcome. I would also like to thank my teachers for help in my English especially my grammar teacher and thanks for reading my letter.

Ricardo Delgado is 22 years old and is originally from El Salvador.

About My Self
Sumaya, Fridley

My name is Sumaya. I'm from Palestine, Jerusalem. I have been in the United States since 2000. I am a professional for haircuts and hairstyling. When I came to the United States, I thought I could have a business as my career, but it was a big surprise that I could not work with my certificate that I got overseas. So I have to study to get my GED, and after that, I have to go to college to study for my career.

I have three kids who are in school, and I have a big family in Minnesota. They help me when I need help. I love my own family and my big family, and I have a very nice relationship with some friends. Sometimes we visit each other and we share a lot of things about family, or schools, and how difficult it is to raise kids and at the same time go to school.

I enjoy going to school, and I try hard to finish my GED. It's not easy, but it is not impossible to do it. It has always been my dream to finish college. "A journey of a thousand miles starts with one step!" And my achievement is coming soon with some persistence.

I have a very nice husband. He is helping me a lot for so many things. If anything in the house is broken or the car needs fixing, he tries to fix it or calls somebody to do it. He helps my kids for doing their homework and doctor's appointments. I am very proud of him and don't know what I would do without him. May God bless him.

Sumaya is originally from Palestine-Jerusalem.

My Name
Phoy Kongkeo, Minneapolis

My name is Phoy
I have two sisters in Laos
I have two older sisters in Laos
I left from my country in 1975
In Thailand before I come to United States

Phoy Kongkeo is originally from Laos.

The Beautiful Seasons in the USA
Ana Oviedo, Hopkins

I came to the USA in 2002 full of dreams to learn English to show my friends when I returned to my own city. I was also planning to come back as a lawyer. Some of my ex-teachers of the University were waiting for me. My grammar was excellent so my Spanish was so beautiful, but I also wanted to know the language that everyone wants to talk: English. In that way, my future was promising.

My name is Ana, I'm 32 years old, I'm from Colombia, South America, and I didn't return. I think I went a different way. I forgot good Spanish because if I want to communicate with other Spanish speakers in the day to day, it requires using Spanish words not existing in the Royal Academy of Spanish, and English has been very hard for me.

I fell in love with this country, with the culture, with the weather…I have not finished yet learning everything about this country. When I think it's time to go back, something new comes that I want to know.

These people are so organized, the schools, the streets, etc., and most of them follow the rules. That's new for me. In my country, it's the opposite. The weather - oh! I love the weather. Four seasons, that's amazing. Summer is so hot and so humid. There are many activities outside, you can lose weight quickly, barbecues, families and friends meet. In the Fall, the colors of the landscape in this season are beautiful, yellow and red predominately, many leaves on the streets like the rivers. Winter looks like a movie, and the predominant color is white. The best description of this season is white, the color of peace. Spring is predominately light colors like pink and purple. We call cake colors (colores pastel).

This country is like traveling around the world. It is not necessary to spend much money really doing it because all cultures are living here together and the knowledge is rich. I learned some words in others languages and different religions. I never imagined how important this topic is for humans, we are so different, but so equal.

The only thing I know in this moment is I'm a better person now, and I am going to learn all I can.

Ana Oviedo is 32 years old and is originally from Cali, Colombia.

The Nicest Gift
Vesna Ellingson, Coon Rapids

My son made the decision to go into the U.S. Air Force. His choice was a shock for me because I didn't like for him to be in the military. Many times, I tried to talk with him to change his decision, but he didn't. I was sad and crying. My son came to me and told me how I have to be happy because he is smart and strong. He made me a promise. When he comes back, he would like to buy a boat and take me with him to travel on the ocean. I stopped crying and started laughing. I remember the time when my son was a child and he would cry for something. My son has grown up. I am happy for him. It is for me, the nicest gift in my life.

How I Was Born
Doaa, Coon Rapids

In 1992, my parents decided to have a baby. They wished to have a girl. Their wish came true, and they were so happy when they had me. But the day that I was born, my uncle, Hussein, died. My uncle was shot by his friend. They were joking around. My uncle's friend was holding the gun, and he shot him by accident. That day was really sad for everybody. They didn't have time to celebrate my birth because they had to plan a funeral.

By the time they had to pick a name for me, everybody was fighting. Each one of them wanted the name that they had chosen for me. My uncle, Hassan, came up with a name for me—Doaa. My parents liked this name. My name is a popular name in my country; my name means to "pray to God."

Doaa is 19 years old and is originally from Iraq.

I am Very Happy
Halima Farah, Waite Park

I come from Somalia. I lived in Mogadishu. I have a big family. They're still in Africa. I miss them, but

I can talk to them on the phone. Some of my children are still in Africa. I live in Saint Cloud, but my daughter lives in Virginia. I came to America to see my daughter. There was a job for me in Saint Cloud. I still work at the same job. I am very, very happy.

Family

Memories
Rosa Cipriano, Minneapolis

I have the fondest memories of my mother. She came from Guatemala by herself in her late twenties. She had to flee from people that wanted to hurt her and take her little girl away. Mother's in-laws hired these people. Margarita, my mother's friend and mentor, helped her get away from them. When Margarita had a chance to come to the United States on a diplomatic visa, she gave her place to mother instead. So, Mother came to work for a diplomat's family. This family promised to reunite her with her daughter after one year. Mother didn't know how to write or read. She had to trust that the family would file the needed papers to bring her child to the United States. Mother worked seven days a week and long nights in order to make the family happy so that they would bring her little girl to her as they promised.

Years went by. Every time Mother asked if they were bringing her child, they would say they were working on it. But eventually Mother was forced to fly back to her country to get her daughter. She was not allowed to take her daughter out of the country without the father's permission. Therefore, a signature was forged since permission from the father was out of the question. They left Guatemala City on a diplomatic visa.

Many years later, Mother re-married and had two wonderful daughters, but her marriage ended in divorce. She raised them by herself. She took them to work with her. I'm not sure how she did it, but she did. Mother helped all of us, and still found time to learn to write and read English. She always encouraged us in everything we wanted to do.

Mother died at the age of sixty and she is buried at the "Gates of Heaven" in Maryland. Before she died, she learned how to write and read. I have a book she read to me and I find her writings in small places. I will finish my GED and become a writer because of Mother.

The struggles and obstacles she went through makes me the strong woman I am today. For all she accomplished and for all the love she gave, we hold her dear to our hearts. I know she watches over us, and is very proud of us, just as I'm proud to be her daughter.

Rosa Cipriano was born in Quetzaltenango, Guatemala. She was 10 when her mother brought her to the United States. Rosa worked as an administrative assistant for Ourisman Honda and raised three children before moving to Minneapolis two years ago. She has two grandchildren and one on the way. Rosa is very happy to have found Northside ABE, where she says the teachers have been so supportive. Her dream is to become a writer.

My Family
Der Yang, Minneapolis

My name is Der Yang. I'm from Laos. I got married in 2007. I came to the United States about three years ago. I live in Minneapolis with my husband and his family.

When I first came to the United States it was difficult because the United States had snow. The snow looked very nice and I liked the snow. At that time I didn't know how to speak English or drive. My husband had to take me to school.

I am thinking about my country, my mom, my dad, my brothers and sisters. My family lives in Laos. They didn't come to the United States. I have five brothers and three sisters. I miss them a lot. One of my sisters and I are the only ones that came to the United States. She came to the United States about eight years ago. She lives in Wisconsin. She has one son. Right now I know how to drive and speak English little bit.

A Long Time Ago
Nhoua Lee, Minneapolis

When I was 13 years old, I always saw a ghost in the dark night for one year. I remember I was sleeping with my grandma and I had a bad dream all night long. I saw a handsome man come to play with me every night. He told me that he needed me to marry him but I told him that I had to ask my mom first. So I woke up one morning and told my mom that he asked me to marry him. And she said, "No, I won't let you go." Then she did something for me by giving me some Hmong medicine. And I had dreams about him for some nights, but not as much as before.

I know my grandma loves me so much; every night she gets something to protect me and lets me sleep between her and my sister. My grandma gives Hmong medicines to put around inside the bedroom. She has medicine to make a necklace to tie around my neck, too. She puts the medicines around everywhere. I was not scared about my dream. Right now I know that my parents love me very much. They did a lot of things for me, but I don't have anything special for

them. Since I got married, I have not dreamed about my handsome man at nighttime anymore. But in 2007, I dreamt one time about him, and when I woke that morning, I felt sad and lonely for many days.

My Important People
Nor Lor, Minneapolis

Important in my life is my mom and my older brother. My mother was the person taking care of us only because my father passed away when we were still little. I don't know what my father looked like. I grew up seeing only my mother and my older brother. I didn't know if I had a father or not.

Once, when I went to play outside, another kid was yelling, "This kid, she doesn't have a father so we can follow her and hit her. Nobody helps her because she only has a mother. Nobody help. Nobody care. Don't be scared. Follow her. Hit."

I ran home. I asked my mom, "Mom where is my dad? Why don't I have a father?" My mom said, "Daughter, your dad passed a long time ago." I said, "Why?" My mom said, "Your dad died in the world." After that, my mom said, "Don't go outside alone because people can be very mean. They don't like kids who don't have fathers, and only have moms, ok?"

I am very sad, but I think one day I should grow up and not be sad about this time.

My Hero
Pakuda Xaykaothor, Brooklyn Center

In my young life, there are many people whom I see as heroes. One person who stands out from the rest is my father, Bounher Xaykaothor. He inspired me to be a good student. He taught me about life and responsibility. He instilled morals and ethical values, which shape me to this day. He is my Hero.

My father inspired me to be a good student. He taught me how to read and write, how to study the right way. He said early morning is the best time to study, because you can remember everything you study. My father taught me how important a good education would be in my life. He said, "Ones who have education, no one can steal from them, and they can do great." He explained how he was separated from his father as an infant. His mother remarried and he grew up in poverty. He was a good student and got a scholarship to study mathematics in Vietnam. Later he got a successful career. This experience has helped him, and he wanted me to have the same.

He taught me about life and responsibility. He said, "As a person born in the world, you have to be responsible." He took responsibility seriously. As a military officer, he taught the young army officers how to be good leaders, he had a responsibility for them to survive in the battlefield. Also, he raised six children, all to be responsible people.

Moreover, my father taught me about moral and ethical values. He said, "Treat other people with respect." Also, he said to do your best to be a good person; do not steal or cheat through life. He taught me to forgive other people. He told me that he once wrote a letter to his father forgiving him for not being there for my father when he was young. He told his father that it was not his fault but the politics of the time which made the relationship impossible.

Everything my father taught me was important for my life. A good education, life, responsibility, ethics, and moral values have helped me to become the person I am today. I hope to teach the same lesson to my children.

My Parents
Anonymous, Minneapolis

My mother and father are important people in of my life because my life depends on my parents. I take part all my life with them until the last three years because the last three years I live with my husband in the United States. My brothers and sisters grew up hard. When my country had a war, we went to Ethiopia as refugees. First time we went to Ethiopia there was a lot of rain. Also there was no shelter, food, water, clothes, health. It was so hard for everybody there.

After three years, we came back to my country. I love my mother so much because I live with her a long time in my life. I am very sad to miss my parents. I like to call my parents every day. Because we are a big family, we live together and loved each other. When I came to U. S., I missed my family and I didn't forget them. Because I live alone I didn't know English and didn't drive a car until now in America. Sometimes it's very hard for me. In my country before I used live a lot people. I never forget my family.

Spring
Eric L. Childs, Rockford

April showers and May flowers. It's time to get ready for Spring.
We make our list and check for everything that needs to be clean.

We prepare the house by cooking food, getting ready for Easter Sunday
with lots of good smelling food. I hope everyone comes hungry. Everything
looks right. Family's here and there.

Smiles are bright with so much joy in the air. Makes me happy that family is here.
It's springtime. The flowers are blooming, the trees are green. The wind is blowing while we sit enjoying a good wonderful day watching the kids laugh and play. It's time
for the best for today. We hid the eggs. Now the kids have to find where they lay.

It's Easter time so have fun. Go play and help the little ones out, those who can't find a thing.

As the day comes to an end we are grateful for this Sunday and spending it with family and friends until next year comes. Again, enjoy Spring knowing summer has yet to begin.

My Life in the United States
Anayeli Contreras, Minneapolis

Hello, my name is Anayeli. I came to the United States in the year 2007. For me, it was very difficult because I never went out of my country. That day I was very sad because I left my mother and my sisters to come alone to look for a better future. In the passing years, I have found that I'm working, I'm married and have a beautiful daughter. Now I don't have my mother and sisters, but I have a husband and a daughter. Soon we will be with my family in Mexico, and we will be a great family. Everyone will be united and be very happy.

Anayeli Contreras is originally from Mexico.

Fun Times
Le Trinh, Owatonna

Every weekend is important to my family because during the week we don't have very much time together, but we try to spend a lot of time together on the weekend.

My husband works at a factory downtown during the week, but he doesn't work there on the weekends. I work at a salon by Wal-Mart, but I don't work over there on Sundays.

We have a little girl who is seven years old. She goes to Lincoln Elementary School. On Saturdays, my husband and my daughter make pie, bread, and sometimes they cook on the grill while they wait for me to come home. After dinner, everybody goes down to the basement because we have family room with an entertainment center.

Sunday morning we go to church together, and after church we always go out to eat! According to me, spending time together on the weekends is very important.

Le Trinh is 50 years old and is originally from Vietnam.

My Crazy Life
Marisol Jacinto Vasquez, Shakopee

I have three boys. My oldest boy is 14 years old and is a teenager. He is difficult and has difficulty with his homework and does not like to study. He wants to play video games, watch TV, and to play on the computer. Maybe it is because he is teenager that my life is crazy.

My middle boy is six years old and is in first grade. He never sits down, not even to eat. He is very imperative. He is fast. He runs all day and sleeps little. I don't know how to help my son. I don't understand my son. I wish I could understand. My life is crazy.

My youngest son is four years old and is in preschool. He learns bad things from his brothers. Sometimes he is willful and wants his own way. My life is crazy.

My three boys care for each other. They protect each other. Sometimes my little boys help clean the house, organize their toys and books. The house only stays nice for one hour, and then the toys are all around the house. My life is crazy.

My oldest boy helps me to care for the little boys when I am working. He helps sometimes to organize the house and to play with his brothers. He reads to his brothers at night before bedtime. Sometimes my life is not crazy.

I work in the afternoon and don't have time to spend with my children because I need to work. I would like to have more time with them, to teach them some activities and to share moments together. My boys are the most important people in my life.

Now my life is crazy, but I think my life will not be so crazy some day.

Marisol Jacinto Vasquez is originally from Mexico.

My Big Family
Silvia Selvas, Shakopee

I arrived in Minnesota on November 10, 2005, with my three kids. I was four months pregnant with my fourth boy. Three happy years later, I was pregnant with my daughter. I'm very happy with my four boys, but I wished for one girl. My one girl is special because everything is different. Her body is different, her clothes are different, and her hair is different. She is much more affectionate. My boys say, "Mom, I love you," but my one girl says, "Mom, I love you," with a big hug and many kisses. My one girl is more interested in the family. The boys just play. My daughter pays attention to where everyone is.

In Mexico, there are many morals. One moral is: the small family lives better. I don't like this for my family because my family is big. Another moral is: where they eat four, they eat five. This moral helps to explain my big family to others. I like the moral: because there is no fifth bad one. It's perfect for my family.

Before my daughter was born, I saw everything in blue because of my boys. Today, I see everything in pink. I am very happy with my family. Every day I give thanks to God.

Silvia Selvas is 33 years old and is originally from Mexico.

The Saddest Time of My Life
Asha Ashur, Rochester

The saddest time of my life was when I came to America five years ago. That was when my sister got cancer, she got very sick. Then she left Columbus and came to the Mayo Clinic, so I wasn't able to see her every day. That was very sad. My sister was a very good person, and I never saw her before I came to the U.S. It was sad. My sister was 30 years old. My sister was a very young woman. She had three kids. My sister died in 2008. I miss my sister, but I'm lucky to get to see her kids every day now. I hope my sister will go to paradise. That was the saddest day of my life.

Asha Ashur is originally from Somalia.

Wonderful Trips to the Beach
Anny Reimer, Saint Louis Park

I grew up in the mountains of Costa Rica. Every summer, my family planned a trip to the beach that included up to forty family members. The trip would last a week.

The journey began the night before the trip, packing the pickup truck and also dressing up in layers before bed. First I put on my swimming suit, then a pair of shorts and a t-shirt, and finally my pajamas.

The next morning we got up at 3 a.m. We all jumped in the pickup truck bed, which was already packed with a mattress, suitcases, and all the necessary stuff for the trip.

The driving time was around three hours. We needed to leave so early because in Costa Rica it is illegal to ride in the back of a pick-up truck, so we needed to pass the police department before they started work in the morning.

On the drive to the beach, we sang, slept, ate, and talked in the truck.

By the time we got to the camping area at the beach, we already had only our swimming suits on— ready to jump in the water!

During those days at the beach we spent most of the time in the ocean, body surfing, learning how to swim, and trying to have as many people as possible holding hands and floating at the same time. One of my favorite games was to build a body tower in the water. We played volleyball and soccer in the sand. We ate fried fish most of the time and drank coconut milk. At nighttime, we sat around a campfire and sang for hours and also listened to stories. When bedtime came, we slept in a huge tent that the adults put together with a big canvas.

The only restrictions that my family had at the beach were that we couldn't be in the sun from noon to 3 p.m., and children couldn't be in the ocean without adult supervision. From noon to 3 p.m., we stayed at the campsite having lunch, taking naps in hammocks, and playing games.

When the time to go back home came, we packed our pick-up and headed home late at night so we could pass the police department after hours.

I thank my family for giving me these wonderful memories.

Anny Reimer is 32 years old and is originally from Costa Rica.

My Life in the United States
Jesus Ramirez, Saint Louis Park

I have been in the United States since March 1997. When I came here, I didn't have friends or family. The first two years here I didn't speak English and it was difficult for me. I was thinking to go to Mexico because I missed my family so much. I felt that I couldn't take it anymore, but after a few months, I found that I had a cousin living here in Minnesota, so I called my family back in Mexico and asked for his phone number so I could call him. Yes, in two weeks I moved into his apartment, and he helped me find a job where he worked in the restaurant. In the restaurant, I met my future wife. I have known my wife for 13 years and we have a daughter together. Looking back, when I first came, I didn't know what my future held, but now I look forward to every single day to go to school and play with my daughter. I'm enjoying every moment.

Jesus Ramirez is originally from Mexico.

My Family
Monica, Blaine

My name is Monica. I came to the United States in 1999 alone. I had to leave my family in Mexico when I came here. I have a dream to buy a house for my mom, and I promised her to come back to Mexico after I bought her a house. But I got married here, and I have two extraordinary kids and my husband. So now I have my own family, but I still miss my mom a lot. I wish one day to go back to Mexico with my family. My mom is one of the best people in my life. She taught me how to be a better person, and I hope one day we will be together as a big family.

Interesting Girl That I Met
Marilyn Lodermeier, Saint Louis Park

My story is about the young girl that I met at the Philippines airport back in 2005. I sat in the waiting area for my flight going back to South Korea. I saw a girl sitting next to my mom and talking about where she was going and what her job was going to be in Japan. She kept talking and talking and suddenly she cried out. I found out she was going to Japan to be a dancer and a prostitute. She said her agency and her mom had an agreement about her job in Japan. "I don't have a choice," she told me, "and my mother doesn't care about my life or my future. She must be crazy about the money that I am going to make in Japan. Whatever happens to me, I hope God is watching. That is why I cried when I saw your mom. I was jealous that you have a mother who cares about your life."

Marilyn Lodermeier is originally from Philippines.

I Love My Family
Anonymous, Minneapolis

I like my family. My family is a mom, dad, three brothers and two sisters. We live in different states in the United States. My mom is the best mom in the world. She is the cleanest and the most honest woman in the world. My dad is a hard worker, and he has raised us well. He showed us the importance of studying and learning skills. He has experience as a machinist and mechanic. He had a garage to fix cars for 15 years. I love my family. I am proud of them for how they have prepared me. As I am talking of myself, I have three children. They have good behavior and are good listeners. Their health is good. Also, they can write and read languages well. That's good for me. Thank God, and God bless everyone in the world.

People I Would Like to See Again
Nan Pyar, Saint Paul

In my future, the people I would like to see the most are my parents and my grandmother because they are part of my life and are important people to me.

I would like most to see my parents and my grandmother because I haven't seen them for 16 years already. I miss them so much. I want to talk to them, but it's hard to connect with them. My parents are working in the jungle and they live there, too. The place that they live in has a lot of mountains, and they don't have phone connection there. Once in a while, they come back to the city and we can talk to each other. My grandmother is living in Burma, and I don't have a connection with her either. Sometimes I miss her and I try to call her, but she lives very far from a place with the phone renter and has to ride on a motorcycle to come talk on the phone. She is too old to ride a motorcycle, so we haven't talked to each other yet. The location that she lives in is a small city. Most people use only a motorcycle, but if you want to rent a car, you can and it's expensive. I don't want to bother her too much. They are part of my life and are the most important people to me since I was born. They raised me up until I was 14 years old and taught me how to be a good person.

In the future, I would like to visit Burma to see them again. I would be very happy to see them whenever I can, and I think they feel the same about me, too. Every time my parents call me, they ask me when I will visit them and they tell me they miss me so much. My mom tells me that my grandmother asks about me all the time, and that she wants to see me. In my mind, I always think about them, miss them, and I always ask myself how can I see them? First I need to finish my GED, get a certificate, and get a job. Then I will try to save money the best I can, and when I'm ready I'll go to visit them. I always think about them, and I will help them to pay for the cost that is expensive. I will send money to them as I can do it. I love to see them happy.

Nan Pyar is 31 years old and is originally from Burma.

An Important Time of Day
Adelfa Paz, Austin

Many people have an important time of the day. For me, it would be at 4:00 p.m. in the afternoon. This is the time when my whole family is home.

To me, eating with the family is very important to have better communication with my children. Sadly our kids spend more time in school rather than in the house with the family. It is sad to think there is only a matter of hours that we spend family time together. Because it is when we can ask questions about their homework or what's happening in their lives. We can ask them about their goals or talk with them about their everyday life.

I would like to know more about the lives of my kids, like their friends, confidants, and their feelings. I would like to have good conversations that make our relationship strong. I want them to learn values, respect, discipline, and self-control. It would make any mother happy to know what's going on in her children's lives, to have a good relationship and to get to know them better. When they visit their friends, then I worry a little because sometimes their friends' parents know about the visits in their house or they do not know. Now I have learned more about my children, and their friends and now ask them first or call their parents' friends.

The family never abandons anyone. The love of the family keeps us together forever. It is very important to meet as a family.

With God's Help
Mireya Alonso, Shakopee

This past summer I traveled to Connecticut to spend time with my sister. We spent two wonderful months together. It was a very happy time for both of us. But two weeks after I returned to Minnesota, she suffered a stroke and was not responding to treatment and was in a coma. The following is from a letter I wrote to my sister last summer.

Dear Amazing Sister,
I am very sad. I pray to God to give me the oppor-

tunity to see you again. I feel a strong pain in my heart. I am upset and scared because I may not have the opportunity to tell you how much I love you and how much you are important to me. Day by day it is difficult to know if I should travel to see you. I call every day to find out how you are doing but I think it would be better if I could stay with you. Some days are good and some days we lose hope for you. My children are having a sad time, too, because they know I am very upset about a dear aunt. My family helps me so that I will not lose hope and you will respond soon.

Finally, in the darkest tunnel, a bright light came and the news is very good. The doctors were surprised because they told us you are clinging to life. They explained they had other people with the same problem but you are lucky to be one that is recuperating very fast. I knew you always were a brave and strong woman. I remember when we were children that you were the bravest sister. Now, I want to tell you thank you for demonstrating your courage one more time as you fight for your life. Very soon I hope to stay with you and tell you face to face that I love you so much my dear sister. Thank you, God, for letting my sister live.

Everything is now good for all of us. My sister, Esmeralda, is only 42 years old and has a beautiful future with her three wonderful children whom I love.

Mireya Alonso is originally from Puebla, Mexico.

Our Blessed Family
Norma Ortega, Richfield

My name is Norma. I came to United States in January 1997. I feel so blessed to have a very special family.

I married a great man and exceptional father. He is my best friend, my support and my soul mate. We have a beautiful girl, she is 11 years old, and a very special boy, who is four years old. My son is very special because he was born with a birth defect called spinal bifida.

Spinal bifida or Myelomeningocele, which is the correct medical name, is basically a hole in the spine's neural tube. Where the hole is located affects how much of the body a person can use. My son's opening is further down the spine, so he has use of his arms but limited use of his legs. Some other complications are hydrocephalus, neurological bladder, club foot. There are more complications, but each case is so different.

It was hard to know that our son had a defect, but we always prayed for him, even when the doctors said that my son couldn't walk and may have to use a wheelchair. My son is walking with crutches or sticks (what he calls them). Although he has had many challenges, he is a very happy boy, sociable, joyful and has a very strong spirit.

We always treat him like a normal child, showing him that he can do anything, just in a different way.

Even for my daughter was hard to know that her little brother was different. She helps a lot and protects her little brother. She knows how important is working together. I think she is a very kind and sweet girl, always caring for others. My husband and I are very proud of our children and love them with all our heart.

It's been a very busy four years between doctor appointments, therapies, school, and work, but all the efforts that our family has made are paying off. We learned many things from our kids. We learned to be patient, to enjoy simple moments, to smile more often and to never give up, no matter how hard the goals or how much time it will take, never give up. We know that each family is different, and has different traditions, rules, and cultures, but what make a family are the love and the respect they have for each other.

Norma Ortega is originally from Mexico.

Role Models
Abraham Hernandez, Luverne

My best role model was my grandmother because she showed me how to respect others and to be polite with all people. She also showed me to use good manners and how to be responsible with all the work in the house and in the school.

I had other good role models like friends that

showed me how to be a good parent when I grow up. Some of them showed me how to handle problems in the future; even some showed me how to be a good husband. However, there were some that wanted me to do wrong things but I really wasn't interested because I learned from other good friends that teach me all the good things.

So because of my grandmother but also to some of my family members and friends I am who I am now and still learning from others like my children, friends, and teachers.

Abraham Hernandez is 33 years old and is originally from Mexico.

My Family
Mai Hang, Minneapolis

My mother had 11 children. I have five brothers and five sisters. We were a family before in my country. We lived together in one home, but right now my mother, father and brother live in Thailand. I am thankful for family in my country. I am sad. Why? My mother, father and brother are far away. I miss them very much.

Mai Hang is originally from Laos.

It's All About You
Maryan Mohamed, Minneapolis

It's all about me. I was born in Somalia in 1979. I have five brothers and four sisters. We used to live together. Then our country had a civil war and was not peaceful. So we left to go to Kenya in 1992. Then I got married in 2003. I liked to go to the United States. My husband went to the United States and sent me a visa but I couldn't come. Then my husband came in Kenya. After three months he went back to the United States. Then he sent me a visa again, but I had a baby, so I waited. Finally we got the visa in 2009. At that time I had two children. Then in 2009, I had a third baby, but it's so sad that I left him in Kenya. I came with my two older children to the United States. And I hope that I can have my baby here in the future.

Oh Mama
Sedera Brown, Minneapolis

Do you have a mom who would drop everything for you, and know she will be there for you? The best thing in my life is my mother. My mom was always there for me when no one else was. A mother like mine is one of a kind. I know when I cry she would hold me, and when I was down she was there for me. When I was ten, I got hit by a car. I thought I lost everything, but God said, "No, this is not your time." So when I got out of the hospital my mom was there for me. A good mother should love, give, care, help and listen to you. A mother should be your best friend, and possibly the only real friend you will ever meet. She will never tell your private stories or hurt you in any kind of way.

When you lose your mom, you will have so many things going through your head. Why do I say that? Because I lost my mom on January 23, 2011. I was only twenty-one years of age. I had just became a woman in my mom's eyes. So how do I feel very, very alone? When I saw my mom in her pretty pink casket that my family and I picked out for her, I cried and cried all day, all night, all year long, but when she went down in the ground all I could say was, Oh Mama. Rest in Peace, Mama.

My Best Gift
Tha Mee, Saint Paul

The best gift I ever received in my life is my children because they are so lovely and so cute. One thing I'm proud of is how they love me so much and they know I am the best gift for them. They always understood me like I understand them. In school they try to be the best students in their class. They study very hard in their class. My oldest daughter is a leader in her classroom. The teacher said when she asked any question my daughter knows all the answers. But my middle son is a little bit lazy in reading. My youngest son is so smart, he is three years old but he learns very quickly and knows how to speak politely to people who are older than him. Sometimes he doesn't want to listen when I tell him to do something. However, I love them the same and I love them so much because they all are my special gifts I have ever received in my life.

Tha Mee is 27 years old and is originally from Burma.

Understanding My Mom
Miriam Rivera, Shakopee

When I was a child, I had two sisters and a brother. My big sister took care of my little sister and me because my mom needed to work. She needed to buy food and save money for necessary things at home. She didn't have a husband. She worked hard to take care of four children. She worked washing clothes, cutting sugar cane, and making food for other women. My big sister was nine years old. She needed to care for us. She was very young and learned to cook and make many things at home. Also she needed to go to elementary school. She finished elementary school.

My mom worked so hard. She saved money to pay for Junior High School for my big sister. My sister went to Junior High School for two years. But she left school with her boyfriend a couple of days a week. When mother had a meeting with the teacher, the teacher said that your daughter only comes to school a few days a week. When my big sister returned home from school, my mother hit her a lot. My aunt defended my big sister. Sometimes, when my mother was hitting my big sister, my little sister and I went in front of my big sister so my mom wouldn't hit my sister. My sister returned to school, but she was absent many days.

When the teacher gave out report cards, my big sister knew that her reports were going to be bad. She preferred to go away with her boyfriend. That night I was sad because my big sister didn't return home. My mother cried a lot. She went to my big sister's friend's houses. She asked them about my big sister, but they didn't answer. My mom returned home. She started to drink beer and alcohol. For me, everything was

difficult because I needed my big sister. Some days I said, "God, I want a different mom because my mom always hits me."

When I was a teenager, she changed a lot. When I talked to her she listened to me. Sometimes she said, "I love you." My childhood experiences made me think about marriage and children and what I wanted in my life. When I grew up, I understood my mom because she had so much work and responsibilities by herself.

Miriam Rivera is originally from Veracruz, Mexico.

My Family Came to the U.S.
Hue Her, Minneapolis

When I was coming to the United States, I felt both excited and dejected, but I was not sure if I was happy or sad. I was happy because I would be going to the U.S. and taking my family with me to the mighty nation. My children could study more English so they could help themselves, then they could find a better job for their future. And I was so sad because I will be leaving some of my family back behind; my mother, two brothers, a sister, and my cousins.

The first day I came to the United States, when I arrived at the airport in San Francisco, I didn't know which part of the United States we were in; I just knew we were in the United States. I was afraid because my group had three families, but nobody could speak English; I just knew a little bit of English. I knew what they were talked about, but I could not answer yet. I thought I was very lonely, but we were lucky because the guy who came to talk to us was Lao, and I can speak Lao. Then I was happy and not afraid. They took my family's picture for ID94 and got it for us.

When my family arrived in the airport in Minneapolis; my brother-in-law, my sister, and my cousin to came to receive my family. I was happy again. I never before thought I would be in the United States.

Hue Her is 38 years old and is originally from Laos.

I Remember
Akech Majok, Coon Rapids

I remember my cousin, his name was Solomon. He is important to me because he grew up with us. I remember lots of things he did for me in time of need. I was young but I still remember some of them. For example, he was my strong teacher and taught me geography and math. He left in 1982 to fight in the war that started in 1983. He became a general in the political army. The last time we talked to each other was in 2008. He told me he would come to the United States for training last month. He got sick and then my aunt called me to tell me. I've tried to call him, but sometimes the network is not good. This November 2nd he passed away. He had five kids, two boys and three girls. His son is here in the University on a football scholarship. Another son is in college in Uganda. I am sorry that I did not talk to him before he died. I planned to visit him next year but God had a different plan. I will never forget you. I will still remember you.

Akech Majok is originally from South Sudan.

What My Father Did For Me and Me for Him
Naima Ali, Minneapolis

In 2005 I was a teenager but my idea was like a 40 year-old's. I was the problem-solver in my family. My family has eight kids but my parents loved me more than the others, I grew up like a queen.

In 2005 my father and I went to Kenya. In 2006 I fell in love with a young man who grew up like me but he didn't have smart ideas like me. We loved each other and decided to marry. I forgot my dad for few days, but he heard about it. When I came home from school my dad was unhappy. He felt sick and he didn't talk much with me for three days. The fourth day was on a Friday when everyone usually is happy. I felt shy to talk with him and I got an idea to make him talk. I stood in front of his room and sang a song about dad. Then I went back to my room and laid down on my bed. He came to my room he asked me what was going on between me and that man. I said, "Nothing, the people have lied to you." He said, "Are you sure?" I said quietly, "Yes", but I had lied to him. Until now I don't want to remember that day, it was my enemy day. I loved my dad, and I loved the young man. Because I was a teenager, I didn't listen to any one.

The next day my fiancé and I were walking in a park. My little brother saw me and told my dad. Then my fiancé's uncle told me that my dad was really angry. My family was searching for me for 24 hours. Finally they found me. I came in front of my dad. "I didn't want to go around you. I'm going to tell the truth. No one is close to you except me and no one is close to me except you." I was crying. He put his hand on my arm. "I left all of my family for you and I swear to God if you are going to die, I'll die because of you." I got down with my forehead on his foot to ask him forgive me. He accepted my apology. We made peace. I stopped loving that man because of my dad.

I Missed My Family in Laos
Pasoua Yang, Minneapolis

I came to the United States on October 22, 2005 to marry my husband. I packed two bags. The most important things I packed were my family pictures, Hmong clothing and my jewelry that my mother gave to me. When I came to Minnesota, I lived in Brooklyn Center. The first week my husband went to work and I stayed home. I felt so lonely because I missed my family and my friends. Now I feel so happy because I have friends and my children.

Pasoua Yang is originally from Laos.

Dear Grandma
Lakkhana Robinson, Big Lake

When I see elderly people I am very sad, because sometimes it makes me think about my grandmother. People call me Anny here in the United States. I came from the northeast side of Thailand, called "E-San." We lived in a big family in my country, and the young ones took care of the old ones. I was very close to my grandmother; we spent most of the time together before I moved here.

I remember when I was a child we used to hang out a lot. We went out to the rice farm to dig out frogs and crabs, brought them home, and cooked them for dinner. She was the most excellent chef in the world. She cooked traditional "E-San" food and it was the most delicious food that I ever ate. I took care of her when she got sick. I bathed her, fed her and slept with her. I miss her so much since she passed away in 2006 and I wish I could see her and talk to her before she passed away. Unfortunately, I couldn't do anything since I moved to the United States in 2005. I didn't even go to her funeral because I came here in a really bad situation. Nobody in my family even knew how unhappy I was. But I have a loving family now and have a two and a half year old daughter. My life is fulfilled and complete.

One thing I would like to do the most is to help old people because they remind me of her. I just wish she had known that she was the most beautiful, loving, caring and generous person. I hope I will be born to be her granddaughter again in the next life, I love you so much, "Na-Na."

Lakkhana Robinson is originally from Si Sa Ket Province, Thailand.

My Family
Josee Defly, Saint Louis Park

My family's name is Defly and we are from Africa. Our first language is French. My family is composed of six people: three daughters, one brother and our parents. My father is a teacher and my mother is a seller. We have many friends. My family likes parties and surprises. Sports are our first distraction. I like my family and I will never forget them.

Josee Defly is 30 years old and is originally from Togo (Afrique).

My Dad
Zalina Khan, Brooklyn Park

I remember my dad every moment in my life. My dad passed away June 28, 21 years ago. Dad was a very special person to me. He wasn't just a dad to me. He meant everything to me, because he never gave up hoping that I could improve with my disabilities. He used to wake up at night to make sure my body didn't curl up in my sleep. He let me lie down straight while I was sleeping. He used to make everything at night to help teach me, like toys I played with during the days. My dad came to the United States and two months later, he passed away. The sad part is I remember that he went home in a box with a cover after only 65 days in the U.S.

The last thing my dad said to me at the airport was, "My daughter, tell me goodbye." I told dad Asalam-walanikum. I love my dad! My uncle told me during those 65 days, my dad wrote letters about me and sent them to nine hospitals. My uncle then told me that five hospitals had written back, but it was after my dad passed away.

Zalina Khan is originally from Alness, Guyana.

Isabel Suazo, Shakopee

Living

A Trip along the Route of My Life
Claudia Varela Howard, Minneapolis

Every morning, I take the number 6 bus to get to my English classes so I can speak this new language and learn this new culture. I enjoy this 30-minute trip the same way I am enjoying this new journey in a new country. My favorite part is when the bus goes around the beautiful Lake Calhoun. I also like to observe the many different people who are going different places. Everybody is so different that it is fun filling in the details and imagining their lives. I look at strange hairstyles, a man with his dog, intellectual-looking people, a man with his walker decorated with a fashionable scarf, different languages and accents. People don't detect my observation other than answering my looks with a smile. Sometimes I feel that my actual life is a dream, because I'm in a faraway country, with my family distant, another language, a new culture and new friends. It is difficult to believe all these new changes in my life in such a short time. But the reality is that I'm here because I choose to be. Now is the moment to live, love, learn and take all the opportunities. Including bus rides.

Claudia Varela Howard was born in Cali, Colombia on April 15, 34 years ago. She grew up in a supportive and loving family, and arrived in the United States on Nov. 8, 2011, shortly after meeting her true love. They married one month later. Claudia volunteers in a hospital and attends classes at Lincoln Adult Education Center in downtown Minneapolis to improve her English.

Life
Rachel Hakanson, Buffalo

Life is a game
You must roll the dice
Hit, miss, and feel the shame

Life is a carnival ride
The ups and downs
Shift and shake your insides

Life is a road
There's twists and turns and
Trying to rush it brings on some burns
Some ways are narrow and some are wide
But you only stumble because of your pride

Life is a flower
Only when you are fully bloomed
You see your colors set apart from the rest
Have you grown strong enough to withstand the test?

Life is a drug
The older you are, the harder they get
Whether it's the end or not is any man's guess

Sometimes you aren't the only one to know yourself best
And you're NEVER the one who gets to decide the day you rest

Life is fleeting
May you cherish today
If you wait 'till tomorrow

Suburbanism
Kadu Tomita, Minnetonka

When I arrived in the Twin Cities, I noticed a particular feature of its urban organization. People live in big suburbs, around two central business districts. Most travels are made by car, and take an average time of 15 minutes and most local businesses are located in strip malls. This is way different from what I was use to where I lived in Curitiba, Brazil. There, a big percentage of the population lives in apartments, in mixed residential/commercial and walkable neighborhoods, which are served by public transportation. The American model has some positive points: the population lives in big houses with huge yards, composing a big green mass around commercial areas. On the other hand, people become car-dependent, due to long commute times and low usage of public transportation.

Kadu Tomita is 18 years old and is originally from Brazil.

Minnesota's Day
Anonymous, Saint Louis Park

I have been in Minnesota since 2009 with my family.
When I was in Japan, I was worried about coming to Minnesota for the first time.
I was afraid of Minnesota's winters.
But I didn't need to worry.
Minnesota's winter is beautiful.
Indoors is warmer than a Japanese house.
I have studied English.
I made many good friends.
I am used to this life now.
I can spend happy days.

Driving in Winter
Paula Ruiz, Saint Paul

This winter is better than last year because it's cold in the morning but the rest of the day it's okay until night. Last year at this time we had a lot of snow. But this year I'm so glad because I drive every day with more tranquility; It's safer for everyone. The snow provokes many accidents. I've been so scared when the snow is so bad because I never know who will hit me. Some people drive bad because they drive fast. I drive slow because I feel scared to drive fast because before I had an accident. That's why I don't like the winter time because we have to drive very carefully all the time because other people don't, and we never know when something will happen to us when they drive.

Paula Ruiz is originally from Mexico.

Memories of Home
Sergio, Brooklyn Park

I was born in a little town called El Tanger, Mexico. When I was a little child, my favorite hobby was to ride horses. While others boys played games, I always looked for a horse to ride. Sometimes wild horses would drop me, but I still loved to ride them.

I liked to help my older brother with all the field work on the farm. When I was just eight years old, my uncle and I worked in the farmland for harvest. He connected the mules to a plow to dig into and turn over the soil to plant the seeds in the ground for harvest.

Then after a few years the government helped the farmers with a new tractor for a group of nine people per tractor. I stared to drive the tractor at the age of 13 years old. Since it was the first time I drove, I was very excited to drive. I worked on the land day and night; unfortunately, the part of Mexico where I lived is a remote and dry land and there is little rain. I decided to immigrate to the United States, where there were a lot of opportunities to have a good life. When I was 16 years old I came to the United States and started a radically new life.

Minneapolis
Chris Acres, Minneapolis

I love living in Minneapolis. I love learning about its history, going to its sports centers and learning about the people living here. For example, I have learned the Foshay Tower was built in 1929 and it has 32 floors. It was the tallest building in the Northwest. I also have learned that Lake Nokomis originally was called Lake Amelia. I have learned that there are lots of different cultures in the city. When I am downtown in Minneapolis, there is always a variety of food you can smell and the foods are different and tasty. I also notice this when there is an event like a sports game. I realize and have seen a variety of cultures coming together that I truly believe is a good thing.

A Memory of My Life
Cristian Guaman, Minneapolis

When I was 16 years old, I came to the United States in hopes of following my dreams and reaching my goals. My first experience when I arrived was in a program called, South West Key, which was for kids who came to this country illegally. It felt like a jail because you could not do anything without permission, and if you broke the rules, there were consequences. I had to wait there for months; scared of being deported.

Then one day a lawyer named Abigail came in to talk to me. She asked me questions about my life growing up in Ecuador. She told me that there was a chance of getting a green card, so I decided to answer her questions. I told her that my childhood with my mom and stepfather was horrible. My father died before I was born. When I was nine years old, I left an abusive household to live on my own. Abigail thought that because of what I had been through, I deserved a chance to stay in the United States and even become a citizen one day.

After that, my lawyer worked hard to get me a Social Security number and a green card. She took care of me, almost like a son and wanted to help me have a better life. I will never forget all that she did for me and I am very grateful for all of the opportunities I have had since she helped change my life. Coming to the United States has given me the chance to make a better life for myself and my family and to follow my dreams of education and success.

Cristian Guaman is 23 years old and is originally from Ecuador.

Natural World
Ebla Hassan Muhumed, Saint Paul

October squirrel brown and black and white stripes
Soft
Tree black, white, brown
Flowers, yellow green

Life in a New Country
Adrian Rivera, Minneapolis

When I arrived in the United States, the first thing I did was pray to God for everything. After that, my friends and my brother went out to celebrate with me.

We ate a big lunch and I felt like everyone was happy. Hours later, my brother took me with him to shop at the mall. I bought everything I needed, including a PlayStation and 32" screen TV!

That day, I felt like a king of a new world. After a week, I started to work in a restaurant, doing things like hot sauces and cold meats. My first day, an American helped train me and helped me talk to everyone. He explained the rules and processes to follow, but inside I felt alone. I didn't understand the new language.

But I met many people from different countries. Now, I feel very fortunate to be in the United States

Adrian Rivera is originally from Mexico.

A Great Privilege in the United States
Rosalba, Minneapolis

When I was little in my home country, I enjoyed my childhood. But when I grew up, everything changed.

My parents decided to separate and the news was terrible. In my school, my grades went down. But I decided to change my life. I left my country. I decided to come to the United States when I was 16 years old.

When I came here, everything was different. One of the biggest problems was the language. And I had to share a room with a strange person. I had to find a safe place for me. In the end, I found it and started a new life.

Now, I'm married. My husband is from another country. I have two lovely daughters. I believe I have a wonderful family. I am thankful for all the blessings. Thank God for this opportunity.

Rosalba is originally from Mexico.

First Days of School
Anonymous, Minneapolis

My first days of school in the United States were very hard. I was afraid, shy, and worried because I did not understand my teacher. Every day was the same day. I woke up at 6:00 a.m. because my bus came around 6:50 a.m. I had to be there before 6:50 and the weather was so bad, sometimes below zero. I went to school Monday through Friday, but I was not in regular high school. They called it Newcomer's School. I do not know what that means. I stayed there about ten months. After that, they transferred to me John Marshall High School in Rochester, Minnesota. I stayed there for one year. After one year, they said to me, "You are over 21 so you can go to adult school."

The Story about My Arrival
Ahmed Nur, Minneapolis

I came to the United States on June 26, 2011. At first, life was difficult because I couldn't speak English. I didn't understand anything in the United States and I came from Egypt. The first months were hard for me. One day I went to downtown Minneapolis to apply for a job. On my way back, I took the bus with a $20 bill and no change came out. I didn't know how to ask a question or how to ride the bus. I stayed home for two weeks because I did not have a ticket or any money. After three months, I went to school and then got a job. Everything is good in life now.

Ahmed Nur is originally from Egypt.

Alone
Lorena Flores, Minneapolis

Alone since I was twelve years old.
Alone in one place.
Alone when I eat.
Alone when I sleep.
Alone when I wake up.
Alone every time.

Special Olympics
Allen, Coon Rapids

I do many Special Olympics sports. I play basketball and hockey right now. I have also done bowling. I even did downhill skiing one winter. I have done a lot of sports. I did track and field and swimming. After each year, we go to State meets and Nationals. We meet with a lot of friends from other teams. I like the exercise. It is a good thing to do. I have also played softball. One year my whole team went to Nationals in softball, I played left field. We had fun. We won almost all the games and we got a medal. I like playing softball the best because it's during the summer. It is more fun when you hit the ball.

My Life in School
Richard Darland, Minneapolis

As I look back on my life, I think the reason I could not concentrate in school is that family was so poor and we did not have many things that many kids had. We did not have running water so that made it hard to take a bath at night. My family did not have a lot of money, so we did not get the things that we needed to live like some of the other kids. Sometimes in the winter, it got so cold and when we got up to go to school our bed would be frozen to the floor.

The house that we lived in was just one room, we did not have a bathroom, and the kitchen was a small space in the corner. We had to heat the room by wood and the fire would go out at night when we were asleep. Then after we got up and got ready for school, we had to walk two miles to catch the school bus and by the time the bus got there we were so cold. I will never forget how cold we got just getting to the school bus. Then we had a two-hour bus ride to school. It took so long just to get to school, by the time we got there it felt like it was time to go back to bed. Then when it came time to get off the bus we had to get from the bus into the school. I didn't know why but there were some kids that would sit and wait for me to get to school, so they could beat me up and spit on me. Boy, did I hate going to school.

The Best Experience of My Life
Thanh Vy Ho, Ramsey

My best experience was my first time finding a job and working at it in my country. I haven't forgotten the day I went to the interview. I was so nervous that day; it felt uncomfortable for me. I went to the office 15 minutes early, before the interview. After the employer said "hi" and looked at my application again, he had some questions for me. I answered all of his questions. I told him I didn't have a degree or any experience and that this was the first time I ever applied for a job. I told him I thought I could do a good job and that I would study more to do my job better. I felt so happy because I passed the interview and they called me to go to work after the interview. When I went to work, I usually did a good job. That made my boss proud of me, and I felt more comfortable. Later, I had some new work experiences that made my job better too.

Thanh Vy Ho is originally from Viet Nam.

Wintertime
Abdullahi Siyad, Saint Paul

Most people don't like wintertime. People suffer because of the snow and cold. Snow can make for risky driving which causes many accidents. It also gives the opportunity for children to go sledding and have snowball fights.

When I came to Minnesota last year, it was during wintertime. When I came out of the airport, it scared me. The falling snow and cold made me go back into the airport. I was wearing a soft shirt, knowing that my younger brother would be there to pick me up to take me to my wife's home in Saint Paul. When my younger brother saw me in my soft shirt, he said, "Are you crazy?" He removed his jacket and gave it to me to wear. In my mind, I was comparing the snow to my home country, where it is more than 40 degrees Celsius. Here it is 40 degrees below. What a huge gap!

Abdullahi Siyad is originally from Somalia.

Life in Minnesota
Amanda Arévalo, Minneapolis

I went to a Subway restaurant. I ordered a sandwich and the caterer asked me, "What kind of cheese do you want?" I said, "Blanco." I confused the word in Spanish for English. He laughed.

One day I was working in the store. An employee asked me, "Did you see the keys? I lost it." I answered him, "I'm sorry, I don't speak Spanish."

Amanda Arévalo is originally from Ecuador.

Learning More About Life
Anai, Colombia Heights

Hi. My name is Anai. The first time I came to the U.S. the only thing I could say is, "bye" and "hi." My first job was as an office cleaner. It was a hard job to do because it was at night and I was tired. I worked for two months, then quit. I found a new job in a restaurant as a dishwasher. I started to learn a few more words like "plate," "give me," and "I need more silverware." I didn't know how to write but I was around good people from this country. My friends at the restaurant taught me a lot of vocabulary and how to cook American food. I kept getting raises and wanted to learn more. I felt like a little kid when my Mom would give me candy when I do good things. When they would ask me to bring things, sometimes I would bring the opposite. I felt frustrated because I wanted to help but I brought things they didn't need. Sometimes my friends would just laugh at me. I feel so grateful from the bottom of my heart to those people who helped me. I hope someday I can see them again.

It is difficult in this country, but not impossible. Good people exist around the world and God blessed me to have put them in my life. I feel proud of myself and how much I've learned from others. The world would be perfect if everybody put just a little good into others' lives. Wars probably wouldn't exist and everybody would live happily like it's supposed to be.

Anai is originally from Veracruz, Mexico.

How to Succeed in Life
Breann Star Mcglonn, Minneapolis

Life can be hard at times, but in order to be successful, you must keep your eyes on the goal. There are so many things that can bring you back a step or two, but as long you keep pushing for what it is you want in life, there is a big chance you will succeed.

I truly believe that if you believe in yourself anything is possible. You can do anything you put your mind to. Life is what you make of it. So make the very best of every situation. If you think negative, you get negative!

I remember when I was 16. I dropped out of school because of the people around me, at least that's what I made myself believe. But no one made me stop. I did it on my own. It was the negativity around me and I let it feed my soul. Now that I'm much older and wiser I know that no matter what, I do what's best for me! And so now, I keep positive people around me, people who want good things out of life and will work hard. No matter how many hurdles they have to jump, they will not stop till they reach their goal.

I see life from a different view now. I will take a step in the right direction every day

I awake. Life is what you make of it.

Never let anyone tell you, "You can't do anything!" Where there is a will there is a way.

Will power within always works, live life and love! NOTHING WILL WORK UNLESS YOU DO!

Nature
Fakiha Musa Yousuf, Saint Paul

The sky is blue
Grass green
White flowers
The tree…green
Rock and bushes

Africa America
Gelgelu Tona, Minneapolis

Today the most important person in the world is Barack Obama. Even though in the USA slavery ended in 1865 no black person became president. Obama is the first African American president in the USA. After Obama was elected, he did many things - brought troops home from Iraq, closed Guantanamo, and Osama Bin Laden was killed. Martin Luther King dreamed about black people having freedom and becoming powerful. Obama came to power, and he changed many things.

In 1865, slavery in the USA ended. African Americans came to power for the first time in 2001 when General Colin Powell became the first African American Secretary of State. In 2005, Condoleezza Rice became the first female African American Secretary of State. In 2008, Obama became the first African American president. He is the strongest president in the world.

Differences
Ahmed Mohamed, Hopkins

My name is Ahmed. I live in Hopkins, Minnesota. I speak Dutch, Arabic, Somali and English. I come from the Netherlands. My story is about the difference between here in the US and in the Netherlands. It looks like the same weather and culture as I see it, but it is very different. What I miss is walking in the street or taking a train or bus, but here you cannot walk in the street or take a train easily because transportation is bad here. If you take public transportation, it is so bad. In the United States, you have to wait for a bus for 20 minutes or more. I miss the opportunity of getting on a bus quickly. But here you have cars. Otherwise, you cannot go to work because weather is bad sometimes. Transportation is bad and the company will ask if you have a car. If you say yes, you're better than another person because you have a car. But you're not really better than that person. I hope the government makes investments in roads and sidewalks, and makes more ways for people to take public transportation to help us stay more healthy and active.

White Wonderland
Alba Kampa, Saint Louis Park

Everything started when I came to Minnesota in 2010. It was my first time traveling so far away from all that I knew, like home, family, and friends. When I arrived here, it was full of snow and terribly cold for me. When my fiancée (who is now my husband) took me to my new house, I didn't care too much about how cold it was, I just needed to go outside and taste, smell, touch, and play with all that white stuff called snow like a five-year-old kid. I remember that same night making my first snow angel, some snowballs, and even a snowman at two o'clock in the morning. It was such an amazing experience for me, I had been here only a few hours and I was already in love with it. Later that day, we went to the Mall of America to get some warm clothes for me. There was a really nice and big Christmas tree and a lot of people. I told my fiancée, "I have never seen people from so many different countries together in one place." It's incredible how many different nationalities immigrate to the United States. Then we went to a winter shoe store and I tried on some winter boots. It felt like having pillows under my feet. They were so warm I couldn't believe it! So I bought them. This winter we haven't had as much snow as last year, but we have had a few snowflakes. So I am happy living here in the white wonderland.

Alba Kampa is 24 years old and is originally from Cali, Colombia.

Coming To America
Samuel Sanchez, Saint Paul

I am Samuel. I am Mexican, and when I was in Mexico I thought everything was normal.

I went to school, but many were talking about the USA, that it is a really good country. Then I moved to Minnesota. My brother and uncles were staying here and everything was different, the food and the culture.

In the first year, I wanted to go back to Mexico, but my brother told me to wait here for two or three years; that you don't want to go back to Mexico. That's why I'm here learning English because I want to spend more time in America.

A Nice Country For Women
Tomoko Kubota, Saint Louis Park

I found the U.S. is a nice country for women. First, women are treated more equally at home and at work. I met some American families in which the wife works more hours than the husband. While the wife is away on a business trip to another country, the husband does the housework and takes care of their children. I have never seen this type of family around me in Japan. I see some fathers come to pick up their children at preschool here. My husband says that half of his supervisors are women, although that is rare in Japan. Women here have an equal chance with men, or you might put it the other way around and say women are required to expend more effort than men. For example, in Japan a woman needs to come back to her workplace as soon as possible after a child's birth.

Secondly, the society of the automobile that exists here is nice for mothers. I used to use a bus and train in Tokyo because there are traffic jams, and parking fees are charged everywhere. When I had morning sickness, I was afraid of taking public transportation for several months. Many pregnant women have difficulty going to their workplaces if they aren't near home. Also, mothers who have babies use public transportation during limited times of the day because rush hours are terrible. But in Minnesota, I can go everywhere by my car without worrying about the time, the number of bags I have with me, and my condition. Because I could forget my morning sickness while I'm driving and away from home, I have enjoyed my pregnancy here more than the one I had in Japan!

Tomoko Kubota is originally from Japan.

Living in a Different Country
Lici Facio Zepeda, Minneapolis

When I arrived in Minnesota, it was very exciting for me discover that the lifestyle is different than in my country, Mexico. First of all, the people are very gentle and charismatic. If you need help, you can stay sure that you'll be helped. The city is clean with green grass in summer, beautiful sceneries in autumn with the colorfulness of the trees, and in winter with all the white snow. Other things that I love are the bike trails, and Minnesota has a lot of them, so if you need go to whatever place, just take your bicycle and ride! It is fantastic all the nature that Minnesota offers. In many places you can find rabbits, squirrels, deer, ravens, and also if you have luck, eagles. Yes, one time I saw one while I was riding on my bicycle.

For me, it was a little difficult the process of adapting when many changes come in life, like moving to another country and leaving all of my family. I was recently married (just two weeks ago), without any member of my family here, without friends for talk or doing many activities. So when I started my English classes at MLC (Minnesota Literacy Council), it was very good because I made some friends with classmates and teachers, and lost my fears of having a conversation with English speakers. At this time in my life, I'm very glad to stay here and have pleasant moments in every day of my life.

Lici Facio Zepeda is 25 years old and is originally from Mexico.

Alex from Belarus
Alex, Savage

I was born in 1985 in Belarus. I was deaf and in hearing class. I studied like normal. My hobby was rowing, kayaking and canoeing. When I finished school I went to college. In college I learned only a little sign language and how to speak Russian. I won a Green Card and came to America. I lived in Minnesota for six month without a job. I found a Workforce Center to find a job for me, but they didn't find any jobs for me. I found school on the internet from CSD. In school I don't know ASL (American Sign Language). I lived with my friend in an apartment and he proposed me to work as a cleaner for awhile. Now I work as a driver. I can talk ASL with the deaf and speak a little English.

Latin People in North America
Lupita Franco, Hopkins

What is behind immigrant people? Why are they in the US with no permission? Why do they make the decision to leave their countries and their families? Was it easy? Well, I don't think so! I can write and think like many of those people because I'm Latina. I'm Mexican, and I know many stories about us.

First of all, the United States is a beautiful country for everyone. Wherever a person was born, it's a dream to live here. In North America, there are a lot of aspects that many countries would like to have, for example: Everybody shows so much respect for elders and handicapped people, and the government protects children. If somebody calls the emergency number, they react instantly to help you.

There are many opportunities to succeed in your goals, opportunities that you cannot have in Latin America. Every time I see a Hispanic, I wonder what he/she left in his/her country, and how hard they must work to support their families, their children, or a sick relative. You never know! In Mexico, if you don't have a career, it is very hard to get a job, and your pay is very low; like 60 dollars per week in a full-time job, and sometimes you are risking your life. You work to survive, and you don't have time to enjoy your family.

Mexicans don't have many options, but they decide to borrow around $3,000 dollars to pay for some help to cross the desert in three days without enough water to survive. If they have good luck and make it to the US, some of them have to sleep on the streets and get any job to save and get back the $3,000 dollars. Also, they have to confront many difficult changes like cold weather, loneliness, and missing important family events.

Many of them only want to get some money, save it, and go back to their country. They don't care how dirty the job is, they just do it!

Wherever you are, nothing is free, and everybody has to work. If a Latino does something wrong, he/she has to pay for it, but it doesn't mean that all Latinos will do the same.

Lupita Franco is 25 years old and is originally from Mexico.

The Life of Dogs
Khan Win, Roseville

My name is Khan Win. I'm from a Karen refugee camp in Thailand, but I was born in Burma. I came to the United States on December 10, 2009. At that time, I saw a lot of snow. That was the first time I saw snow. It was too cold to go outside, but I liked to go out. I didn't go to school. I just stayed home for three months.

I started school in March 2010. I didn't understand English, and didn't know how to speak it. In December 2010, I changed schools to the Lao Family English School. I really liked the teacher.

At the end of the month in 2010, I took two classes, in the afternoon and evening. One evening, the teacher showed our class about a "Therapy Dog" from the newspaper. I was surprised. I like dogs, but I'd never seen an intelligent dog like that.

In my country, I didn't see people who cared about dogs. People raised a dog, but they didn't care about their dog. They'd give the dog a bone to eat, or they'd give the dog some food that they couldn't eat. If the dog barked day or night, they hit the dog. Eighty percent of the people didn't care for their dog, and just twenty percent gave the dog what it really needed. I want the dogs to feel love and caring from the people in my country.

In America, all dogs get love and caring from people. I'm really proud of the dogs in America. They can help people in many ways. But I feel so sorry for the dogs in my country.

Khan Win is 25 years old and is originally from Burma.

Accomplishment
Chit Sae Vang, Saint Paul

My name is Chit. I am from Thailand. I live in America for five years. What I love about America is freedom; I want to be a citizen and to be smart. What I accomplished in America is having my green card. I now know how to making cake, tri-colors, and Jell-O papaya salad. I am happy.

My Life, My Battle
Hadisa, Brooklyn Park

Seeing my Mom and Dad together makes me smile and feel healthy. We are a total of six siblings. Five boys and I am the only girl. We used to be one of the happiest families in my country until one day war broke out. It scattered everyone and tore lots of families apart. I was about five years old.

I once had a little sister. She died during the war when my family was running for survival. There was no food or even water to drink. She died of hunger.

My parents took the rest of us to a strange land. Growing up in this land was a big disaster for my family. My parents became farmers. As for us, the children, we had to go into the bush to cut grass and wood and then come back to the city to sell it to have money to eat. We had to travel 25 minutes to get water to drink.

My Mom couldn't take this kind of life. She asked my Dad to move to the city but he refused. My Mom ran away to find a better place. Sometimes I would sit and cry for my Mom, praying to see her again. I was by myself most of the time.

One day my Mom came back and tricked my Dad to get me away from him. My Mom brought me to Ghana. She registered me in school for the first time. My friends used to laugh at me because I was 13 years old in the third grade. By the help of God, I was determined and kept pushing myself forward. By the end of the year I could read, write and spell words.

Eventually we moved to the U.S. Experiencing the other side of the world brought me joy and happiness. Some years later, we followed up on my brothers and Father. I found out that my Dad died three years before. I cry because now I live in the U.S. and my Dad is not here to enjoy it with me.

I'm now the mother and father for my brothers. I work to help support them in Africa and also support my mother here. I am a single Mom with a beautiful daughter who looks up to me.

We sometimes fall and rise again, unless we choose to stay down.

God is in control!

Hadisa is 21 years old and is originally from Liberia.

Stay Healthy and Live Longer
Chong Lee, Saint Paul

There are several important things that people should do to have a long, healthy life. Good health is one of the most important things in life, but many people do not take care of themselves. Here are the three most important things that people should do: First of all, people must exercise at least three days a week to keep their body healthy. People should join the activity that they like because the exercise won't make them feel bored for a long time. For example, soccer is my favorite sport, and I play it almost every day.

In addition, people must eat healthy food every day. Vegetables and fruit are very good food and are rich in vitamins. People have to take 3-5 servings of each of them every day. People must eat vegetables more than meat in their meals.

Third, People have to take care themselves all the time. They must clean their body or take a shower, at least one per day. For example, I brush my teeth every time I go to bed, and when I wake up in the morning. Especially in the winter time, people must wear warm clothes. In conclusion, all the reasons above are my important things to keep people healthy and have a long life.

Chong Lee is originally from Thailand.

Mother
Anonymous, Blaine

I remember my mother, her name was Rukia. Every time I wake up, I remember her because I loved her. She was important and although she died, she gave me gifts. She taught me about getting married and taking care of my kids and husband. Some people don't do that. Right now, I'm married and have six children. I remember everything my mother taught me. I will always remember her and never will forget her.

Smells from My Country

Dorian Salazar, Minneapolis

Today I want to introduce to you the smells from my country, Guatemala. If you like to travel, you should consider going to Guatemala, where you can feel the variety of smells we have, depending on the region you are visiting. If you to Antigua, Guatemala, you can smell the flowers, especially roses and corozo. A corozo is like a flower seed from the palm tree. If you go to the North, you will have the jungle smell and you can enjoy the combination of many different kinds of trees and wild animals, too. If you prefer the sea smell, you can go to the South and enjoy the beach or fishing, too; but if you love the coffee, you can go to the East where people grow the top coffee. Or if you like the cows and drink the fresh and pure milk, you can go to the West and you can smell the corn, onions, and tomatoes, too. Also you can enjoy and smell our many kinds of flowers we have all the time, no matter if it is winter or summer time. It is the reason why we have a slogan: "The Country of the Eternal Spring."

Dorian Salazar is 44 years old and is originally from Guatemala.

Life in a New Country

Elpidio de Jesus Cruz, Minneapolis

I am happy for crossing the border. She is a new country. I am sad for my family. I miss the land and my brothers. I think it is good working, sending money for my family in Mexico. They can buy food and clothes, pay bills, energy and electricity.

In the farm, when we finished work, we played cards and played soccer. On a Saturday, we would go to town for shopping for food, chips, snacks and soda. Sometimes I would buy one beer to drink, only in dinner or in lunch.

Three months I worked in North Carolina, harvesting tobacco and potatoes. It was heavy, very heavy work. Now my life is nice. I have my daughter. We play, watch movies, cartoons, and go shopping on the weekend for food and toys, and sometimes clothes or other things.

Elpidio de Jesus Cruz is originally from Mexico.

About My Senses and Tastes in My Country

Gerardo Alarcón, Minneapolis

I smell a lot of coffee in this plantation. This place in the farm is very nice for me because I was born here many years ago. In this place I see many sights in the sky, since morning is still night. For example, I know when it's going to rain. I have a good ear and I hear sounds long distant. I hear the music of my small radio that accompanies me all moments in the farm. I like tropical or Latin music of a different country. I feel very happy, like in the beginning. I feel very near to my family: my parents, brothers, sisters, nephews, nieces and many friends and neighbors.

Gerardo Alarcón is originally from Colombia.

Rachel Hakanson, Buffalo

Summer, My Favorite Season

Anonymous, Minneapolis

My favorite season is summer. Summer is very beautiful because there are many different things like the sun in the lake and different flowers. They grow many kinds of fruit everywhere. The weather here is very warm and makes me remember when I was living in Guatemala. In this country, my family likes to go swimming at Lake Cedar. I like summer because the weather is like my hometown is all the time. Summer is also a nice time to catch up on outdoor activities like play soccer, run, and walk with my family. I think the summer in Minnesota is extremely wonderful.

Working Retirement Time

Messan Megnassasnh, Saint Paul

I believe that working retirement should start at 55 of age instead of 65. We all have experienced how hard it is working at a younger age. Let us think about when people get older and are working. I also believe that, approximately 60 to 80% of old workers are victims of sicknesses and are dying between 70 and 80 years of age. As a result, many of them can't fight off illness because their body started being too weak. For some people after their retirement just started at age 65, they found themselves at nursing homes.

From these experiences, it shows that many workers don't enjoy their retirement time and 401k money. At 55 years of age, every worker should start their retirement, and enjoy their life when they're not too old. This is very important. Also, some elderly men and women need some time to relax, stay with their grandchildren; talk to them, and teach them about their future life.

We also need to be retired at 55 years of age to vacate the offices and give jobs to the next generation and not leave them at home unemployed. Workers retiring at 55 years of age instead of 65 would solve many health problems and avoid early body fatigues, and people could enjoy a little bit of their lifetime before 70 or 80 years of age.

Yer Lee, Saint Paul

Untitled

Bernadino, Saint Paul

During my first weeks and days in the U.S., it was the first time I saw snowfall. It fell for a long time. I couldn't find work for three or four months. I was very worried, but when the spring and summer came all went nice. I knew the lakes, the parks, and many different places. Now it is good. I miss my family, but I am glad because I can help them.

Bernadino is originally from Mexico.

Traditions

Memories From My Grandmother
Lilia Elias, Shakopee

I remember when I was a child in my little town of Tuxpan, Mexico, we celebrated the Virgin on the Talpa on February 2nd. I liked this holiday.

My grandmother had the tradition every year to put an altar of honor in her home because she was grateful for the miracles from the Virgin. She made the altar's roof with palm branches. Inside the altar, she decorated it with flowers and different colored papers. In the center, she put the image of the Virgin. People went to pray and sing for nine nights before February 2nd. My grandmother gave everyone punch made of soda and wine. This punch helped to refine the voice for singing.

The last day my whole family made tamales with pork and chicken for our family, friends and neighbors. Some aunts prepared the masa for tortillas, others cut the vegetables and cooked while others made champurrado, a hot chocolate with masa. My cousins and I washed the leaves of corn and tied tamales.

Everyone participated in preparing the tamales. Even more important, we were together with my grandmother. In the night, we went on grandmother's roof and watched all the people arrive. Everyone sang to the Virgin and we gave tamales and champurrado to all. It was a moment that I will always remember.

Lilia Elias is originally from Mexico. She is the youngest of three sisters and one brother. She finished high school in Mexico and came to the United States eight years ago, where she studied family literacy. Lilia's husband and two children are the engines that drive her. She is excited and grateful for the opportunity to share some of her childhood memories.

Lilia Elias, Shakopee

Hmong Traditions and Customs
Lee M Xiong, Brooklyn Park

In Laos, the Hmong lived in the highlands (mountains); it is beautiful with lush vegetation. During the Vietnam War, the Hmong were forced to move from place to place. In the end, they separated and immigrated to different countries. However, the Hmong maintains their self-identity by keeping their language, traditions and customs.

There are three Hmong subgroups named by the general appearance of their clothes. These subgroups also have different dialects and all live in different regions of Laos. There is the Green Hmong (Hmong Youag). Traditionally, the Green Hmong women would dye their clothes with delicate designs and different colors. The White Hmong (Hmong Der), the women traditionally wore clothes made of un-died hemp fibers so their skirts would always be white. Sometimes the White Hmong women would put designs on their skirts and would wear a money belt in reverse applique with embroidered detailing fringed with beads and Laotian coins and silver bells. Last but not least, there are the Stripe Hmong (Hmong Du or Chai). Traditionally, they wore long black sleeve shirts with stripes half way down the sleeves to show they are from the Stripe Hmong Clan. As you can see, the Hmong people were able to physically differentiate each other by their style of clothing.

All three subgroups do share in some of the same traditions such as; at the end of the harvest season and going into the New Year, the Hmong people have a big New Year celebration (Noj Peb Caug). Hmong families from different villages would all gather together in their finest clothes to celebrate and partake in the festivities. For unmarried young men and women, this was a time for them to meet their potential wife or husband. This was also a time for them to participate in a tradition called ball tossing. The men would form a line and the women would form their own line across from each other and toss a soft ball made of cloth and sing to each other. The ball is a symbol of a relationship between a young man and woman. The ball tossing allows them to get to know each other and the ball tossing may continue for days. If these young adults find a match, many of the couples usually marry following the end of the New Year celebration.

Lee. M Xiong is 30 years old and is originally from Laos.

Spring
Zaman Albdeer, Coon Rapids

There is one day in spring that means a lot to me. Actually, it is a special time and we have several names for the date, March 21 in Iraq. It is called "Eid Alduujal," which means the holiday begins, "Eid Alshgrai," which means holiday for the tree, or even "Eid Norooz" for Kurdish people, which means a new day, or a new light. This holiday is celebrated by people in the southern—and especially the northern—part of Iraq. Usually families go to gardens or a big park on this day. The history behind this day may be due to the observance of the vernal equinox by the ancient Sumerians, who were some of the first to celebrate this day. We wait impatiently for this day every year. We prepare and plan programs, such as eating and dancing. We also wear special clothing. The Kurds in northern Iraq wear amazing clothes with bright colors. The Kurds dance in the street to Kurdish music. At this time, the fruits of the Buckthorn and Lotus trees open and display the Elias, Alaraezki, and Jasmine flowers. This landscape has magic eyes and you know God has created the magnificence of nature.

Zaman Albdeer is originally from Iraq.

Peaceful
Halima, Minneapolis

I am Muslim. I've been here 13 years. I have never been in jail.

I grew up in Kenya. I was the first child my mother had, and now I live in the United States. I'd like the world to stop fighting. Everybody is the same. If you have any culture, it's ok. You don't have to celebrate Ramadan or Christmas. If it's not your culture or religion, then it's ok, don't worry about it.

Customs
Abrehet Haileselassie, Saint Paul

In my country we have many customs. On Ashenda we eat doro wet, enjera, and heshity anbash. We get together with family and listen to Tigrinia music.

Women in Islam
Houda Elaatabi, Apple Valley

A majority of people have the wrong idea about human rights in Islam, especially women's rights. This false idea is a result of lack of information about how Islam truly respects the woman. Islam came to bring justice to all mankind, including woman. While women were treated no better than slaves with no rights in past centuries, Islam is the first religion that provided inheritance rights to women. Muslims believe Adam and Eve were created from the same soul, so man and woman should be equal in all aspects. There is no decree in Islam which forbids women from seeking employment, and there is no restriction on benefiting from women's exceptional talent in any field. The history of Muslims is rich with women of great achievements in all walks of life. Personally, I know many women in Muslim society with the same high status as men. Islamic women play big roles in helping the community in many fields such as medicine, education and business.

Islam considers a woman's role as a mother and a wife as the most sacred and essential one. No one, maid nor baby-sitter, can possibly take the mother's place. It is a noble and vital role, which largely shapes the future of nations.

Islam requires modesty in both men and women. Woman should wear the cover, Hijab, so she can be judged by her mind and personality, not by appearance.

Women in Islam cannot be forced to marry anyone without their consent. They have the right to choose their husbands and keep their last name even after marriage. They also have the right to seek divorce and custody of young children. Also, a woman should be supported by her husband even if she is rich already. Moreover, her share and dowry are completely hers and no one can make any claim to them, including her father and her husband.

Last but not least, Islam honors a woman through all her life's statuses, as daughter, sister, wife or mother, and taking care of her is one of its commandments.

Housework
Luta Tshihamba, Saint Louis Park

In my country, the Congo, a woman has chief command of the house. She works with her children and the relatives living with her in the house. Some women work in the fields, some in the markets and others in the public and private sectors. When they come back home, men's duty stays behind and they come home to relax. Culturally, they are not supposed to work in the kitchen.

Women work in the kitchen with their helpers to speed up the work as a cooperative. Soon the food will be ready on the table. After they finish eating, the women and their helpers will clean up and do the rest of chores in homes.

When I came to America, all my helpers stayed in the Congo. I found myself alone. As a batik artist, if I start a project, I have to continue working on it until I finish that part; so the dye would not dry before I finish the first part of work. It takes many hours of working, which I would stay up until very late in the night to finish. I must concentrate and focus on the object so I don't make a mistake. Above that I started school and had a lot to learn. I was very tired all the time. After my husband saw that I was suffering, he changed his mind about this cultural behavior; he helps me a lot with the cooking. Sometimes he cleans the dishes and does other things around the house. He irons his clothes. This has been a big break away from the cultural behavior. I appreciate his support and wish that other Congolese men would do the same.

Luta Tshihamba is originally from Congo.

My Childhood
Nashwa Ibrahim, Fridley

My childhood was my favorite time for me. When I think about my childhood, it makes me miss that time in my life. My dad, my mom, my sister and I were a happy family. Now, my dad is an old man with white hair, a white moustache, and his smile is very bright. He is a very energetic person and very active. Also he is a morning person who enjoys the fresh air. He used to wake up early when he would hear the azan. Azan is loud in the sky and it means it's time to pray.

When I was young, I could see most of the people rushing to pray. Also I could hear geese, chickens, and hummingbirds. The geese would say "cuk cuk," and the chickens were clucking looking for their mothers; and the ducks waddled down the road with baby ducks behind them. I could smell the garden plants, sunflowers, roses, and rosemary. Hummingbirds and canaries filled the trees with music. After prayer, I saw farmers going back to their farms, teachers going to school and students following them.

Some stores would start to make falafel, beans, and bread for breakfast. My dad use to make us breakfast after he came home and it would help everyone wake up. He would rub my back; it was a good feeling. Then I'd take a shower, put on my clothes and eat breakfast with my family. Then I'd meet up with my friend, Hanna, to go to school. We enjoyed smelling the fresh air and flowers. I miss that life a lot.

Nashwa Ibrahim is originally from Egypt.

My Native Country
Tuoi Nguyen, Brooklyn Park

I am from Vietnam. My country is very beautiful. There are 15 million people, who are very nice and friendly. When we have free time we like to talk, swim and party. There are two seasons in my country, summer and spring. The best time to visit my country is in spring (from December through March). Typical foods in my country are white rice, spring rolls and pho (made with noodles, meat and salad). Some typical jobs that people have are small food businesses, garden work and building houses.

One problem that my country has is no freedom and few jobs. One thing that is better in my native country than in the U.S. is that it is warmer and we never have snow. One thing that is better in the U.S. than in my country is freedom, people have jobs and go to schools and food is cheaper. What I miss most about my country is the food, weather, my friends and the beaches. One interesting thing about my native country is everyone rides a motorcycle.

Tuoi Nguyen is originally from Viet Nam.

Thanksgiving
Donis, Coon Rapids

Thanksgiving Day is an American holiday, but the good thing about this holiday is when you come to America you can enjoy it because they have something very interesting about it. The interesting thing about this celebration is you can celebrate any way you want to. Also, this is an important thing because you can remind yourself about people who are important to you. Thanksgiving sometimes reminds you that friends and family are important to be around.

The Pilgrims and Native Americans came up with a very special holiday. And I like it too, because when we gather we eat and laugh and I see very incredible blessings and I do thank God for everything he gives us. When I start to go shopping for Thanksgiving food, I make sure I list everything I need. I like to buy summer squash, sweet potatoes, lettuce, tomato, cucumber, corn, Bok Choy, and scallions. I also buy fruit too; strawberries, cantaloupe, papaya, watermelon and a lot of other things I like to prepare. Then I start to cook the turkey; after I put the turkey in the oven, then I start to cut up the salad and fruit. When I finish cutting them, I make sure to wrap them and put them in the refrigerator.

So I begin to set up my table and clean my living room. My kids do wonderful work because they help me too. They clean their room and then go to take a bath when they are done cleaning up. So I am thankful for them because they help me a lot. It is good to thank God for whatever you have or own. For me, I thank God each day for my life and for everything God gave me. Also I am thankful for friends and family and everybody around me. God is always there for me when I need it and I am happy when I see my friends and family come together!

Donis is originally from South Sudan.

Homesick
Thor, Corcoran

I was born in a small village in Laos. I grew up in a big family; I have five brothers, three sisters, two brother-in laws, three sister-in laws, and seven nieces. My family owns a store that sells traditional clothes from my country. I have always helped my parents sew, since I was ten years old. Every weekend I went to the store to help my mother and sisters. My family was busy all the time. We did not have much time to be together, but we always had dinner together.

Every time my family had dinner it was a good time for our family to spend time together. We had many different things to tell each other, especially my brother who always had very funny stories to tell, so my family always had fun. But times passed by so fast. I graduated from high school and then attended a University in Vientiane. It was very far from my home, it took ten hours by bus to the University. After that, I only came back to visit my family twice a year, during the Lao New Year and during summer break. I studied at the University for three years and then I got married. My husband lived in the United States, so I moved here to live with him. That is why I am here learning English and I am very happy that I am able to write this letter about my family back in Laos. I still miss my family all the time. I hope that one day I will be able to go back to my country and spend a lot of time with my family.

Thor is 21 years old and is originally from Laos.

Omar Kazem, Luverne

Folktale of Chinese New Year
Wenjing Jiang, Saint Paul

In ancient times, China had a mystery story about a monster. This monster had a pair of horns and it was very violent. It lived in the bottom of the sea and climbed on the land every New Year's Eve. It ate domestic animals and hurt people. This monster is called "Nian." Every New Year's Eve when Nian came, all the people of the villages used to run away deep into the mountains to avoid Nian.

However, one New Year's Eve was very different. When the people of the village were preparing to leave, an old man who looked like a beggar from another village came to the village. He had a silver beard, leaned on a crutch and carried a bag. Some people were closing windows and doors; some were packing suitcases. Everyone was concentrating on their own things, and nobody noticed the old man. Only an old woman gave the old man some food and tried to persuade him to move to the mountains as soon as possible because Nian would come and damage the village. But the old man looked very poised and he told the old woman if she allowed him to stay at her home one night, he would kick out the monster. The old woman couldn't believe him; she just left her house and ran away.

Time steadily passed by, until midnight. Then Nian came to the village. The monster felt that the ambience of the village was so different than before. Nian saw the eastern side of the village where the old woman's house looked strange—a large red paper was stuck on the door and inside the house looked bright. Nian saw the situation and started shaking and roaring and felt angry and stared at the door awhile, then fluttered to the door. Suddenly, he heard some loud noise from inside of the house. Nian began shaking and couldn't go near the door anymore. Nian was afraid of the color red and the noise of fireworks. At that moment, the old woman's door was opened; an old man wearing red clothes was laughing loudly and standing inside of the house. Nian was scared and ran away immediately. When the villagers came back, they found the village was peaceful and they were so surprised. This is why the Chinese celebrate New Year.

Wenjing Jiang is originally from China.

My Home Country Myanmar
Justina, Saint Paul

I want to introduce everyone to my country. The Republic of the Union of Myanmar is a country in Southeast Asia. Myanmar is bordered by Bangladesh, India, China, Laos and Thailand. Myanmar consists of 14 provinces that include seven states and seven divisions. Myanmar has a tropical climate with three distinct seasons: the hot season, the rainy season and the winter season.

Nowadays, the capital of Myanmar is Naypyidaw, which is located in Mandalay Division. Myanmar is rich in history, culture, customs and traditions. The most famous place in Myanmar is Bagan, which has a lot of ancient buildings and pagodas. A pagoda is cone-shaped monumental structure built in memory of Buddha. Bupaya Pagoda, Shwesandaw Pagoda, Minglazedi Pagoda and Shwezigon

Pagoda are the most famous pagodas in Myanmar. The second famous place is Inle Lake where the floating island is located on the lake. In addition, there are also nice, beautiful beaches where people can enjoy on their vacation time. The main religion in Myanmar is Buddhism. People in Myanmar are very generous, hospitable and good natured. As a tradition, they teach the young people to respect and obey the elderly. In conclusion, I hope if you visit my country, you are satisfied and you will enjoy your time.

Tradition
Ana Perez, Osseo

My favorite tradition is July 4th. On that day in the morning, I like to go to the lake with my children for swimming and make a barbecue at the park. At night time, I like to go see the fireworks. I like to be together with my family. I enjoy all day with my children every year. That park is located in Maple Grove. The kind of food I like to make on that day is barbecue, with rice and salad, and I bring it to the park for my family.

Ana Perez is 30 years old and is originally from El Salvador.

Benkei Revenge
Courtney Mason, Minneapolis

On July 27, 1900, in the southern part of Japan, a great warrior named Benkei was born. At the age of five, Benkei was watching his father named Sensei, who was also a great fighter, practicing and fighting at the great Olympics every year. When Benkei was six, his father taught him all the techniques that he knew. Benkei caught on very well, and it only took him one week to know what his father taught him. On one hot summer day, a great invasion happened in his hometown. The northern part of Japan invaded the southern part. When the invasion was done, Benkei found out that his father was dead. Benkei swore to his father that he would get the person who was involved in his death.

Benkei started a group of people who were 21 and up who were willing to help fight for Benkei's revenge. Benkei was the youngest person ever to fight in the war. A month went by and word got out that the people responsible for the invasion of Benkei's hometown were the Wolf Chain Soldiers, and the person who shot Benkei's father was a man named John Smith. Benkei declared war. It was a hard battle for both sides. After March 27, 1927, Benkei's side won. When the war ended, Benkei settled down on the East Side of Japan, and in 1933 when Benkei was 33, he got married. He ended up teaching his three kids what his father taught him when he was young. When Benkei was 57, he opened up a gym in Tokyo and named it after his father, the great Sensei.

The image of the Benkei Warrior is used with permission from the Minneapolis Institute of Arts

Halloween
Lang Nguyen, Saint Paul

Last Monday night many kids came to my outside door and knocked and said "trick or treat." I opened the door and gave them many candies. After that another group of kids came and they knocked, too. I gave again. After many times I didn't have any more candies. I turned off the light and went to bed. They didn't knock up to 11:30. I think now the children went back home. After that I think next year I'll buy more candy. I'll give very much. I'll be happier than now. I was a little sad because I didn't have a lot of candies and because I love the kids.

Lang Nguyen is 64 years old and is originally from Vietnam.

New Year in Iran
Elham, Apple Valley

New Year in Iran is different from the American celebration. New Year starts on March 20 or 21. The whole family puts items on the table. The items are "S" words meaning life. Sabzeh means green plant, which represents rebirth. Samanu means juice of germinating wheat or malt mixed with flour. Serkeh means vinegar, which represents age and patience. Sekeh means coins, which represents prosperity and wealth. Sa'at means clock, which represent time to live. Sir means garlic, which represent medicine. Sib means apple, which represents health and beauty. Scripture means Ghoran, which represents God with us. Ayeneh means mirror, which represents the images and reflections of Creation. Sonbol means hyacinth, which represent happiness. Fish means life. Candle means enlightenment and happiness. Basket of egg means fertility. Dry fruit of the Lotus tree means love. Sumac berries means the color of sunrise. The family comes together and the elders bring money for the family. We eat special food made by women of the family. It's usually rice and fish. This is a favorite holiday in my country.

The Importance of Camels in Somali Community

Khadar Hassan Ali (Aloore), Columbia Heights

The Somali are one of the multi-state communities of Eastern Africa. Somalia is their main state, but they also occupy a large part of Djibouti, northern Kenya and the Southern Ethiopia Rangelands, loosely referred to as arid and semi-arid lands. Camel is the premier livestock of the Somalis that is uniquely qualified to provide sustenance and sustainability in the Somali ecology. The importance of the camel for the Somalis arises primarily from its provision of milk and meat within the subsistence economy, and its use as a beast of burden for transporting milk to the market, water from wells, and household belongings when the families move to new areas.

Basically, camel milk is staple food for Somali nomads, and is considered a whole food. Camel milk is low in fat and sugar; but rich in iron, potassium and Vitamin C, It also stays fresh longer than any other livestock milk. Camels are usually milked twice a day—morning and evening. If the camel is very productive, it takes at least two men to milk it.

Meat is another important source of food from camels. In general, Somali camel herders never slaughter a camel for meat unless compelled by circumstances. Herders will slaughter a camel, especially a male calf, for meat during periods of drought. Other occasions when camels may be slaughtered are during very important religious ceremonies and weddings, or when camels are either crippled by predators or seriously injured.

Apart from their value in terms of milk and meat, and as transport animals, camels are prized according to their role in traditional social relations, e.g. the payment of bride wealth and compensation of injured parties in tribal feuds. In the case of tribal feuds, camels are the only means of payment of blood money to the lineage of the deceased. Of all the domestic livestock they raise, camels are the most highly valued, and have practical uses in their vast oral literature.

In fact, There is no other community in the world where the camel plays such a pivotal role in the local economy and culture as in the Somali community.

Khadar Hassan Ali (Aloore) is originally from Somali.

Vietnamese New Year

Ngoc Tuyet Truong, Columbia Heights

In my country, the New Year is the best holiday in the year. It's celebrated at least three days. In custom, most people begin to prepare everything a few months ahead.

The New Year begins between late January and early February, it depends on the lunar calendar. It is the most important festival of the Vietnamese people. The New Year is a time for people who have worked wherever come back home for family reunion and festival. This reason is why a lot of Vietnamese people are living in the world return to my country for New Year.

In my house, my mother decorated a big branch of apricot blossoms with many small colorful things between two kumquat trees; she put them next to a big table. It was covered with a beautiful tablecloth. My parents placed a big table the front of the altar. On the altar, she decorated a vase of flowers, two watermelons, fried-fruits, fruits, cookies, a sticky-rice cake, two red candles and a censer with incenses. When my mother finished cooking food, she put them on the table: eggrolls, hotpot full of seafood, roast duck, pork stew with hard boil eggs, fried rice, fried sticky rice cakes and some drinks.

When my parents celebrated ancestor worship, first they burned the incenses sticks to pray for Land Genie, because in my country people had believed that Land Genie had permission from their ancestors to come to homes for reunion. Second, my parents (with incenses sticks) prayed for my ancestors to bring my family good luck and happiness. Third, family members followed my parent's ritual. My family had celebrated for about an hour. Next, my family burned the symbolic papers of money, gold, clothes and something for my ancestors. After that, my family and relatives ate dinner together. Then, my mother washed dishes, cleaned the house and finished by 6:30 p.m. Finally, my family gathered in the living room, ate cookies and fried fruits, drank tea, listened to the New Year's music and waited for the New Year come.

Now, my mother is not living. When the New Year comes, I remember my mother, how she was busy, and some families' difficulty in my country for New Year. I miss her so much. I think I am very lucky because I grew up with a wonderful mother.

My Favorite Holiday
Carlos, Brooklyn Park

My favorite holiday is Christmas Day because I'm from a poor family, and when I was growing up my parents couldn't buy me what I wanted. They bought me what they could. I remember when I was ten years old I wanted a bicycle with all my heart. And they couldn't buy it for me, but now I appreciate what they did for me. Now I can buy what my daughter wants for Christmas, and that makes me very happy. And that's why Christmas Day is my favorite day.

Introduction to the Story of Abdi Ali
Ogaso H. Omar, Minneapolis

When storms come across the trees, the hot air is filled with sand and no one ventures out, it is a good time to tell the story of Abdi. He was from the poorest hut in the village, but he rose to power and became the leader of his clan. This is his story.

Abdi lived in the north of Somalia a long time ago. He lived near the edge of the Shebelle River. He was a bright thirteen-year-old boy with a strong, healthy body. His father was a brave man who died during a famine in the village. His father tried to save the lives of his people by fighting a giant lion. Abdi's father was crushed to death during the struggle, but he killed the lion and deer, and the meat from the deer kept the people from starving. Abdi was his only son and he lived alone with his mother. Abdi was a hunter, and he knew how to kill deer.

Ogaso H. Omar is originally from Somalia.

Hmong Clans
Wa Thao, Minneapolis

Many Hmong clans live in the world, but Hmong cannot marry within their own clan group. A marriage partner must be found from another clan. For example, a man in the clan name Thao cannot marry a woman in the clan Thao. However, they are allowed to marry someone from a different clan or their mother's clan. For example, the children of a brother and sister can marry because they would be from different clans.

Traditionally, when a boy wants to marry with a girl he will make his intentions clear and will snatch her during daylight or at night at any opportunity that is appropriate.

Before the boy will snatch her, the boy must give a gift to the girl. Then he has the right to marry her. After a couple of days, the boy can snatch the girl to become his wife. The boy's relatives are sent to inform them of the whereabouts of their daughter and her safety. Before the new couple enters the groom's house, the father performs a blessing ritual. The father of the household moves a chicken in a circular motion around the couple's head. The girl is not allowed to visit her parent's house for three days. Then the parents of the groom prepare the first wedding feast for the guests. The wedding is usually two days.

The couple returns to the house of the bride's family at the end of the first wedding feast and spends the night in preparation for the next day. On the second day, the family of the bride prepares a second wedding feast at their home. After that, they are done with their wedding. The groom and the bride come back home and live together forever.

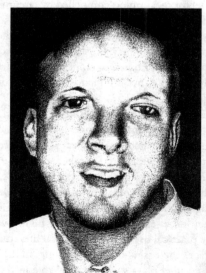

*Self-portrait drawing by
Arthur Duran, Buffalo*

Memories

Wat Tham Krabok
Ka Chang, Mounds View

Hmong Wat Tham Krabok is a small poor village in Thailand. The Hmong lived there from the year 1995 until 2005. It was a beautiful place with many people and with mountains surrounding the village. This place will always be in my heart. All our houses were made from coconut trees and fresh bamboo. At night, we dropped the wax from burning candles on our table and then stood the lighted candles in the hot wax because we didn't have any electricity at night. I liked to watch the stars at night, feel the wind pass me and hear the crickets cry. In the mornings, I could hear the chickens crowing. I also heard the woodpeckers crying and flying around the tops of trees through the blue sky. There were lots of children running and jumping everywhere. I could see the smoke from cooking fires billowing out of each house. In the morning it was always party cloudy, but by eight o'clock, the sunshine came and all the clouds disappeared. It was very hot there in the afternoon. You could see the blue sky so clearly. I would sit on a wood chair, sewing clothes to sell, under a tree near my house. I listened to Hmong music. I also saw the shadows of the trees and leafs falling and even the shadow of myself. I liked to look at my shadow beside me. Sometimes sitting there alone, listening to some music, it made tears come out of my eyes. I hated to see myself cry. When I would feel bad, I would climb to the top of the mountain. On the mountain, I could see monkeys jumping from tree to tree and Kea birds playing. I would feel better at that moment. I would let the cool wind pass me. Right now, no more people live at Wat Tham Krabok because all the Hmong people came to the United States. The Thai people didn't want the Hmong people to live there anymore. Many people from the United Nations came to our village and they talked to our parents about going to America. I miss it a lot and it still lives in my heart forever. I left everything, every moment—good, bad and sad. I left even the happy there. Now I feel like I am so far away from Wat Tham Krabok.

Ka Chang was born in Laos and went to live in Wat Tham Krabok when she was nine years old. She came with her family to America in April 2005 when she was 18. Today she is married and works as a personal care assistant. Ka studies at Metro North in Blaine, working towards her diploma.

My First Time Scuba Diving
Yung S. Yee, Minnetonka

Soon after I took my first scuba lessons, my friend and I went to Cozumel, Mexico for a diving trip. On the first dive, I noticed a sharp hissing sound coming from a leaking air tank on the boat. I was hoping that the guide would be nice enough to use that tank, but he didn't. I got it. I checked the gauge and it read 2000 lbs. of air. I jumped in the water. The water was so clear. I saw many kinds of beautiful fish and coral. My friend saw a king crab in a narrow cave and caught it. He handed it to me and I held it near the crab's two claws so it wouldn't pinch me. By then we were 80 feet down. The scenery was so beautiful. I checked the air gauge. It read 500 lbs. A minute later it read 300 lbs. I thought to myself, "I should go up soon." My breathing was a little difficult and I knew what that meant. I signaled to my friend that we have to go up. He couldn't understand so I pushed the gauge in his face and he saw it read 0 lbs. My friend pushed his mouthpiece into my mouth. By then I was so panicky. I was all set to give up my life. Then I saw a bright light under the water. Soon I realized I was on the surface and I was breathing and coughing constantly. Even with all that commotion going on, I held onto that crab. The dive boat spotted us and came over to pick us up. I threw the crab onto the boat and my friend asked "What was that?" I told him it was the crab he caught. He couldn't believe his ears. I got into the boat and my legs were shaking. I couldn't even stand up because I went through so much.

The guide prepared lunch with our crab and everybody loved it. They all thanked us but no one knew what had happened to get that crab, except the two of us.

Experience with My First Child
Lourdes H., Brooklyn Park

When I lived in Mexico I had my first child. I remember one day my little child, maybe he was four or five years old, and he liked to play with an old tricycle. Sometimes the seat fell and sometimes he played with the tricycle anyway. I didn't see when he took it—I only saw when he tried to carry the tricycle to the other side of the patio. The tricycle didn't have the seat anymore, but it had a little hole and he cut himself on his finger. It looked bad because it was bleeding. I was scared because my mom usually helped me to take care of my child, but that day she wasn't there. So I took my child to the hospital. The doctor said the stitches might make it look worse. Maybe after that the scar will look too big so it is better if you take care of his cut by washing and putting alcohol on and keeping it clean. So now he is 18 years old almost, and he finishes high school this year. So when I see his finger I feel sad because he has the little scar on his finger. I learned if we have any old toys, throw it away.

A Happy Memory
Ilwaad, Minneapolis

I was born in Mogadishu in 1988. When I was 11 years old, I went to Nairobi. I didn't see my mom for years. I miss her. My aunt took care of me because she loves me. I thought I would see my mother someday. Then my mother sent my visa. I felt very happy when I saw my mother again 11 years later.

A Very Embarrassing Moment
Sharon Shuck, Duluth

I am a senior citizen, and frugal is my middle name. I am a hoarder and tight with the purse strings. I have always been this way.

My kitchenette lacked storage space so I used the oven as a hiding place to stash stockpiled canned goods. While preparing for a Thanksgiving feast, I cleaned and popped the turkey into the hot oven. Two hours later, after a short nap, I heard a loud bang from the kitchen. I ran to the kitchen and gasped at the sight of the turkey on the floor under the table.

A gallon can of pumpkin had exploded in the oven. The kitchen smelled of pumpkin, and the contents of the can were scattered on the walls, ceiling fan, floor, refrigerator, and sink. The stove was another sight. The oven door was bent and had blown off the hinges. The racks were mangled.

I immediately called the fire department. They had many comments and laughed, asking if I was serving turkey and pumpkin. It's a good thing I had renter's insurance. Being frugal does not always pay.

A Scary Experience
Lishu Hickok, Owatonna

I had a scary experience when I was five years old. At midnight, my mother was taking care of my younger sister when I shouted - hungry!

My mother told me that I needed to go out and buy food by myself, so I got some money to go out. It was dark outside. When I was walking to the corner, I saw many flashing lights in front of me. Before, I heard about a ghost story, so I thought I saw a ghost in front of me. I was very scared; I cried and ran quickly back home. I didn't buy anything, but I forgot I was still hungry.

The experience frightened me, and I never went outside at midnight by myself until I grew up. As it turned out, the flashing lights were fire flies.

Lishu Hickok is originally from China.

My Life in Laos
Panyia Vang, Saint Paul

This is about my life in Laos. I saw the mountains. It's beautiful in Laos. The Hmong people like to farm. They like to raise cows, chicken, ducks, horses, and pigs. They live high in the mountains. They are poor, but they live a happy life. In the summer, the Hmong village and the mountains are beautiful because the plants are green and many flowers are beautiful. Farmers plant everything that is green and very beautiful.

A Painful Memory
Eh Kaw Htoo, Saint Paul

I want my descendants to know about the night when I had to escape from the Burmese soldiers while they were attacking my camp at midnight. Most of the people were sleeping, and none of the people knew that such a thing would happen. All of the people woke up and ran out of the camp when they heard the frightful sound of guns. When I woke up, my mother held my right hand tightly so she wouldn't lose me as we ran. We ran as fast as we could with a lot of other people. We were like a group of buffalo being chased by a tiger. Many people fell on the ground and were stepped on by other people because it was dark and people were hurrying and scared. When my mother and I ran in the field, suddenly we both fell on the ground. Before I could get up, a heavy metal box belonging to someone else fell on my left leg and broke it. I was screaming and crying because it was painful. My mom couldn't do anything to help me and could not get any help from others, so she carried me to some bushes to hide. Many other people were hiding there, too. My mom put me down there and tried to cover my mouth with her hand so I couldn't scream. I had to suffer pain for a while until the Burmese soldiers left the camp. Then, a few people carried me back to the camp and took me to the hospital. My leg got better, and I could walk well after a couple of months. But I will never forget how horrible and frightening it was to be a refugee in that camp in Thailand.

Eh Kaw Htoo is originally from Burma.

In Memory of Grandma Calenders
Lien Nguyen, Plymouth

Her name was Eleanor Calenders, but my son always called her "Gra-ma Lender" with the incorrect, cute accent of a three-year-old boy who was learning how to talk. In July 1975, we arrived in the United States after the fall of South Viet Nam. Mrs. Calenders was the caretaker of our apartment in Brooklyn Center. This was my first home in our new country. I remember, as we entered the building, a lovely seventy year old Eleanor welcomed us with a sweet smile and with an open heart. Thirty-six years have passed, but I've never forgotten the many ways that she helped me adapt to my new life in the United States.

Today, sitting in my living room watching the snow gently falling outside, I am reminded of the Vietnamese New Year that is coming on January 23, 2012. This is the Year of the Dragon which represents strength and power. Mrs. Calenders didn't have either one of those, but she had a warm heart flowing like a stream to a river. I hope the new year will bring justice and love to everyone in my homeland.

Lien Nguyen is originally from Vietnam.

Still Going
Anonymous, Minneapolis

Our civil war started on a Sunday in 1991, it was sorrowful. When the war started I was afraid of the sound of guns. We got confused because we never saw fighting before. Many people died and were not buried. Many people fled to Kenya and Ethiopia. Somalian people ran to all parts of the world. Some of them don't want the government because they looted many houses and farms. So many want to see peace yet our war is still going on.

This is One Memory
Ahmed, Minneapolis

I am from Somali and I grew-up in Somalia. I moved to Addis Ababa, Ethiopia in 2006. I lived there for four years. I did not have an education because I was scared. I came to Minnesota in 2011. I saw a lot of snow. It was the first time for me. I'm very happy because I live in Minneapolis with my wife.

Memories of Home
Nath Xiong, Brooklyn Center

I have many memories of home and my memories make me miss home a lot. When I lived in Laos, I was going to school in the capital city of Vientiane. It was expected of us to further our education. Although, it took several years before I would be able to come back home, I would always think about what I use to do and plan new things for when I returned home.

I have always planned that when I was finished with college, I would go back home to my village, get married to a nice girl and live with my parents. Basically, I want to start a new life and spend time with my parents. That was my dream because I never had time with them when I was going to school. Being my parents' son I've always wanted to become successful enough to take care of all their needs. I want my parent to retire and rest for everything they've done and given to me. At least that was my plan, until I met my wife and my plans changed.

In order to be with my wife, I had to move to the United States, because that's where she lived. Being in a different country, especially one that is so different from my home country, made me miss home that much more. Although I've made a temporary home in the United States, plans to return to my home in Laos still remain in my heart.

Nath Xiong is originally from Laos.

Cambodia
Dyna Sok, Saint Cloud

My name is Dyna Sok, and I am from Southeast Cambodia. In Cambodia, there is a small city called Pouthisat. There are many people in Cambodia. The population is about 15,000,000. I am from Phnom Penh, the capital. Phnom Penh is in the east on the Mekong River. Phnom Penh is a big, busy city. Cambodia is hot in the summer and warm in the winter. The people in my country are busy, happy, and friendly

My Recent Trip
Wilson Bohada, Austin

At Christmas, I went to a place that I miss a lot. Recently, I went back to my home country and I was very excited. The last time that I went to Colombia was three years ago. For that reason, I enjoyed visiting my family so much and sharing with them. Especially during Christmas and New Year's Eve, because it is a good time to share with family and friends.

My recent trip to Colombia was nice. The weather was a bit rainy, but okay. I took advantage of my visit and went to different places such as the malls, towns around Bogota D.C., and to see Christmas lights. Also, it was a good opportunity to buy some inexpensive things to take back to decorate my house. I did many activities that I have not done for a long time such as going walking. Also, it was a good opportunity to take a bus and go around the city. However, I had to stay a couple of times a long while inside the bus because of the rush hour.

Going to Colombia during Christmas is a good opportunity to be with family and friends. It is the season when everybody gets together. The days before Christmas, we get together at my aunt and uncles' houses. Besides gathering for each of the days before Christmas, my family has a big celebration for Christmas and New Year's in my grandmother's house. After Christmas and New Year's, there is a barbecue with fresh beef, corn on the cob and ripe plantain. All those things were the same as when I was young, and for that reason, I enjoyed them so much.

Another thing that I missed a lot was the food. Some of the food I can find here in the United States, but some traditional foods are impossible to find here. Colombia's food has a variety of flavors, tastes, colors, and smells that are unique. For those reasons, I enjoyed eating traditional food from my country. Moreover, when I visited my family, they pleased me with delicious food including the traditional fresh homemade fruit juice of guava, mango, suorsop, passion fruit, and banana passion fruit. Because the food was so good, I ate a lot and gained a little weight when I was in Colombia.

To be in Colombia was an opportunity to visit some places in Bogota. I enjoyed the weather, seeing the Christmas decorations, eating and drinking traditional foods and juices. Most importantly, it was a good reason to be with my family. Ultimately, I am very happy here in Minnesota, but I would like to visit my home country and my relatives more frequently.

Wilson Bohada is 31 years old and is originally from Colombia.

After 23 Years...
Victorya Sinelnikov, Plymouth

Each person remembers their childhood. Many people remember their first friends. Very few people are able to manage their childhood friendships through their whole life. There are many reasons why this is difficult.

I am from Kiev, the ancient and most beautiful city in the Ukraine. It is not close to the sea, however. My parents considered the sea air useful and took me to the Black Sea every year as a child. We rented a room at the same place every year. There was a girl who lived there that was my age. We became very good friends. Every year we impatiently waited for summer to meet again. We grew and continued to be friends—we wrote letters, visited each other and phoned each other. When we each got married, we still stayed in touch. Then I left the Ukraine. It was 23 years ago and we were lost from each other. I very often remembered my friend. I showed my children photos of her.

Suddenly, two months ago, I decided to go on "Russian Facebook." There I saw a letter from her. Now we talk every week. We have plans to acquaint our children. This is the best thing that can happen to a person! It was like we were never separated for 23 years!

Victorya Sinelnikov is originally from Ukraine.

One Day of My Life
Amina Aden, Minneapolis

One day of my life in 1991, the enemies came to attack Somalia. Everybody yelled and started running. While my family was running away, my father was out of the city. We had two nephews. Their mom and dad had passed away. The oldest nephew was two years old and the younger was one years old. My mom had the second youngest one who was very sick. When the enemies started firing at innocent people, my mom and the rest of the kids left. The one year old was left behind. I ran back and carried him on my back for three days until we came to a refugee camp in Kenya.

Amina Aden is 32 years old and is originally from Somalia.

Life in Sierra Leone
Charles Wright, Brooklyn Center

Moving to Sierra Leone was a bad idea. When I was five years old, my sister and I moved to Freetown, Sierra Leone with our Aunty Grace to visit our grandparents. We were supposed to stay in Freetown until school started but unfortunately things didn't go as planned. Three days after we arrived, a war broke out that made our stay longer. It was bad for me because I couldn't return to Liberia to start elementary school. But what I went through during the war was really sad and scary. It wasn't only the sounds of the gun but the number of dead bodies and the way people were killed that really frightened me.

As we were trekking from place to place trying to avoid being killed, there was a town we went through that was really sad. People's houses were burned down, crying kids were left behind by their parents along the street, and dead bodies were everywhere. Up the street, down and across everywhere there were dead bodies. I saw a body lying on the sidewalk with no arms, legs, or head. It made me really scared and sad that I had to experience this. Going through the war in Freetown was not part of the plan.

Charles Wright is originally from Liberia.

My First Time at the Mall of America
Oscar McGrew, Minneapolis

I went to the Mall of America for the first time on a hot summer day in June with my aunt. Lego Land was so fascinating to me. I felt I had died and gone to heaven.

After that, my aunt wanted to get my ear pierced. I told her I really didn't want my ear pierced.

Then she said,"It won't hurt, and it will take but two seconds." So I said okay.

The ear gunner said, "What side do you want it on?"

I said, "The right."

Then she had a curious look on her face. She proceeded and – voila! She was done. The pain only lasted two minutes. I told my aunt I never want my ear pierced again.

She laughed and said, "Boy, you are silly."

After that, we walked around the humongous mall for hours. I felt like I was lost because there were so many stores and venues. Before we left the Mall, we stopped at Cinnabon to get their world famous cinnamon rolls. That was my favorite day of my life besides Christmas.

The Birthday of My Daughters and Me
Rosa Ruiz Meza, Elk River

In December 2010, there was a party for my daughters and me in Mexico. My daughters Johanna and Karina and I all have birthdays in December. Johanna's birthday is December 1st, Karina's is December 20th, and mine is December 18th. The party was in a meeting room. We invited lots of family and friends. We had mariachi music, food, drink, cake and candy.

Rosa Ruiz Meza is 41 years old and is originally from Mexico.

Revolution Time in Togo

E. Awoudi, Minneapolis

This memory marks the most important time of my life. It is why I came to the United States and how my family and I came to immigrate here.

The International Conference of Baul (French) was in 1989. The conference was recommended to all African countries to practice democracy because most African country leaders were dictators. After the conference, revolutions began everywhere in Africa. For my country, Togo, it was exceptionally hard and very difficult because it was the 38th year we had the same President. The country was very painful to live in with people dying every day. It was totally depressing.

To be safe, I left my country in 1997 with my family to go to a refugee camp in the Ivory Coast. The Ivory Coast was the only country in West Africa at the time that wasn't going through a revolution crisis yet. We stayed in the Ivory Coast for three years.

In 2001, the U.S. Embassy in the Ivory Coast (Department of Immigration) summoned us for an interview. Nine months later, we received a letter that we were accepted as refugees to immigrate to the U.S. Immediately, we started all vaccinations and all processes we needed for the trip. Once all was done, we left the Ivory Coast for the U.S. the same year. It was a three-day plane journey.

When we got here, the first thing that happened to us was to sleep. We slept as if we were still in Africa. The second problem we had was English. There are seven people in my family but nobody spoke English, and nobody knew the value of the money we were supposed to be using. After we got our Social Security Cards and I.D.s, the kids started school. Six months later they could translate for us what people were saying. The adaptation was hard for the first years, but we finally made it.

E. Awoudi is originally from Togo (Lome), West Africa.

Journey to the South

Regina Monegan, Minneapolis

One day, my mother, my Uncle Carl, Uncle William, and I decided that we all wanted to take a trip to see our family down south for one week. Everybody who was going met in front of my house to load up the three cars that were going.

Uncle David was driving one of the cars with my three cousins, Uncle Kenny, and me. My Uncle William was driving the car with my mom, my older cousin Tawana, her son and her nephew, Uncle Archie, and my sister Christine. Tony drove the last car with Uncle Carl, his wife, and their daughter. We all said a prayer and headed out for Greenville, Mississippi, leaving Minneapolis at around 2:30 p.m.

Our first stop was at a Wendy's in Iowa. We took up one corner section of the restaurant. The woman taking our order got frustrated when her cash register wouldn't let her ring up past $300 dollars. We spent half an hour ordering in groups by which car we were in. The woman didn't know what to do. We sat, ate, and laughed about it before loading back into the cars.

I can't tell you what was going on in the other two cars, but the one I was in was really quiet. I stayed on my cell phone the entire time talking to my friend Sincere, looking at the sights, playing games with my Uncle Kenny, and posting on Facebook how far I was from Minnesota.

When we made it to Greenville, our family that was living there was excited to see us. We stopped at our cousin Pumpkin's house before checking into a hotel. Everybody met at the Huddle House Restaurant for breakfast. They put us all in their party room.

Greenville was very small and relaxing. Every corner had a Double Quick gas station selling food and beer. None of the liquor stores sold beer, just hard liquor. That was weird to me. Later in the week, we went to a restaurant that just appeared out of nowhere. I thought we were going the wrong way and had to do a U-turn. When we turned around the restaurant was right there all lit up like an episode of The Simpsons. We spent over $400 on dinner.

On our way home we listened to the song "Mississippi Blues" every time we entered a new state. This was one of the best vacations that I ever took.

The Death of My Father
Sahra Abdirahman, Saint Paul

My father died September 11, 1992, in our house in Somalia. My father use to love me and play with me, and I loved him too. My mother told me later that when he tried to go out I used to go crazy. He would take me whenever he walked out. He took me out to Madrasa to learn the Quran, but whenever I came back home I would look for him in the house. If I missed him, I use to cry and ask my mother where he was because I wanted him to play with me.

One day while I was in Madrasa, my father got sick. He had asthma and died with the disease that day. When I ran home from Madrasa, I saw a crowd of people crying and jumping. My mother and her children were among them. I looked for my father in the crowd, but he was not there. I asked my mother where my father was, but my mother did not reply. I cried every evening, and always looked in the rooms whenever I came from Madrasa.

Sahra Abdirahman is originally from Somalia.

About my Country - Iraq
Ahlam Toma, Saint Paul

Hi, I am Ahlam. I'm from Iraq. I'm going to tell you a little about my country. My country is located in the Middle East. People in Iraq speak Arabic. The weather in Iraq is so nice; in the winter the weather is cold and rainy. However, it doesn't snow. In the summer the weather is hot, but it is not as humid as it is in Minnesota. Fall and spring in Iraq are very moderate. As you notice, we have four seasons. This weather has influenced us in so many ways. That is because it has made us able to plant a lot of different kinds of crops. Having good land and these crops make our food so cheap. The agriculture in Iraq has helped its economy by trading with other countries. It also offers many jobs to people. From our crops we have discovered so many medicines. Iraq is very famous for its petroleum. In conclusion, I love my country, and one day will go back to visit my family.

My Native Country
Zahrah, Coon Rapids

My native country is Iraq. My country is beautiful, with many mountains and rivers. There are twenty five million people. People in my country are very nice and they help each other. When we have free time we like to go fishing and cook outside. The weather in my country is very hot in summer and cold in winter, but there is no snow. The best time to visit my country is in March because we celebrate spring day. During this time, all the people cook and grill fish and kebabs outside. Typical food in my country is Almeskuf. That means grilled fish on the firewood. Some typical jobs that people have are soldiers, doctors and teachers.

One problem that my country has is more than one war. One thing that is better in my native country than in the United States is that people don't have many bills and most people have a house. One thing that is better in the United States than in my country is peace, and my children are safe. What I miss most about my native country is my family. One interesting thing about my native country is that when a man wants to marry he can marry four or three women and they can live together.

Zahrah is 47 years old and is originally from Iraq.

Honduras Beaches
Luiz Avila, Inver Grove Heights

Honduras is a tropical country placed at the heart of Central America. It has coasts in the Atlantic and Pacific oceans. The most beautiful beaches are at the north of the country. Roatan belongs to the bay islands and here is where everyone can enjoy West Bay, which is considered the most beautiful beach in Central America. Tela city is on the north coast with beautiful beaches too and close to the exotic national park, Lancetilla. Ceiba city is 60 kilometers away from Tela with the largest beaches and the most exciting carnival every May.

Riding Bulls

Charles Burroughs, Saint Cloud

My name is Charles Burroughs, and I always wanted to ride bulls. I was afraid to do it because I was raising two sons, and I was scared I was going to get hurt and I wouldn't be able to take care of them. So I waited until they were in college and they could take care of themselves.

It was 1986, and I was living in Oklahoma. My friend's dad asked me if I wanted to ride a bull, and I said, "Yes." He said, "I can teach you." He put a barrel on a rope and said, "If you can stay on this barrel, you could ride a bull." He shook the rope. I stayed on for eight seconds. I rode at least seven bulls and then I went to the championships in Las Vegas. When you ride bulls, you are competing with other riders for money and prizes.

At the championships I won $10,000.00. I rode for about two and a half years. Then one time a bull threw me, and I was knocked out. My back and my wrist were injured. That's when I quit.

I Come from the Biggest City in the World

Luis Rivero, Minneapolis

My name is Luis Rivero and I am from Mexico City, a beautiful city. It's really big, like Los Angeles and New York together and probably a little bigger than that. Mexico City has 20 million inhabitants. It is the capital of Mexico. It was also the capital of the Aztec empire before the people from Spain come to America.

I lived there for 24 years and still remember so many things, the streets, the subway, the zoo, and the schools I went to. I especially remember the college (University of Mexico, in Spanish UNAM). It is a very big, big city and a big college. But really the thing I miss most from Mexico City is my family, my mother, my brother, and my two children. One day I will go back to Mexico City.

Umphiem Refugee Camp

Eh Htoo, Saint Paul

There are many refugee camps which are located in different countries, but there is one of the refugee camps named Umphiem which is settled in Thailand. It was established in 1999. It combined two different refugee camps, Maw Kew and Hway K'lop. Our Umphiem camp was quite big and wide, and was surrounded by a forest and mountain. In front of the camp there was the main road that we could use to visit Mae Sod and other villages. Also, on the other side of the main road there were forest crops, a mountain, and a hill. At the top of the hill there was a lonely and peaceful cemetery which was surrounded by short and tall green oak trees. Then, at the back of the camp there was a mountain, cliff, hill, forest, crops, waterfall, and a spring. Moreover, there were many wild flowers and plants which gave different fragrances. Other things in the forest we could find were some vegetables such as ferns, bamboo shoots, mushrooms, and wild banana buds for the meal. Near the camp there were two or three Hmong villages and a lake. In this lake, we could go fishing. In our camp we also grew bamboo and eucalyptus.

We also had many NGOs, Non-governmental Organizations of the United Nations, the ARC, American Refugee Committee, Community Health, Education, Water and Sanitation. There were high schools, post-ten schools, vocational training courses, churches, hospitals, temples, a monastery and a mosque. More than that, there were many ethnic groups such as Karen, Mon, Chin, Kachin, Karenni, Burmese, Rakhine. I think even though our camp was not as developed as other communities or cities, it was wonderful and had natural beauty that could persuade a person's heart and mind. If people traveled across or walked along our camp without looking back, they wouldn't be dissatisfied because the camp was very interesting.

Eh Htoo is 24 years old and is originally from Burma.

Sweet Land of Liberty
Judah C. Batener, Circle Pines

I'm from dust and heat
I'm from mango trees
I'm from playing in the rain
I'm from barefoot in the sand
I'm from hand pumps and wells
I'm from washing clothes with hands on washing boards
I'm from a house with double porches
I'm from no electricity and unfinished buildings
I'm from 24th Street with kids playing in the dirt
Boys playing soccer and girls jumping rope
I'm from single mothers cooking and cleaning
I'm from rice every day
I'm from a tiny kitchen with everything in it, dim lights and very comfortable
I'm from a large family
I'm from respecting my elders
I'm from people dying prematurely every other day
I'm from traumatized families
I'm from loss of loved ones I'm from broken hearts from the wars
I'm from war and more war
I'm from a happy neighborhood with loud talking and hardworking people
I'm from everybody trying to get through the day alive and peacefully
"Go to school and learn, become a better person, always put God first"
Is what my parents say
I'm from church every Sunday and Wednesdays
I'm from growing up with the teachings of Christianity
I'm from Liberia
The Sweet Land of Liberty

Judah C. Batener is 18 years old and is originally from Liberia.

Upstate New York
Deborah Avery, Minneapolis

I am originally from Upstate New York. I was raised in the Adirondacks, a quiet and peaceful environment, beautiful in all seasons. The place where I lived was away from city life, enough to be comfortable. In the morning I would always try to wake before dawn to hear the birds sing their song, to see the sun appear from the dark to lighten the day. Even the rainy days were peaceful, to hear the rain falling from the roof, hitting the rocks, splashing in the puddles. I have enjoyed walks along a quiet road listening to nature to guess and discover what the noise was, where it came from. I would often take a walk through the woods, to see what nature had for me to see. I also enjoyed the quest for wild strawberries, blueberries and raspberries for making pancakes and muffins. I enjoyed sitting in the backyard, relaxing, and tuning into nature. Hear the wind blow, know the direction it comes. The air smells so fresh—so calming. To hear a grasshopper hopping in the grass, a cricket chirping, and wondering where it is hiding. Hearing a peaceful creek flow, a crackle in the woods, wondering what it may be. A deer or a bear could just be your cat or your dog. Ha ha. The beauty and tranquility is always a peaceful memory to ponder in stressful times.

My First Job in the United States
Roman Llapa, Minneapolis

Hi, my name is Roman Llapa. I am going to tell you about how I started working in this country. First, I have lived in Minneapolis since 2001, when I decided to move from my country. I was a little worried and afraid, thinking about what my first job was going to be. I started work in a restaurant. My duty was to wash dishes. I had never been a dishwasher. It was very hard and difficult for me because it was a new country, new people, and I didn't speak English. Also the weather was so bad at that time. Later, I got accustomed to this country, this culture, and the kind of life they are accustomed to living here. However, I will always remember that first job.

Roman Llapa is 35 years old and is originally from Ecuador.

I Remember My Country
Faduma Barkhadle, Saint Louis Park

Somalia is located in the Horn of Africa. It lies along the Gulf of Aden and Indian Ocean. Also, it has two main Rivers, Shabelle and Juba. The weather is not too hot and not too cold; it's just perfect, like paradise. I was born and raised in Mogadishu. It's the biggest city in Somalia. It's famous for many things, like bazaars, historic buildings, and its beautiful beaches. I remember my childhood when my friends and I went to the beach to swim a lot. I loved the fresh air, and I loved the fresh food, such as meat, milk, fruits and vegetables. Unlike here, I did not have frozen food. I wish I could go back there someday and see the rain fall. I love it. When it's safe, I'll go back.

Faduma Barkhadle is originally from Somalia.

My Story
Mu Htoo, Saint Paul

My name is Mu Htoo. I was born in Burma on January 1, 1969. My village is Saw Eh Doe. I have one sister and one brother. I am the youngest. Because the Burmese Army attacked our village, we were running in the forest. We didn't have food, clothing, or medicine. We were very poor. There were always soldiers walking around our area. My mother and father, my brother and my brother-in-law were all killed by Burmese soldiers. I was very afraid.

In 1999, my family crossed into Thailand. It was our second country. We lived there for 10 years. We lived In Mae La Oon Camp. We were supplied many things by the Thailand-Burma Border Consortium (TBBC). We had the food, clothing, medicine, education, everything, but because we didn't have the Thailand Population ID Card we didn't travel outside the camp.

On May 12, 2011, my family moved to our third country, America. We live in Saint Paul. I like Saint Paul. Now I attend VSS school. I have been here at VSS six months. I know a little more English. I like all my teachers and everybody. They work hard for me.

Mu Htoo is 43 years old and is originally from Karen State, Burma.

My Life
Moo Mu, Saint Paul

My name is Pla Moo Eh Khu Soe Kaw. My nickname is Moo Tha Lay. I was born in Burma on November 25, 1992, Sunday afternoon. My parents' names were Saw Tamalar Htoo and Naw Aye. I have two brothers. My older brother's name is Ner Kaw and my second brother's name is Say Taw Kaw. I'm the youngest, a sister.

In 1998, the Burmese soldiers came to my village and killed my parents. My brothers and I did not die because Karen soldiers had us. On December 25th at night we moved to Thailand. My brothers and I lived with somebody. When we missed our parents, we cried. We wanted to go to school but we didn't have money.

One day we saw my grandmother and my grand mom took us to her home. She asked me, "Do you want to go to school?" I said yes, and she said to me, "You want to go to school. I will change your name to Moo Mu and your date of birth to October 1, 1990 because you are very young, so you can change your name and your date of birth. You can go to school with your brother." I said, "I want to go to school. I will change." My brother said, "Why do you change your name? You are very young." I said, "I know that, but I'm going to school with you. I'm happy." My brother said, "You will be happy in your life." I said, "No, I will never be happy in my life." All night we prayed to God and we slept. I knew one day God will have me. I believe him because I have a new life and a peace for my life.

Moo Mu is 21 years old and is originally from Karen State, Burma.

Memories
Chit Chaw, Saint Paul

In every moment, there is something happening in our world. I'd like to share a personal story that taught me to show loving-kindness toward everyone I meet. I don't ever want to feel sorry again about being too late for someone. So we need to show our love when we live together and when we are alive and in love with each other as best as we can. Don't feel sad after someone who we love is lost, because we don't know the future.

She was my childhood friend and older than me by almost five years. She took care of me more than my sister when I was a little girl. She always had patience with me, encouraged me, and forgave me for everything. She was my greatest and kindest friend. When I played with her, I always wanted to win, and she let me. I didn't like her when I was young because I thought she was a tight-wad but she never got angry with me. She smiled all the time. I didn't know that her parents were poor and couldn't afford for her to go to school. So she had to work for her family.

After I finished high school at the age of 15, I went to Bangkok. We didn't see each other for two years. I couldn't believe all that had happened very fast in two years. When I knew enough about her, I felt I wanted to apologize to her. One day, I wrote an apology letter and sent it to her but she received my letter on the same day she died. I felt very sad, and I spent my time crying for a long time. After that, I understood that you could die even if you are young or old. I knew I'd never see her again for my whole life. She died from gastric disease.

It was too late to apologize to her. I wanted to tell her, "Thank you for giving me the experience of life and how I received love from you." I wish I could meet her one last time, but I know it never will be. Even though I never see her, I'll always remember her, and she'll stay in my heart until my life ends. The other fact she added to my life is how she taught me to show love to others.

Chit Chaw is 23 years old and is originally from Burma.

Surprise and Happened
Pattama Littana, Otsego

Hi my name is Pattama. I want share my story. I know the women in the world want your husband and boyfriend to surprise you and give you something for Valentine's Day. Me too. Every year on Valentine's Day, I tell my husband buy something for me but he's not. He told me next time.

Last year, my husband and I went out for dinner on Valentine's Day at a restaurant after he was done from work. My husband and I drove the car to go to my sister-in-law's house to drop off my kids for her to take care. My husband and I went to the steak house in Coon Rapids. In the restaurant a lot of people I wait for line about two hours. About two hours I looked to my husband. He had two hands in his jacket pockets the whole time. I didn't know why because it was hot in there. I thought he was hiding something in his pocket. I put my hand in his pockets and felt something like a small box. After we were at a table, he opened the box and I saw a diamond ring for me.

When I looked at my cell phone, I saw I had missed calls from my sister-in-law. I didn't want to call in case she was going to complain about how long we were gone. I went to her home and opened the door and saw my daughter crying. My sister-in-law said my daughter had gotten hurt. My husband took her to the hospital and I waited from 9:00 until 3:00 in the morning.

It was such a happy and sad day on Valentine's Day.

Pattama Littana is 36 years old and is originally from Thailand.

My Journey
Mee Vang, Minneapolis

In my life and family journey, I have lived with my mother and father. We worked in fields and farms in Laos for a living. We didn't have any electricity there, and we lived in houses made out of bamboo wood.

Mee Vang is originally from Laos.

My Hero
Soudsakhone (Sue) Chitmany, Elk River

It was late at night. My two sisters and I got woken up. The adults put us in a cart. In the torchlight, I saw a lot of people running, screaming, crying, pushing and shoving. My father held my little sister. My mother stayed behind.

We stayed for six months in the refugee camp in Thailand called Na Pho. There wasn't much food. I remember my father trapping huge rats and birds. He would sell them at the market. He did all he could to feed his children.

My father was a Thai soldier who later joined with the United States Army to fight with the Vietnamese Communist. They had to do everything to survive, even drank from the creek. My dad also worked with the U.N. We had it good. My father would bring boxes of noodles and canned foods.

The time came to come to America. I'd never seen a bus or airplane before. We didn't speak English; my father knew a little. He had to go to school to learn so that he would be qualified to come to America.

When we arrived in New York, my father had said to me, "This is the land of opportunity and freedom. That's why we're here."

Looking at my father's army picture every day, and seeing what he had to go through to come to the United States, helps me appreciate everything I have and stay strong. If he could do it, I can do it. Most of all, I thank him for what he did for me, and for others, to have freedom. He's my hero whom I can look up to. I'm thankful I have father like him.

Remembering
Hamdi Mohamed, Minneapolis

I remember where I used to play when I was young. I also remember a lot of things I used to do when I was young and back home. I remember our house back home and the neighborhood. I remember childhood friends. Now I am homesick because I am missing a lot of things.

New in Minneapolis
Anonymous, Minneapolis

It was Monday. I woke up at 7:00 am. I looked out my window. A lot of snow had appeared in front of my home. I had a job interview at 9:30 am. I was a new in Minneapolis and I hadn't even seen snow before. I didn't have a car at that time. I was going to ride the bus, but I didn't know the bus schedule. So, I stood by the side of the road.

I couldn't be there for long because it was too cold. Then I saw one of my friends driving a car. I called him, but he didn't hear me. I ran after his car and everybody was surprised and looked at me. Fortunately, he stopped at the first light. His car was the second car from the light and I kept chasing to reach my friend's vehicle, but I could not get to him.

After a while, I almost gave up getting to my destination. I thought about how I would get to the job interview. I attempted to walk and passed three or four blocks. I was tired and I felt very cold. I thought I might die. I entered a coffee shop and ordered cup of coffee. I drank my coffee quickly. I become energized to keep going on my journey. Finally, I got there at 9:33. Three minutes passed the appointment. But I am lucky and I got hired.

A Scary Memory
Adelanke Akinneye, Forest Lake

A scary memory before I was ten years old was when I got lost in the woods. I went with my grandma to the farm. I was so carried away with birds and interesting leaves, I kept going until I couldn't find my way back. It was starting to get late in the evening. I was so scared when I heard the voices of the crickets and wild animals. I started crying and screamed so maybe someone could hear me. Luckily for me there was a hunter man that came to my rescue, and he brought me back to the village safe and sound. Then I found out that the villagers had been looking for me already. Since then I have been very careful anytime I went to the woods.

Adelanke Akinneye is originally from Nigeria.

My Grandpa
Iliana H., Wyoming

I have a happy memory when I was a young girl. One morning when my grandpa was eating breakfast, I woke up so I could eat with him. Then when my grandpa was going to work, I felt sad; I wanted to go with him to work. My grandpa said not to worry, I will be here for dinner, and we can eat together and talk about school and my work. After dinner he said, I want to tell you something: you and your brother are going with me to my Christmas party at work and meet my friends.

My grandpa always was funny and friendly, so when he took us to the store he always bought something for us. He always was there when we needed him. Grandpa was so close to me growing up, but when he passed away I was very sad because I was not there with him and couldn't say good bye. I felt like the world fell on my head. I went to Panama for his funeral, but the airplane was late. I could not make it and I felt so sad. The next day I went to say good bye to him in the cemetery. In my heart grandpa knew I was doing everything so I could be there with him. I know that he will always be with me in my heart.

Iliana H. is 40+ years old and is originally from Panama.

Goofy is His Name
Chelsea, Wyoming

My happiest memory was when I got a cat from my mom's old boyfriend. I remember this little kitten, he was so cute. I remember asking my mom if I could keep him, but she did not want a cat because he would make a mess. I told my Mom that I would take care of him, so she let me keep him. That made me so happy. I had to think of a really good name for him, so my mom and I were thinking of names for him. My mom wanted to name him Boots because he has white paws, but I did not like that name for him. I was thinking of a name, and the name Goofy came to mind, so that became his name. Goofy has been a wonderful cat over the years, and he is still goofy!

A Scary Memory in My Life
Sony, Forest Lake

My scary memory before I was ten years old was about when I used to pee in my bed. That usually happened when I was dreaming about using a big blue bowl to pee. The next morning I realized I wet my bed again. My dear brothers always scared me and said I was found in the dump and my parents adopted me. I saw they enjoyed making me sad and scared. They were so tired doing laundry and cleaning my room almost every day because my mom worked and they took care of me. They changed the strategy and started with a new plan. They said they were going to push me in the water from the top of the bridge if I don't stop pee. This scared me so much. From that day I started thinking what can I do to stop wetting my bed and also make my family proud of me.

Sony is 30 years old and is originally from the Dominican Republic.

My Native Country
Amenyona, Coon Rapids

My native country is Togo. It is a small country by the ocean. There are about seven million people; they are nice and caring. When we have free time, we like to travel or visit family. The weather in my country is nice and beautiful. The best time to visit my country is from December to May. Typical food in my country is flour cornet Mack. Some typical jobs that people have are taxi drivers. One problem that my country has is no jobs. We don't have enough money for food and everything is expensive. One thing that is better in my native country than in the United States is no stress at work, you are free to do anything you want and every month you still will get paychecks. One thing that is better in the United States than in my country is that when I send money back home, the exchange rate is higher. What I miss most is my family and friends. One interesting thing about my country is the beach. You can have fun with friends and have Christmas together with family and friends.

Amenyona is 33 years old and is originally from Togo.

A Memory of Lydia
Toke Adegoke, Ham Lake

My scary memory is about a girl living in our neighborhood. Her name was Lydia, but we called her Mama because she called her mother Mama. It happened long time ago when I was age seventeen. Lydia was a childhood friend of me and my siblings. We loved her so much because she was a friendly and loving girl. We played together, and sometimes she stayed overnight at our house. At other times, we stayed at her house, too. One day Lydia fell sick and was taken to the hospital, but five days later she died. When we heard about her death, it was very painful. We cried because Lydia was a very sweet girl. Her death was a shock to me and my siblings, especially me. I remembered her all the time. I couldn't walk alone at night. It seemed to me as if she's coming towards me. Her death was scary to me to the extent that I couldn't sleep alone in my room. During the day I used to be very happy, but at night I was not happy because I knew I would not be able to sleep. I would remember her and become scared. One day I concluded in my mind that I will stop thinking about her and that really helped me and stopped my being scary about her death.

Toke Adegoke is 31 years old and is originally from Nigeria.

A Scary Memory
Phuong Green, Wyoming

I have a very scary memory from when I was three years old. A military camp about three blocks behind my house was full of weapons, and it exploded. Someone wanted to open the bomb to get the iron, but he didn't work carefully. The bomb began to explode and burned all my neighbor's houses and my house. My sisters, my brother and I ran away from the fire. Because I was the youngest, my oldest sister carried me. I still remember my older sister fell down many times. She was only five years old, too young to run for her life. It was lucky that nobody got hurt that time. It was too scary to forget, even though I was just three years old.

Phuong Green is 38 years old and is originally from Viet Nam.

My Special Cat's Life
Corrina Kubitz, Burnsville

My cat's name is Goofy and I have had him for nine years, since he was 6 weeks old. He died eight years ago. I surely missed him a lot. He had kidney failure and I had to feed him with I.V. fluid everyday.

He was the most special cat that I ever had because he saved my life while I had an insulin reaction and he knew that I had diabetes. When he sensed that I had an insulin reaction, he jumped on my bed or on my couch and he sat on my chest and licked my face to wake me up. Sometimes, he ran to my boyfriend for help. He followed him toward to me. After that, he went everywhere. I could even let him outside and he wouldn't run away. When it was time for him to visit the doctor, he knew. I took his favorite blanket and put the blanket around him while I picked him up to the car. He stayed inside the blanket while I drove to the vet. When I brought him to the vet, he really hated the doctor, so he crawled into my jacket and hid. When the doctor finished checking him and I picked up his favorite blanket, he saw me and meowed, then crawled to the blanket. I went to the car and he still stayed inside the blanket until we got home. He knew the road and he came out from the blanket. He stood up by the window and said "MEOW," and was excited to be home.

He was an amazing cat.

Myself
A. Mohammed, Minnetonka

I was born in Somalia. I started going to school when I was seven years old. I've educated myself ever since. I finished high school when I was nine years old in 1980. After that, I got married, opened a store, and started my family. My daughters, Asha and Saynab, were born, so I had to work harder to provide for them. A sad memory was when my daughter Saynab was born. She soon passed away and I was I left with Asha. I loved her dearly regardless. My wife left Asha and me after that to go to America and file for us to come, too. In the end, we did. Now I will continue my education in America and get a good job that will support my family and me in the future.

My Happiest Day
Abdulwadud Amin, Minneapolis

My happiest day was when I got approval for my interview with the I.N.S. (Immigration and Naturalization Service) in Kenya. What made it my happiest day? Was that I got settlement in the United States of America. In 1993, I escaped from Ethiopian Colonizer to neighboring countries, Djibouti, Somalia, and Kenya. In January 1999 I went to Nairobi, Kenya. After two weeks, I applied to the U.N.H.C.R (United Nations High Commissioner for Refugees) in Nairobi, Kenya. After one week, I got an approval letter from U.N. H.C.R. After four months, I received a letter from J.V.A (Joint Venture Agreement) - United States of America for interviews. I passed the interview with J.V.A, and J.V.A. transferred me to I.N.S. The next day the I.N.S. made an interview with me. After a few months the I.N.S called me to its office and gave me an approval letter that said, "You have passed our interview, and you will go to the United States of America." This is significant for me because I will become an American citizen and I will have the right to live in the United States of America. I can't go back to Oromia until the Oromo people get freedom or get independence.

Abdulwadud Amin is 57 years old and is originally from Oromia Horn of Africa.

School Story
Qadan Ashur, Minneapolis

I started school in Somalia when I was little. It was hard for me to read books, but I liked playing with children outside the school. I had a lot of fun when I was young. I used to color something everyday. I used to have many friends in school, and I played with them.

A Little Girl Without Her Snow
Taquila James, Minneapolis

I was born May 7, 1983 in Minneapolis, Minnesota. We moved to Coppers Cove, Texas in June 1988. I was five years old. It was so amazing, the sun always shining, and parks with swimming pools everywhere. We would stay out late, just plain old fun. I loved it. I never wanted to leave my family and friends, but change is always good, at least that's what my mom used to say. Days, weeks, months had passed and things were going good. Getting a little homesick, but I was a big girl—I could manage. I started kindergarten and met a lot of new friends, but could think of nothing but my friends and family in Minneapolis.

More time passed and seasons changed and I became more homesick. My mom would say, "Don't worry, Christmas is coming." You see, I loved Christmas; I loved my new toys, and my new dolls, which I referred to as new friends. More importantly, I loved the snow. Seeing the snow brought out the joy in me. You see, living in Minneapolis, you get used to things like snow and cold winters, and snow is one that I have grown to love. I could do without the cold.

Only two weeks to go and still no snow, and not only was I sad, I was worried. "Mom, when is it going to snow?" I asked. She looked at me with sad eyes and said, "Sorry, sweetheart, but it doesn't snow like back home." My heart was broken. I felt tricked. I would have never come if I had known that. Christmas was two days away and my mom tried her best to make me feel better. She even tried to make our house look just like our house back home. It just wasn't the same.

"Christmas is here, Christmas is here," my little brother shouted.

"So what, there is still no snow."

He then jumped on me and said, "Is there something in your eye?"

"No."

"Can you see?"

"Yes, why?"

"'Cause you said there's no snow."

I jumped up and ran to the window, and to my surprise it was snow. The first time Texas had seen snow in a long time. That's why I love the snow.

Use for a Rooster

Xee Lee, Minneapolis

When I was young, I lived in Laos. My father and mother, they didn't have a watch to know the time when to wake up in the morning or go to work at the farm. They only used the Rooster to tell the time: what time they can wake up, when it was too late for them, and when to go to work.

They would hear the Rooster sing for the first time at 3:00 o'clock in the morning. The rooster sang, "Cock-a-doodle-doo!" And when my mother and father heard Rooster sing "cock-a-doodle-doo" one or two times, they would wake-up quickly to cook and prepare food for their family to take to work on the farm. Boil some hot water to boil packing food. Boil some vegetables, peas, carrots, meat, salts. Fry meat, peas, mushrooms, scallions, garlic, tomatoes. Make some hot peppers with chili peppers, garlic, scallions, tomatoes. And she served some fruits on the table, too. My father would chop some grasses, served to the Cow and Horse.

After they finished their jobs, we ate together and went to the farm. And another thing, when my father and mother worked on the farm, they also used the bird for telling the time to know when to come back home. When the bird sang a lot nearby or around the farm, my mother and father understood that it was about time to come back to their home right away. If the bird sang and sang a lot and they couldn't go home, later it would be dark coming home.

At this time, the Hmong people were still living in Laos or villages, they always use a rooster like in this story. So the Rooster served as a natural alarm clock for people.

Xee Lee is 50 years old and is originally from Laos.

From the Long and Thin Country

Ximena Vicuna, Saint Louis Park

My name is Ximena Vicuña. I was born in Santiago, capital of Chile. I love my country; there you find practically all climates of the world. The north is the driest place on earth, in the central region you find more places to enjoy, like big beaches with soft sand to relax on a sunny day. Also in the south you can enjoy an infinity of lakes, rivers, lagoons and the Pacific Ocean that offers us a wide range of possibilities to practice fishing along Chile. It is amazing that just one hour's drive from the capital you have a mountain to ski on in winter.

When I arrived at Minneapolis, Saint Louis Park, I looked for a connection with the nature and I found beautiful places: lakes and great parks that I visited with pleasure; running, working and biking while I was seeing the lake. Those are unforgettable images.

I came to the United State for three years; my husband was elected to work in a Mining Project in Ely, north of Minnesota, because of his vast experience mining in Chile. The first year was difficult for me; adapting to the extreme cold was not easy, the snow in winter put the streets more slippery and dangerous to drive. My great difficulty was not speaking English, but I found an appreciated opportunity to learn English in Community Center of Saint Louis Park. The program of study has been excellent for me, and the teachers have been highly motivating in their teachings.

To have been in a classroom with classmates of different countries and cultures has meant an appreciable experience for my life. I will keep in my heart forever Minnesota.

Ximena Vicuna is originally from Chile.

Moving To America
Ghavin Marryshaw, Bayport

When I moved to the United States of America, life for me was difficult but still somewhat easy. I used to go shopping with my mom. Every time she shopped I noticed, and after a while, I was driving her to the store. Where I lived, there was a pizza place right next to the apartment building. But because I had no friends, I started missing the friends I had back home and my country even more.

I started going to school for a better education. I then noticed the difference in the classroom; here they are very small and you have to share a table, but back home they are large. It was different in the way they taught, and in the way they used their words. I had to adjust in order to learn especially in speaking proper English because back home we speak a dialect we call Patois or Creole.

After a few months, I came to realize that I liked it here quite a bit, and that home wasn't on my mind like it was a few months prior. I had quit staying home and just staring out of the window all day, feeling sad and lonely. It was a good new feeling. Thanks for reading my story.

My Wonderful Country - Somalia
Anonymous, Minneapolis

Somalia has many wonderful things. First, Somalia has the largest ocean coastline on the Indian Ocean, which Somalis get seafood. Somalia has two big rivers, Jubba and Shabelle. The water of the two is used for farming and irrigation. Somalia has four seasons, summer, autumn, spring and winter. Finally, Somalia has one of the best agricultures in the world. Somalia has nice temperatures ranging from 30C to 40C. The climate in Somalia is extraordinary.

The Best Doctor
Gududow, Minneapolis

In 1977, when my cousin's wife went in labor, they took her to the hospital in Mogadishu (the capital of Somalia). She was unable to push the baby out, so the doctor had her go into surgery.

During her second pregnancy, when she was in her ninth month, her husband's mother requested him to bring his wife to her house. When she felt the pain, she went to the hospital near her house, and she was not able to push the baby out again. The nurse saw that she had had surgery so she told the doctor and took her into surgery.

Then the husband's mother requested to see her. The mother understood that she was not able to push the baby out, so she stuck her finger down the woman's throat to make her gag. As soon as she gagged the child came out! The nurses said, "You are the best doctor!"

Gududow is 78 years old and is originally from Somalia.

My First Visit Home
Shua Yang, Corcoran

The first time I went back to my country to visit my parents everything had changed. My brothers, sisters grew up and my parents were older than I was there. I was feeling that everything in the world had changed and never returned the same as it was. I spent a month with my family, but it wasn't enough for me. I wish I was a son, never leaving my parents. If I was a son I'd get to stay with them and help them with everything until they're old and they will have time for resting.

After one month, I came back to the United States. I hope I will go back my country again soon to visit my parents.

Shua Yang is 31 years old and is originally from Laos.

Who Is Important In Your Life?
Bria Yang, Minneapolis

The important people in my life were my parents because when I was born to live in a small house in Thailand of our village. They tried to take care about me and teach me to get a healthy life. When I got sick and ill they were worried so much. In my family we had more children and needed more food than before.

My village was near the mountain my parents and I went to carry wood for fires and bamboo to make food. Sometime we bought mango at the mountain for low prices. When I went to school, I had many friends and teacher. My friend and I would clean room and sometime we would clean bathroom too. After lunch we brushed teeth and went to room for learning. We like to read book at the library near the class but I like to read story and my friend like to read poem.

My Travel to the United States
Carmen Collaguazo, Golden Valley

I remember when I was ten years old. My godmother wanted to bring me to the United States, but my parents didn't want me to go with them. But I really wanted to go to the United States. I had a dream to go to the United States for twelve years. I decided to come to here because it was my dream. I traveled Ecuador to Mexico. When I was in Mexico, I went to visit the Basilica of Guadalupe. I prayed and told her to help me to come to the United States without any trouble. I live in the United States. Then ten years passed. I was happy I could go to Ecuador and came back when I got the chance. I achieved my dream.

A Happy Family Memory
Anonymous, Minneapolis

I remember when I was young, my father and I went to the playground. When I was playing, my father was trying to run with the ball and hit the goal. My younger brother hit him and he fell down. All the young ones laughed at him. My father said, "Hey, why are you guys doing this to me like this?" We were all laughing and so he left. When we came home, I told my mama what happened in the playground, and she also laughed.

My Earliest Memory
Mariam Abdullahi, Minneapolis

My earliest memory was moving to my grandfather's house. My grandfather's house was a farm. He was ninety-one years old and he liked to drink camel milk so much. One day he called to me and he said to close the window. But I did not understand what he was saying to me. I called my mama and I said, "Help me." My mama understood what my grandfather was saying. My mama closed the window. I was happy because I didn't want to make him mad with me. That time I was five years old.

Airplane
Plaw Doe, Saint Paul

Until I was 24 years old, I never flew in or saw an airplane. When I came to the United States, it was the first time I saw an airplane. When I neared the airplane, my heart was very excited. I asked myself, How do people fly? I didn't know how to go into the airplane. When I flew, I was thinking, "If the airplane is broken, what can I do? We will all die." But many people stayed in the airplane.

Learning

King of the Animals

Uchenna, Plymouth

Once upon a time, animals decided to have a King of the Jungle. There were so many animals that they decided to have a meeting to find one animal to be the king.

During the meeting, two animals, a tortoise and a lion, came out to take the position. There was a disagreement among the animals because they wanted only one animal to become king. Therefore, they asked the tortoise and. the lion to fight, and whoever won would be their king. The fight started and the lion carried the tortoise six feet in the air and threw him down. The tortoise's body busted and scattered into several pieces. The animals started picking up the tortoise, and they declared the lion the winner of the fight and King of the Jungle. After they picked up the tortoise's body, they glued the pieces of the tortoise back together. That's why a tortoise's body has split marks; and each time you come in contact or across a tortoise, he always hides himself inside his connected body thinking that the lion is coming again to start a fight.

Uchenna O was born in Nigeria. She studied accounting at the School of Polytechnic and graduated in 1996. Uchenna came to the United States in November of 2004 and became a Certified Nursing Assistant and Home Health Aide in 2007. During an adventurous trip to Minnesota, she fell in love, got engaged and decided to live here. Uchenna currently attends the Osseo Adult Basic Education Program.

If You Don't Know the Language, You Get Pushed Around
Dunia, Fridley

When I came to the United States in August 2001, I spoke little English. I started working in October, so I was afraid to communicate with the people I worked with. One woman told me to do her job that the boss had said for her to do. She was lying.

One day after my English got better; I was training one other lady. The woman came and told me to do her work again. Then I told her, "I can't, I am training someone!" She said, "If you don't do this, I will tell the boss." I said, "Tell the boss five times! Not only one time." She apologized to me. She said she would not tell the boss. I thought, "I am not going home today until I talk to the boss." At the end of the day my aunt came to pick me up. I told my aunt what happened, and we talked to the boss. The boss told me to write everything down that she did to me. Then I wrote it down, and he told her, "Do your work and leave Dunia alone!" At last I had my rights. My English is much better now and I am still going to school.

Dunia Gure is a student in the Metro North ABE Program, Blaine Learning Lab. Dunia came to the United States in 2004 from Somalia as a refugee through Kenya. She lives in Fridley and works at Crestview. Dunia wants to go to college to become a nurse.

Childhood
Rashida Khan, Minneapolis

I grew up in Somalia. I was living with my parents, siblings, aunts, uncle, and my grandmother all together in a one big house. I went to middle school with my sisters Monday through Saturday. My middle school was six kilometers from my house.

Boys and girls went to separate schools that were close to each other. My favorite subject in school was science because I liked learning about plants and animals. I was also very good at mathematics. We used to wear uniforms to school and teachers checked our hygiene every day before class. School started 9:00 in the morning to 3:00 in the afternoon. After coming home from the school, me and my sisters and my friends would go to the park and play together after playing for two hours, we would go and do our homework.

A Great Lesson for the Rest of My Life
Maria Herrera, Austin

When I was ten years old a girl who lived next to my house stole my doll. I started to mourn, but my grandma told me, "You will not fix anything if you keep crying." Then she took me by the hand and led me to the girl who stole my doll, and told me, "Now I want you to fix your problem." She also said, "You are ten years old and I know you must defend yourself because throughout your life you'll find all sorts of people and perhaps I will no longer be there to defend you." My grandma taught me many things, but above all she taught me that I have to use words to express what I disagree with.

I've always been shy, but when I see something wrong I can't stay silent, thanks to my grandma. I think she has been the wisest person I have known because although she is no longer physically with me she is still part of my life.

Learning Continues at Any Age
Debra D Greer, Brooklyn Park

As an older student my life is continuing to grow, some of us may blossom at twenty while others may blossom later in life, but no matter what stage life may find you, life will continue to grow as long as you continue to live it…I visualize myself as a relentless flower forcing its way through harden desert soil…soil that been fossilized through the changing climate of time.

My life has taken me on many journeys, each journey was a stage set into action for the next phase of development and growth with perseverance interlocking like a hand and glove…one is needed for stability, while the other is needed for protection Each is needed to co-exist together as one. Perseverance has taught me to never give up on my dreams, believing that I have more to give to myself and others; life is a lesson and my life is full of lessons. I now realize that I'm not just existing in this world, but an individual who has so much to contribute to its community, and willing to share my lifelong experiences that hope and dreams are not just another word added into ones vocabulary, but words full of true meaning if I attach its meaning to my spirit….

What I have learned over the years can be unitized in my career development. I have learned to be organized, detailed, and to communicate well with others. These skills have given me the opportunity to be exposed to a diverse background that will be very helpful in the near future as I pursue a degree in Health Information. Persistence is the key to success if I continue to believe that success can be attainable, and if I never give up on my dreams that success is mine.

"To accomplish great things, we must not only act, but also dreams: not only to plan, but also believe." - Anatole France.

The stage is set and the opera is still in session, it's not over until the Fat Lady sing; and I will continue to sing until I have taken my last breath.

When I Write
Robert Amos, Lindstrom

When I write …
    ….I get lost in words
    ….my heart becomes my hand
    ….my eyes become my ink
    ….the mic becomes the paper
    ….now listen to what I speak
    ….I know the paper is listening
    ….I don't have to ask twice
    ….I feel alone in a place full of people
    ….I just know the pen is stitching up the world.

My Destiny
Dawn Young, Minneapolis

I have learned to take control of my destiny, and in doing that I will have to be in a place where my mind is open to the new things in life. I have not always had this mindset, so for me it is important that I have control of the way my life should go. I believe my Savior guides my destiny. He is first in my life.

I have made many choices in life that have not allowed me to move forward, but now it is time. I have many goals that I must complete and many who will help me get there. First there is my daughter Divia and my son Eugene, and of course there are my Pastors, Dewayne and Parthia Hill, who have had a great part in helping me. I have always dreamed of getting my GED and to one day go on to college; I will get there. I also have a great dream to one day open my own business to help people that are less fortunate than me. My dream is to help people that have been on drugs and who have been homeless. I would like to see them have a chance in life; I have been there myself. Sometimes we go places in life that we have chosen for a period of time and it takes people that have a heart to see us make it. Giving them transitional housing will help give them an incentive to be with their kids, and also help young ladies that have babies to learn to take care of themselves.

I thank God for my destiny, goals and dreams. They will not just impact my life, but all that is a part of my destiny.

School Time
Carrie Swor, Duluth

I'm forty years old and decided to finish my schooling and graduate from the Adult Learning Center in 2012. The teachers were totally awesome. They helped me a lot, especially my reading and literature teacher and my math and science teacher. I am very thankful for all their help and support to help me graduate and to be able to go on to college. I couldn't have done it without their help.

At forty years of age I made an example for my daughter Jamie, my niece Baylee, and my nephews Levi and Jaden. Jaden is three and really wants to go to school. My daughter, niece, and nephews saw me going to school every day. I hope that gives them the incentive to graduate on time and that I've made a good example.

I'm so excited.

The U.S. Changed My Life
Eri John, Elk River

Living in the United States, I have learned that sometimes I take things for granted. I was nineteen years old when I came to the U.S. It took me three years to understand English, but sometimes I didn't go to school because I was too lazy. Then one day I thought that I have to do something with my life, so I started going back to school.

I'm working on my diploma. It is tough. I try not to complain, but I have to be strong with myself if I want to succeed in this life. Being positive, I mean when I open my mouth, I speak positive. It helps me.

Halimo
Halimo Sheikh, Minneapolis

Halimo likes her family
A lot of hope for my country
Like to visit my sister
I like important English everyday come to school
My children are happy; I like to see them every day
Ok because I study English
Halimo

My First Day of Cooking
Sapna Kumar, Roseville

I am the dearest daughter of my parents because I am the one sister with four brothers. My parents love me a lot. They didn't want me to do anything with my hands. Everything was given to me. Therefore, I didn't know how to cook and clean until I got married!

One week after my marriage, my mother-in-law asked me to cook something for them. I was scared. I wanted to tell her that I didn't know how to cook, but I couldn't say it to her. I went to the kitchen to see what I could cook for them. My whole body was shaking. I couldn't think of one thing. Then I called my mom and asked her to help me. She gave me one easy recipe and said to me, "Best of luck!"

I asked my God to help me, and then I started to cook. When I served my dish to the rest of my new family, they were laughing at me because of my nervousness. They liked it and said they appreciated me. I happily said thanks to God. When the others got busy, I told my mother-in-law that I didn't know how to cook. She smiled at me and said, "Why didn't you tell me before? Now it is my responsibility to teach you how to cook."

Right now I'm able to cook because of her. I will always remember that day because it was very important for me, and I never want to forget it.

Sapna Kumar is originally from Pakistan.

Waiting for a Call Back
Alvaro Barrios Sarmiento, Minneapolis

What should we do when somebody does not answer our letters, phone calls, e-mails, and cell phone calls? Sometimes I feel that sending a message is like putting some words in a bottle, and then setting it adrift in any sea of the world. My mind just wonders who will be able to read some of the words that one day I had written in a moment of solitude. Maybe words turn old like a genie in a bottle or a leaf still waiting to revert to green again.

Alvaro Barrios Sarmiento is originally from Colombia.

Single Mother
Gloria Montoya, Shakopee

I am a single mother of three boys who are 14, 12, and 5 years old. My life is not easy because I have to be a mother and a father at the same time. It is hard. One day, I made the difficult decision that I am better off without my partner. This decision affected my children, but it is for the best. Sometimes my kids have no understanding of how big an effort it is to earn money, to take care of the house, to fix the car, to help with homework and cook. My big effort is coming to learn English so that I can help with homework and possibly to get a better job with my improved English skills. Sometimes it is not easy when they have questions about their body changes and when they have "guy" questions. I think I don't have the correct words to talk or to answer their questions. My priority is my children because I provide the necessary needs. I love my kids. When I look at my kids, I smile and I forget everything. I am a single mother, and I am very happy.

Gloria Montoya is 35 years old and is originally from Mexico.

Lessons and Dreams
Patrick Newson, Minneapolis

The one lesson I learned in life is that breaking the law gets you nowhere, except for making minimum wage at a fast food restaurant. After rerouting my life I've chosen a direction: from now on I'm going to stay "sucka free," be good, don't break the law, stay out the game, stay law-abiding and don't get locked up, go to school every day, and obtain my G.E.D.

After a good education, I will be taking pictures showing my portfolio to creative, artistic people. The direction I'm heading is exciting. I plan to do big things: take pictures of movie stars and celebrities, and places around the world. Rerouting my life has been very soul searching and an experience.

A Special Blackboard
Anonymous, Minneapolis

There are two blackboards in my class and they contain characteristics of knowledge.

They are rectangles, four sides, two long sides and two wide sides and they are located on the wall of the class. They are built of wood, are colored black and clean. They are full of beauty and give an impression that everyone who has seen it must be impressed by all the time. They contain a lot of knowledge and rare resources that humans cannot see, catch or touch. Sometimes students with ideas or questions write on them, but the teacher usually writes on them every time she teaches us. She writes some important information about the teaching plan or general knowledge in the world. These two blackboards can be a good way to indicate to every human and to us, how to meet the civilization and a cheerful future that we have never seen before.

These two blackboards have a lot of advantages and they are very valuable to us. They also are the property of school and us, so we should keep them clean and very nice. Like this day and forever so that the next generation might use and inherit them from us in the future. Also I expect that the new generation is going to use them worthwhile and in useful ways in order to bring the generation to meet the progress of science and knowledge and to understand more about the living things in the world. The blackboard will help to recreate, build and teach the generation to become clever students and to have an important backbone and strong country; that they will discover some new advantageous things and bring those new things to develop and serve society. The country and the world in the right way with good quality can conduct the country to enlightenment.

My Dream is Coming True
Manuela Alejandra Pinto-Jacobo, New Hope

My dream started when I was at the University of Guadalajara studying to become a veterinarian. I wanted to study English as my second language. My veterinarian studies took all of my money. I had no mare funds left to take my English courses.

After graduating from the university with my veterinarian degree, I began working with the government and pork producers. I helped to control two special diseases in pigs. I loved my job. It allowed me to focus on my dream and I began studying English. I took English classes for only two months, because I travelled a lot for my job.

One day a friend of mine told me about an agriculture program at the University of Minnesota. My friend Bernardo helped me to fill out the application because I didn't know any English. I had to lie and say I spoke English fluently when I applied for the program. Fortunately, the university accepted me. They sent me all the paperwork that I needed to apply for a student visa.

When I came to Minnesota I was a little worried because I didn't understand any English, but I was sure I was in the right place to pursue my dream. I met a woman that spoke Spanish and explained my new job and courses, which helped me to adjust to my life.

I met an American man and we started dating over a year ago. He speaks only English and that is a very good way for me to improve my English. I got engaged this past Thanksgiving Day. We are planning our wedding now, and will be married soon. I'm very excited for the future. Finally my dream is coming true. I feel blessed by all that has happened in the last few years.

Manuela Alejandra Pinto-Jacobo is 30 years old and is originally from El Rincon, Jalisco, Mexico.

I Am Happy for the School Opportunities in the U.S.A.
Cecila Cifuentes, Austin

My name is Cecilia Cifuentes. I have been living in Minnesota since November 28, 1998. I am originally from Mexico. At that time I didn't know anything about this country. I was kind of scared, because I didn't speak a word of English. But my goal was to go to school to learn the language. That way I can find better work opportunities, either here, in other places or other countries.

At first I lived in Marshall, Minnesota for about three months. After that I decided to move here to Austin which has been my home for thirteen years. I am so thankful for the big opportunities in this town that I love. I am also thankful for the people who have helped me to find classes. I remember my tutor who helped me a lot with my reading. I also went to River Land to study ESL (English as a Second Language) and computer classes. At that time, it was a little hard because I was going to school in the morning and working in the afternoon.

For a few years I quit the school. I started a family. I have a husband and four beautiful kids. But I never gave up. I just followed my path thru them. That's why I am here today. I am following one of my biggest dreams. The experience has been great, especially because I have met very good people in this city. Those few years in the school and some other years of practicing with friends and coworkers, has been helpful for me to become a better English speaker and reader. I hope a lot of people can learn from my experience. It is never too late if you have a dream. My dream was to learn to speak and read English and I am still working on it. I think there is always something new to learn, especially in this beautiful country, the U.S.A.

Understanding English
Edwin Sinche, Minneapolis

When I came to the United States, everything was different. I came here in the winter. I had to work for two weeks. Every night, I dreamt about my family. When I got my first job, it was washing dishes in a restaurant. I remember when my boss asked me my name; I didn't understand what he was saying. I said, "Sorry, but I don't understand English." It was very hard for me to learn English.

But now I'm here in this country for two years. I understand English and now I speak it. My dream is to someday be a teacher, but for now I'm studying really hard.

Edwin Sinche is originally from Ecuador.

Education
Josue Palacios Lopez, Minneapolis

You are the ocean full of life.
You are the sun that gives me light.
You are the treasure that is not hidden.

Without you, poets do not have words.
Without you, a stanza would not make sense.

You are the journey to wisdom.
When I learn about you, I realize that I need you even more.

Josue Palacios Lopez is 27 years old and is originally from Guatemala.

I Am Student
Ah Tah Mon, Elk River

My name is Ah Tah Mon. I come from the country Burma. Before I came here, I never studied English in school. Now I am living in United States for almost six years. I had many troubles in the United States, but I have some good friends for me. Whenever I have trouble, they will help me. So now is first time I am studying English in school. I hear my teacher talking English to me, so I am proud to be a student in the classroom and to hear English words.

Ah Tah Mon is originally from Ye Township, Burma.

A Boy Named Ton
Kia Vang, Minneapolis

Once upon a time there was a boy named Ton. He went to play. He saw an old man wearing glasses reading a book and the boy was so happy. He went to the store to buy glasses so he could read a book like the old man. Later he got so mad at the salesman. The salesman asked why. Ton said, "Because when I wear your glasses I still cannot read." The salesman wondered why the boy said that and then the salesman asked Ton, "How many years did you go to school? Do you know how to read?" The boy said, "I never went to school. I came here to buy your glasses so I can read." The salesman laughed at this and told the boy, "You need to go to school to learn how to read. When you get too old and you cannot see, then you come back to buy my glasses."

Learning English is Important and Difficult
L.V.A., Minneapolis

Learning English is terribly important and difficult, because learning English takes place inside and outside the classroom. It is important for these reasons. First, it is necessary for communication, to get better jobs and to achieve our goals. The second reason is to have a better and easier life in America, because without education life is very hard.

The English language is difficult to learn, especially for people who are non-English speakers and for people who are older than 25 or 30 when they first come to America. The older we are, the more difficult it is to learn. Before I came to America, I said to myself the dream of my life is to go to America. I heard from some people that life in America is beautiful and heavenly. Then on August 27, 2000, I came to Minnesota and for the second time in my life I said to myself, finally, my dream came true. A few weeks later, I started working and two months after that I was thinking I will never forget how badly I wanted to come to America. I never realized how difficult it would be to adjust to life in America.

L.V.A. is 40 years old and is originally from Valle de Santiago, Mexico.

When I Came to the USA
Victor L., Maple Grove

When I first came to this country, it was very difficult for me to understand English. I remember when I use to go to the grocery store; I could not use proper words to ask somebody a question. Also, it was so hard to take the bus because it was winter and very cold. I decided to take the test to get my driver's license. When I got my driver's license, my cousin told me I could buy a car. I bought a new car and was so excited that I could drive my family to Saint Paul. It was not easy to drive in the snow; it was very slippery so I was very nervous. When you are driving, you have to pay attention to the road signs so you have to know English. For me, it is very important to learn English so that I can communicate and at the same time have better opportunities.

Keep Growing
Teo Silva, New Hope

It's never too late to learn something new. Every day is different because you make the difference. When we had one or two years we learned to walk and from there our minds began to learn everything we need. The mind is always hungry for knowledge, and then we grow up doing many things because the mind is fresh all the time. If we want to do or learn something new, we must be persistent and never give up, put into practice all we know, and continue to learn more things. No matter what happens in our lives, we need to continue growing. If we can't do something the first time, we must try again and again and ask ourselves every day, "What did you learn today?" That is helpful.

Improving Oneself
Anonymous, Minneapolis

My motivation to keep improving my writing in English is to think. Every time I keep coming to school, I learn more towards that goal. I would like to improve my education in the future. Everyone in this school wishes to get their GED. That is what I would like too but it is hard to do.

I can suggest to everyone who goes to school to keep doing it. Learning a new language could have many benefits. It's easy to understand everywhere in the country when you travel around the U.S.A.

Most people who come from other countries are immigrants. Some of them get married and they have their own family. Some of these people don't speak English and sometimes the kids speak just English. It's so difficult to understand each other because we are speaking different languages. I think it is best if we speak both languages then we can understand each other well.

Classmates
Lourdes Godinez, Bloomington

Today we say goodbye to some of our classmates and friends as they begin a new stage in life.

The experiences we have lived during this time fill us with enthusiasm to move forward.

For it is here that we learned not only a new language but tools that help us to have a better quality of life.

Also during this time, we have learned the meaning of friendship, solidarity, companionship, happiness and trust.

Thank you, teacher, for your time, your patience, and above all for sharing with us your knowledge.

Classmates, this fight is to be better human beings, better mothers, and to learn every day that which encourages us to be good women.

Lourdes Godinez is originally from Mexico.

Studying English
Rosa E., Coon Rapids

I started studying English in Minnesota, in the U.S. in 2011. I remember the first time I came to school to study English, I felt excited. I would to like to learn as much as possible. The first time I was very nervous. Now I feel better because I can do everything with no help. I learned a lot from my job. I remember speaking my first words in English at my job.

English is difficult because words are written, pronounced, and read in a different way. I think the hardest thing for me about learning English is to speak it when I do not spend any time studying at home after school. I speak more English than Spanish. I usually don't have a problem when I speak English; I have more problems writing it. I practice by reading it more; I like to read a lot. I only have problems when a person is talking to me. I don't understand them because they are not speaking clearly. Learning a second language is easy. I think it's easier when it's between the ages of three to five years because at that age a child is like a sponge. The mind is clean and it grabs everything it needs to know and absorbs it.

The best advice I could give to someone who is going to study and learn English is that it's not too late to learn; it all depends on the person. When I first came to the United States, I didn't know English at all. I only knew how to say yes or no. It didn't matter if it was something good or bad, I always said yes or no. Now it all depends on the question and I can give a good answer. When I compare the little English I knew back then to the English I know now, I feel so sure of myself to know more. I feel free and I'm not embarrassed to speak. In the past (and present) I have made mistakes with verbs. I understand when a person talks to me. That way I try to get another person to understand my English.

My dream is to speak, read and write well in English. Little by little I know I will achieve it. I don't know how or when, but I know I will. I like to think positive.

Rosa E. is 53 years old and is originally from El Salvador.

Learning English
Hussein Hussein, Coon Rapids

My name is Hussein Hussein. I moved from Iraq to the U.S. in July 2008 with my family. When I first came to the U.S., I didn't understand English well. When I went to the doctor, I needed help. I didn't understand what they wanted me to do, so I wanted to learn English. Right now, I go to school because I need to learn more English. After three and a half years, I am able to understand English. I feel happy when I speak English. Today I can talk with the doctor and I can help others. When someone asks me a question, I can answer. I want to teach other people in my country how to speak English.

Opportunities for Education
Marcos Higuera, Saint Paul

Minnesota has excellent education and second language programs. I have been studying here for almost six months. This program has free tuition and classes, but most importantly is their teachers; they are graduated and volunteers. Students can receive classes in comfortable buildings with great facilities. Students from around the world can come to school and share their experiences, culture, traditional food, and so on. Amazing people become a multicultural class in the ESL (English as a Second Language) schools.

Marcos Higuera is 37 years old and is originally from Venezuela.

My Life Goal of Learning English
Anonymous, Minneapolis

My goal is to learn English. I started my class in the year 2005. Since that time I am interested in learning English. It is not easy for me, but I have to achieve my goal. When I came to Jamie and Whitney's class I understood more than before. Although it was very hard for me the last four years, now I understand better. Before it was very hard for me to write a paragraph but now I can write and read. I will not lose hope. I will keep up and do my best to come to school and accomplish my goals. I hope my dreams come true.

My Friend and My Family
Mohamed Ali, Fridley

Thank God! I've never had problems in my life. Even when I was little and even now; only the home I lived in Somalia was not good. I am thankful to my parents for giving me good advice. They taught me to pray and respect others. They also taught me how to help the needy; so, I admire them greatly. I have many friends but I have one best friend, and his name is Ali. He is 50 years old and he lives near me. He has four children, two girls and two boys. He is a taxi driver. Every night we meet together, we chat about our future and events. We watch T.V. and we enjoy sports; Soccer is our favorite. We were in the same class in our country and we love each other now. We both got married in the same year, in 1969. In Somalia, my friend had a store and sold different foods such as rice, sugar, pasta and other small things. My friend was very smart, because he knows how to manage a business.

Mohamed Ali is originally from Somalia.

A Little Bit of Me
April Tucker, Saint Cloud

My name is April. I am 32 years old. I had four months left of my twelfth year in high school in Long Prairie, Minnesota. Because of health reasons and family issues, I was told I couldn't catch up and graduate with my class, so I basically gave up on going back to school even though I wanted to. It burned inside of me the urgency that grew year after year. It took 13 years of job searching and being overlooked by almost all of the jobs I applied for. I kept telling myself, oh, I will go back, and never did anything about it until now.

I have made mistakes, and was separated from my kids. This if my number one reason for me to do something with my life, so I can be stable and get my family back and own my own business. Then I will eventually have something to hand down to my kids. Getting my GED is so important to me, and I want to thank all the teachers for all their support and positive reinforcement, as well as my family and friends. Thank you.

My School
Rose M. Elhaj, Coon Rapids

When I started my nursing classes, I first went to Anoka County to take a test. I failed. That time of my life was not good. I went to south Minneapolis for business school. I met the teacher and I studied classes there. I got sick and I had surgery. My doctor told me to stay home for six months. I left my school after I paid all the money and I stayed home all these months taking my medication. I didn't know how to drive at the time and whenever I took the medications I didn't feel like myself and I could sleep all day long. I stopped taking these medications without the doctor knowing and went back to school. I took my classes for one month and three days, and then I signed up for the state test in Saint Paul Community College. I was so nervous. I felt like I failed the test. All the other students when they took the test it was their second time. It was my first time and so I didn't know how it went, but I prayed to God that everything went well. I was so happy that God answered my prayers.

After I passed the test, I got my certificate. Because I was so happy, I got sick and I had a headache. I couldn't sleep for three days. If I would have failed the test my life would have ended because I wouldn't be able to work in a company. Now I'm so happy I have a full time job and I am a certified nurse.

I give thanks to all my teachers in south Minneapolis and my teachers in Metro North Adult Education. Thank you all for helping me. Now I know that I'm a strong person.

My True Story
Maryam Ahmed, Minneapolis

My first day at my first job was very difficult for me. I work with seniors. The first day, I didn't understand how to follow directions. I drove my car for more than three hours. After that, I called my manager. I told him I was lost and I'm not going to my job. He told me, "Why you didn't call me?" I told him, "I'm sorry, but I can go tomorrow." He said, "You be careful tomorrow. Go early." I said, "I will be careful tomorrow." The next day I went early, more than two hours before the job started, so I made it on time.

My American Dream
Abdullahi Said, Minneapolis

My dream in America is to take part in the land of opportunity, such as in education and other social matters. The dream in this country is that you must be a man who knows what to do. I should support my community and my family for a better life and a better education. My point is to change lot of things about this world. That is why I came to America and started learning this hard language. My dream in America is not only to support my community but support other communities too. My dream in America will come true.

Studying English
Gena, Coon Rapids

I started studying English in the United States in 2009. The first time I came to school to study English, I couldn't understand the people. Everything was new to me. English is difficult because there are so many verb tenses and the spelling, speaking and grammar are very different from my native language. The most difficult thing about learning English is speaking. I do speak English outside of school. In my daily life, I have the biggest problem communicating in English when I talk to neighbors, doctors, or go to the grocery store.

I think learning a second language is the easiest when you are five or six years old because at this age you have a better memory. The best advice I can give someone who is going to study English is to learn a lot of words, listen and practice speaking, and to not be afraid to try. When I came here, I knew 20 words in English. I feel like I have progressed because when I first arrived here, I began to understand a little.

Accomplishment
Khou Lee, Saint Paul

My name is Khou Lee Moua. I am happy to see 2012 New Year. I got my green card. My husband and I had a child together. His name is Alexander. I am happy to learn and speak English. My teacher is very good.

First Day of School
Abdinasir Tobe, Saint Cloud

When I was six years old, I remember my first day of school in my country. It was very difficult for me to get up early in the morning. I hated to go to school because I couldn't sleep late, but now things have changed. I like school.

I remember one story my dad used to tell me when I was a kid. The story was about two men, one of them was a rich man the other one was a poor man, but the rich man didn't have any education at all.

They traveled together one day. The rich man came to the poor man and asked question.

"Did you travel this way before?", the rich man said.

"No, it is my first time,," poor man said.

"Do you have enough money?"

"No, I don't."

"Today you will lose half of your life because you have nothing to eat," the rich man said.

After a little while the poor man saw water coming inside the boat. He came to the rich man and said: "Since we started our journey you questioned me so I'd like to ask you one question. Do you know how to swim?"

The rich man said: "No."

"Today you will lose all of your life! My parents didn't leave money for me, but they gave me their knowledge and skills, my friend. The boat is going down and now your money will not save you today. Bye." said the poor man.

The rich man was dead and the poor man survived. So any time I remember this story I like school more than anything because to have education is important.

Why I Come to School
Sadia Yusuf, Minneapolis

I want to study English and more speak words. I want to read new words. I need more writing. I want to study a lot English. I want to talk to people. I need new words and lot of speaking. I want a better job and understand co-workers. I want to understank my friends at work. I want to speak English because I understand my boss. I want to study more English.

A Lesson I Learned From My Child
Blanca Villagomez, Brooklyn Park

Everyone has to learn their own way. Sometimes we get a surprise from someone that we never expected, like our kids. I have three girls, Jazmin, Stephanie and one that is on the way. For a long time I thought that I was the best mother they could have. However, yesterday I took Stephanie to a physical examination and almost everything went well, except she had one little issue that we needed to work on, her organizational skills.

The Doctor suggested that we get a calendar and put a sticker on every day that she had done a good job. The Doctor told her she is very brave,of course, being her mother, I was very proud when Stephanie asked, "What if I get a prize at the end of the month?" The Doctor said, "It was a good idea." I agreed and asked her, "What do you want?" Stephanie replied, "I want to spend more time with my mommy." I was very upset. I thought my girls had enough time to spend with me. I thought to myself; why would Stephanie say such a thing? When I suddenly realized we were spending time together, but it was not quality time together. It was true we spend so much time doing things and we never stop to enjoy our time together. I remember my grandma telling me, some people are always trying to catch ants instead of elephants, now I understand what she meant.

Days of Our Life
Anonymous, Brooklyn Park

Last year, many people I knew passed away; a baby, co-workers, friends, and finally my own miscarriage. These events have made me look at life differently. I have learned that you have to live each moment at a time. You try to make the right decisions because each day is uncertain; tomorrow may have trouble of its own. You may not always win the temptation of the day, but you can learn from it and live with the decision you made. I know I can't do it alone. I need God. No one can live your life for you, but you can share your life experience with your partner, family, and friends. And lastly, don't forget to enjoy each moment as it comes.

I Am Bilingual in Mexican and American Sign Language
Federico P., Saint Paul

I am from Mexico. I live with relatives, a deaf uncle and deaf aunt. My dad plays three different Mexican vihuelas (guitars). I heard mother wanting to move to Minnesota for many years. I started to look up where so I could join the Saint Paul school with deaf people, HUBBS Center Adult Basic Education Program. My brother drives independently outside in the bus, where I learn improvement by enjoying the trips everywhere we go in school. My brother doesn't worry, I will want to go to school to try to learn, read, and write, by seeing my deaf teacher using ASL (American Sign Language). I learn to watch her ASL. My ASL skills have improved, but not my Mexican Homemade language. I love ASL better than Mexican Homemade language. I also try to write English. Mexico and Minnesota are different because of the deaf community in Minnesota that is better than Mexico's due to no Deafies around me there.

My Writing is Education
Rukia Osman, Minneapolis

My name is Rukia. I am from Dire Dawa, Ethiopia. I used to live with my family of sisters, brothers, and parents. I remember the first day I came to the United States on July 16, 2008 to Washington, D.C. It was nice weather. When I left the airport and went outside, I said, "Oh my God."

My writing is about my English. I like to speak English because I hope it is better and I hope to learn more English. Education is important to everyone to get jobs and to have a better life. I also hope to get a good education for my life because when I came the first time, it was difficult for me to understand people and the way. Now, thank God, even though I don't speak good English, I understand more than before, and that's why I go to school.

The Importance of English
Anonymous, Minneapolis

The American Dream for every person when they came to this country is to get a better job and a better life. The first little thing is to learn how to speak and write English because that will help at the beginning of their life here. It will help to make conversation with people, to make appointments with the doctor, to talk with the police if something happens. English is very important.

My Story
David Williams, Sauk Rapids

I started off in Chicago, where I was born in Cook County hospital. We lived on the south side of Chicago. My sisters, brother and I were raised in the beginning of our lives in the projects. Later we moved to Mississippi where my mom and dad are from.

My dad is from Holly Springs, Mississippi. It's a small town and home of Rush College, an all black college. It is the poorest college I have ever seen in my life. We lived in Holly Springs for quite some time where we farmed. It was really different from the big city. My dad and his family have 100 acres of land there. We went to school in another small town called Posse Camp, Mississippi. That is where I ran in the Junior Olympics. I won first place in the Sprint Race, second place in the Shot Put, and third place in the Long Jump.

Down in the Delta, now that's where my mom's from, I love it. She's from Arcola, Mississippi. It's a small town in Washington County. I use to go back there every February, that's when the sunshine is very nice. I have never been to a town where nearly everyone is kind of related to you, and I do mean that. We moved back to Chicago later in my life. When I turned 18, I came to Minnesota.

My Lovely Country
Abdulaziz, Plymouth

I have been living in the U.S.A. for one year. I began my stay in Arizona and then stopped in Minnesota, which makes me feel that I'm missing where I came from, Saudi Arabia. I'm not from there, but I would love to be from there because I was born over there. Originally I'm from Djibouti and that means that I speak two languages, Arabic and Somali. English is my third language. In my opinion, English is an easy language and I'm enjoying learning English. But I'm missing both countries I came from. However, I'm living a wonderful life in my third country, the U.S.A.

I'm half way to accomplishing my goal of learning English, studying more English, and then moving on to become a dentist in the U.S.A.

Abdulaziz is originally from Djibouti.

I Was Crying
Irma Romero, Hilltop

I came here 11 years ago. I'm from Ecuador. I remember my first job was in Edina. I was working the third shift and I was a janitor. I was cleaning the carpet and touched the alarm. And in a few minutes, many, many police officers came to the mall. I was scared because I don't speak English, but my friend Kevin Lindberg helped me. I love him because he teaches me many things. He tells me about this place for my learning English.

Irma Romero is 50 years old and is originally from Quito, Ecuador.

Teach Me
Paw Htoo, Roseville

So much depends upon
A beautiful teacher to
Teach me more English
In my classroom

Paw Htoo is originally from Burma.

Learning English
Cecilia Garrido Alcaraz, Austin

The hardest thing about coming to a different country is the language. My first English teacher helped me so much to learn English as my second language. I always thought, "How can she be that patient with all of her students?", since we all were beginners, and didn't understand much. At first, I only knew a few words. I always wondered how I did on that very first placement test she gave me. So far, I have had many English teachers. I know I've been so lucky because I have had the best English teachers there are. I'm very grateful to all of my teachers because I've learned a lot from all of them.

An English-Spanish dictionary was my best friend at that time. It helped me to translate all of the many papers I got from my son's school every day. I noticed that by translating word by word not everything made sense. Sometimes I got disappointed because even spending a lot of time with the dictionary; I still didn't get what the letters said. Then I found out about English classes for adults, and I didn't hesitate to register.

I remember being afraid of going to the store to buy groceries. I just hoped that nobody would ask me any questions. Once at a supermarket at the checkout, I paid for what a bought and the cashier asked me if I needed "Drive up" and I said, "No, thank you." Then she said, "You want to carry it out, right?" I answered, "No." Then she looked at me with a strange look. At that time, I knew I had answered wrong. I should have answered "Yes" to one of the questions, but to which one of them? Now, I know how to answer the questions because they still ask the same questions at the checkout in that grocery store.

I'm still in the process of learning a new language. Even though the path is sometimes rough, I'm determined to reach my goal. It will take time, dedication and a lot of effort, so I'm willing to do all that in order to succeed.

Cecilia Garrido Alcaraz is 43 years old and is originally from Mexico.

My Car
Hassan Liban, Minneapolis

My favorite Car is a Honda Civic for a personal reason. I like it because it is a two door sports car. It has the red rims, runs very fast, and does not finish gas quickly. Therefore, I purchased a Honda Civic for $6000. It was beautiful, and so comfortable. When I drove on the street the people said, "What a nice car," especially girls. However, one day some terrible incident happened to my car. I drove to Rosedale Mall for shopping and parked my car in front of J.C. Penny's and went into the mall. I spent about one and a half hour. When I came out, my car was not there because someone stole it. I was so shocked. I called the police immediately and reported it. Then my friends gave me a ride home. After two days, the police called me back and asked me if I wanted to see my car. Then I went to see my car, and I found it. It was so messy, and the window was broken, and they removed the tires and the rims. They took those away. I learned from this lesson; don't leave my car again without alarms.

Hassan Liban is originally from Ethiopia..

Funny Story
Nancy Tamayo, Minneapolis

After I came to the United States, I went with my son one day to deliver newspapers. That day, it was raining a lot. When the old woman opened the door, my son gave her the newspapers and she said, "Bad day." I said, "You, too!" because I didn't know much English. My son asked me, "Why did you say that?" I told him, "I thought she said 'Have a nice day'!"

Nancy Tamayo is originally from Ecuador.

Driving in the USA
Gang Li, Austin

I came to the United States on June 29, 2011. Before that time, I knew some things about America from TV and books. I was interested in everything that I saw and listened to, and wanted to see more. So after I came, getting a driver's license was the first thing I had to do.

In America, after I passed the knowledge test, I drove my own car for several weeks and got the driver's license after the road test. In China, you must go to driver's school to learn how to drive a car. After that, you have to take a knowledge test. If you pass it, there are three road tests waiting for you. It took me about half a year to get a Chinese driver's license.

It is different between China and America to drive a car on the road. There is no speed limit in Chinese cities. Many people drive fast. They will maintain speed when they see pedestrians wanting to cross the road because they think the pedestrians will stay back and let the cars go. It is very dangerous. Now, in America, when I took a test for the license, the officer said, "You must stop the car for pedestrians, if you do not stop you could get in trouble."

Another thing that is different is there are no stop signs in China. Almost every intersection has a traffic light because many bicycles and cars would make traffic jams if there was no traffic light. So when I drive a car and go through the intersection now, I usually want to stop even though there is no stop sign.

By the time I go back to China, I hope there will be more and more people in our country that drive carefully. The safety for people is the most important thing for us to do.

Love

Jelly and Peanut Butter Sandwich
Leo Lara, Columbia Heights

It's interesting when we compare cultures and traditions. We often find similarities and differences amongst each other, especially when it comes to food.

This passage of my life initiated and evolved in Ecuador, South America. At that time I was in my mid-twenties and a "starving musician." (jajajajajaja!) I met Kathy—a "gringa" working to build a music program at a center for street kids—through a mutual friend at a concert hall called *La Casa De La Cultura Ecuatoriana*.

Just a couple of days later, was when I initially began seeing her. (Well, she says two days, although, according to my memory, I was at her door a couple of weeks later.) I continued to visit her more and more often, partly for my "enamoramiento" (courting), and partly for the enticing food she offered me.

I realized that those incredible jelly and peanut butter sandwiches and the chocolate chip cookies she prepared for me were something that put me in heaven. Never in my life had I eaten such a strange but deliciously sweet sandwich—and the cookies, mmmm, they melted in my mouth. I was used to eating the basics of rice and beans and fried yucca. These novel things that she would do with food won my heart.

Kathy and I married six months later and migrated to the United States to raise our family of five children and make a career together of musical performance and cultural education. Our home has become a magnet for family and friends to enjoy the multicultural conversations, musical gatherings and banquets. Our kitchen now smells of the combination of cultures, from the Ecuadorean foods of rice, beans, and yucca to the sweet aroma of snicker doodles and chocolate chip cookies. Of course, those delicious jelly and peanut butter sandwiches are still a special treat for me.

Leo Lara is an Ecuadorian of African and Indigenous descent who has played music professionally since 1971. As a member of Jatari, in his native Ecuador, he investigated native musical traditions through performances aimed at reclaiming cultural identity. Leo moved to the United States in 1978, founded the Minnesota Committee for New Song, and now performs solo, with an Andean ensemble, and with his wife, Kathy. Leo and Kathy have five children and three grandchildren, and are committed to building musical bridges of cultural understanding. Leo currently studies at North Metro ABE in Columbia Heights.

Daddy's Girl

Domingo Zambrano Ramirez, Claremont

I dedicate this to all wild parents who lost a child in adolescence.
Unexpectedly, you feel rejected by the Lord, no longer in His presence!
Trying to understand why the man upstairs could let this happen.
I feels like He doesn't even care about what's happened.
Sit'n back in heaven laugh'n!
I know He can hear me rapping!
My beautiful creation,
It hurt when your last breath was taken.
I spend every wake'n moment trying to live it down.
My baby was dying and He was nowhere to be found.
As I try to hide the pain inside, I come to realize,
I'm going crazy, losing my mind,
Messing with this pen and pad to pass the time.
Trying to get to death quicker.
Drowning my sorrows with a bottle of liquor.
As the pressure grows thicker,
I remember praying for my baby to live!
Asking if He was able to send me an angel but He never did.
Holding her close to my heart from the start.
Remembering the day we had to part.
Even though you're gone, I'm still a daddy in this world.
Your memory lives on because you will always be – Daddy's Girl!!!

Tun Aung, Saint Paul

The Happiest Day of My Life So Far

Houa Vang B., Minneapolis

Now, it was about twenty years ago. I remember my girlfriend and we were in love with each other for a long time. Everything was going well and we hoped to create the future together with the bright earth.

One day, I asked her to marry, but she apologized that she can't marry me. The problem was she had been betrothed with another boy while they were both still little children and they will have a wedding soon when they're ready. There's one thing she couldn't be obstinate about. In Hmong culture, children must obey their parents. Mostly the children must agree with their parents without choices.

Since that day, she was not quite seeing me as before. She pretended she didn't know me when I saw her. I was down hearted and became obsessed with worry about my true love that I gave her already.

Then I was sad and I wanted to go far away because I didn't want to see her wedding. "Why does the earth seem too narrow for me?" I thought and I yelled inside of my heart. I went to school hopelessly, even though my ears heard the teacher, but my brain and my heart had gone far away somewhere else. I learned nothing from school because I always thought about her. My friends also consoled me, but it got worthless. I couldn't pass out of my memory; I felt exhausted and darkness in my life.

About two months later, but it felt like two years, I was still sad and lonely when she came and told me that we were winners. She's ready to marry me anytime because both sets of parents canceled the engagement. "It's so cold I couldn't stay alive without you; please embrace and clasp me to your chest and let's go together my honey," said her soft voice that I never heard before and I wished for. I was so happy that tears dropped, but I was not sad. Then it made me start seeing the earth become brighter and brighter.

Actually, the earth was as wide as I see at the end. So I will never forget her forever, the lady who is "my wife now."

Houa Vang B. is 30 years old and is originally from Laos.

My Life Is Complicated But I'm Thankful

Jonah T., Minneapolis

I was born deaf. I am an only child and my real parents are also deaf. They couldn't handle me when I was two or three years old, so they decided to send me to a preschool in Faribault at a deaf school. Later on, my real mom wanted me go to deaf school, so around 1990, I entered school. I don't know who anyone was there. I was a little boy who was shy and quiet.

A few months later, my teacher spoke to me. The social worker explained to me by saying, "Your mom and dad decided to send you to foster home." I was confused and I asked "Why?" My social worker wanted me to understand. My parents struggled with money and couldn't afford to help, but they did the best they could. My parents made mistakes. They made a decision to send me to a foster home for a while. I was unhappy for a long time because I felt no love and was lost. My foster home was not enough support for me. Every Christmas I prayed so hard because I was looking for new family. I needed new feelings of love, kindness, support and the ability to settle down for good. I graduated high school in 2005. I went to school programs in Brooklyn Park, Minnesota. I kept going to school every day and I did not give up. I'm looking for a new life and career.

In 2008 my friend and I went to a church in Minneapolis. I wanted to meet new friends because I was homeless for several years. I felt funny, but I knew something would happen. I found someone who understands my life, what I have been through because I suffer. I met someone, his name is Jim. Jim is kindness for me. He saved me a many times and is supportive. I like him as my dad. We have known each other for four years now. Also I felt we were connected in oneness. Like always, we are bond. We felt a spiritual reconnection. On Thanksgiving Day 2011 he told me that he wanted me to be his son. I felt speechless on that day, making me smile again with love, kindness and support. I love you dad in all my heart.

Time Does Not Wait

Malee Vue, Minneapolis

The earth has four seasons.
It is winter, summer, spring, and fall.
The earth moves around and around every day, and we can feel like it still moves
A flower grows up beautiful, but the flower dries up and dies.
The time does not wait for you if you want to do something good for your life.
Begin right now; do not wait. If you want to reach your dream, continue, do not stop.
We don't know if tomorrow we will still be alive or not.
If you want someone to stay with you forever, you have to love him or her from your heart.
Love means do everything good to the person you love.
Even though you love your mom or your kid, you must tell them from your attitude or from the work you do.
True love is not jealous (in Hmong language) Hlub tsis xam khib
True love does not discriminate (in Hmong language) Hlub tsis ntxub ntxaug
True love means not staying angry.
True love is honest (in Hmong language) Hlub ncaj ncees
True love is patient (in Hmong language) Hlub ua siab ntev
True love is respectful (in Hmong language) Hlub ib leeg hwm is leeg
If you have complete love all of the above is with you.
No one who you love can leave you.

A Good Relationship
Laura Concepcion, Crystal

There are a lot of different kinds of relationships. To have a good relationship, both people have to be honest and trust each other. Both have to agree on what they plan to do. For example, if they are living together, the expenses—such as rent, electricity, gas, telephone, and food—should be shared equally. A good relationship is also about sharing activities like joining a club, bowling, exercising, or jogging. A relationship is nice when each person understands that when one has a problem, the other has somebody with whom to discuss it. Most of the time, a good relationship is better with someone outside your own family. There are a lot of different kinds of relationships in life, and I will be very happy when I find someone that I can trust, enjoy, and be comfortable with.

Laura Concepcion is originally from Dominican Republic.

A Lovely Friendship
Marina Jones, Saint Louis Park

Bear was a four-month-old dog when the police found him lost on the street. He was a cute black lab that needed a new home. The cops went to a bar and asked if someone there was interested in adopting a new puppy. That night they found him a new place. His new owner, a single young guy, brought him home without predicting how hyperactive he would be, and all the changes that would happen in his life with a new family member. Despite shoes, clothes, books, papers, and some more things destroyed at home, they became best friends. Bear was a joy in his owner's life. They would walk, run, and have fun together for many years. Everybody called him a crazy dog because of his eternal puppy behavior, but his owner loved him and enjoyed their adventures. Unfortunately, after almost ten years of lovely friendship, Bear passed away, but he is vivid in his owner's memories forever as his happy dog.

Marina Jones is 27 years old and is originally from Brazil.

My Grandmother
Marwa Abubaker, Austin

My grandmother was a special person to me. She always offered love and kindness. She often made you feel so confident and strong. Her arms were always open no matter what you did wrong. She always smiled, she never got mad, she never screamed at me.

I loved the times when she told me stories about Aladdin and the Arabian Nights. She also told me stories with chorals. All of hers were better than any stories I ever read. Also she gave me advice and told me about her experiences in life.

When I was sick she took care of me until I got better. She didn't take me to the hospital. She used her own medicines like honey and lime for colds, or she covered my body with an herb called Neem to reduce the fever. Also she put the sesame oil on my body for muscle aches.

My grandmother lived a long life. She died at 120 years old, and she was like a reference book to my entire community because she knew a lot of information about our history. My grandmother went away from us, but we still remember her. I wouldn't be the person I am if I did not spend time with my grandmother.

My Children's Dreams
Magali Garduza, Fridley

My name is Magali. I came from Mexico, and I have ten years living in Minneapolis, MN, but I am not alone. I feel happy because I married and have two precious boys. When I stay at home, I like to take time to ask them about how their day in school was, what they learned, what they liked the most, and what their dreams are for the future. My older son wants to be a doctor when he grows up. My little son wants to be a dentist; since they were little they said that. I feel motivated with their dreams, and I really hope to help them to reach their goals because I love them with all my heart and I give thanks to God for having them. I feel that they are the most important thing in my life.

Magali Garduza is originally from Mexico.

Goodbye to Nasra and Me
Seti Harusha, Coon Rapids

I married my first wife in 2003. Her name was Sabimana Tielive. She was pregnant during the middle of the year 2003. She was very sick and stayed in the hospital on and off for six months. One day she wanted to throw herself into the big hole we had dug out of red clay to make bricks. When I got outside, I caught her hands. She screamed loudly that night. People came and asked her what happened. My wife told them, "I want to die! I want to end my sickness."

About a week later, we had a baby girl. I named her Nasra Habonimana. Both of these names have a meaning. Nasra is an Arabic name that means "One who survives death or an accident," and Habonimana is my mom's sister's name that means "Allah" or "God sees." After having a baby on May 19, 2004, my wife came home. She stayed just two weeks at home before she got sick with a fever. I took her to the hospital and she had drips going into her arm, but she didn't get better. She stayed two months at the hospital until she died on September 11, 2004. At that time my daughter was only three months old. I took care of my daughter by myself until we came to the U.S.A. in 2006.

Now my daughter is seven and she asks about her mom. But I keep telling her, "I will explain to you later." She tells me, "I know my mom has already died because I never talk to her, even on the telephone." I told Nasra, "I will tell you when you are old enough to understand about sickness and death."

Even now I still miss my first wife a lot. Before she died she told me, "Don't give permission to anybody else to take care of Nasra." After that she shook hands with me and said goodbye, but her heart was still beating slowly even though I couldn't see or hear it. Later, she died when I was at the Mkugwa Refugees Camp. The Islamic Community had given me money to buy soap and other things. A woman stayed by my wife's side in the hospital. The woman told me before she died, she said "Amina," which means Amen.

I still cry sometimes when I see my daughter, Nasra, because she reminds me of her mother's life.

Seti Harusha is originally from Tanzania.

My Mother is Special
Mahmood Hassan, Inver Grove Heights

My mother is my special friend; my mother's name is Hinifa Begum. She was born in Calcutta, India. When my mother was 16 years old, she studied in Calcutta, India. She went to a convent school and met my father; they fell in love with each other. They decided to move to Pakistan and never go back to India again. My mother's family all live in India and my father's family all live in Pakistan. While my father went to England alone, my mother lived in Pakistan with my dad's sister. However, she could not speak Urdu; she spoke only English. I came to America and I am staying in this country. I called my mother and she has decided to come to America. She has found a job in the factory.

Mahmood Hassan is originally from Pakistan.

Ribbons
R. M. Taylor, Blaine

Multi-colored glitters in her hair,
fluttering wildly in the sweet, sweet air.
Flashing brightly into the deep red sun,
moving lightly in the sky.
Wrapping in around her in gentle grace,
not a one out of place.
Moving in silently,
reflecting in the air the love they shared.

Best Mom
Fadumo, Minneapolis

My name is Fadumo. I am from Somalia and was born in a small city. I have five brothers and three sisters. I grew up with a large and happy family. I am the only one who is friendly with my mother. I think my mother is the most amazing mother in the world. I remember how she fed me and how she held me. She told me I am with you even if I am gone. I have a lovely mother and often dream of her. I hope we live together again.

Love and Understanding in Elderly Care

Carmen Mairena, Golden Valley

The love and understanding of the elderly in the nursing home is very important. It helps them make an easier adjustment when they are transferred to their new life.

When an elderly moves to a nursing home, he or she leaves behind almost all the things that formed part of his or her life: friends, family, independence, possessions, pets, social activities, personal customs, and routines.

The caregiver with love and understanding can help the elderly to face all these drastic changes. One of the first steps to take is to introduce themselves to the elder and tell them why they are there. Then to take the time to make them feel welcome, comfortable, secure, loved and confident. Finally, telling them, "I am here for you. I am here to help you in all your needs and provide the care that you deserve."

Showing love and understanding in all the moments of sadness, discouragement, and loneliness helps the elderly to feel better, more comfortable and helps in developing a relationship of trust with the caregiver. Consequently, the life in a nursing home becomes pleasant during the last moments of his or her life. This is the important job of the elderly caregiver.

Carmen Mairena is originally from Nicaragua.

For Those I Love

Ashlie Arnold, Brooklyn Park

For Those I Love: I want you to know that I may not know how to express how you all make me feel, but if you were not in my life, I would feel broken. My sisters and my best friend are the only people I can be myself with when I'm around them. When I'm with them, I don't have to act or prove anything to them.

My sister Larisa is someone I fight with all the time, but at the end of the day, she's still my sister who I would fight for life.

My baby sister Kenya is two years old. I'm closer to her because I basically raised her since she was born.

Kenya means a lot to me. When I look at her, she always makes me smile.

My best friend Shay was always there for me through our childhood. Shay is someone I can really look up to. She is a special someone I can go to with my ups and downs.

These three girls are those I love the most in my life. Personally, my best friend Shay was one of those kids back in middle school that wasn't very social with other students in class. She's Indian and kids would judge her because of her race. But I saw Shay as just a normal young girl that just wanted someone to talk to and be her friend. Her family wasn't always around that much, and she didn't really get along with her mom, brother or sister. Most of them lived up north, so she stayed at my house all the time during the school year and in the summer time. We would always call each other sisters because we always stayed together. I love Shay like I love my other two sisters. They will always be those I love the most till death do us part.

My Mother

Henna, Blaine

I remember my mother. Her name was Aisha. She is important to me. She was a special person. She was very patient and kind. She taught her kids about what to do with problems. For example, she taught me all the time, to be patient. She always told me that if someone wants to be an enemy, to be nice; don't be the same as them.

We came to the United States in 1997. That's when my mom started to get sick a lot. It was very painful for all the family, because she was spending most of the time at the hospital. She was in a coma for three months. When she woke up her brain was changed. She was like a different person, she forgot some things. After that, she lived about two years; then she passed away. We were all very sad and we remember her every day and night.

Henna is originally from Somalia.

Don't Wait Until It's Too Late
Francisco Hernandez, Minneapolis

This is a story of a young couple that really loved each other. The man was in his 20's and the girl was 16 or almost 17 years old. The young man was a singer. One Saturday evening this singer was performing a concert when he saw this extremely beautiful young girl. His voice started to shake, and he felt as if it was the first time he had ever performed, but this time she was the only person who mattered and could change his emotions, his feelings, and his mind. He could no longer concentrate–he almost forgot the song. Of course this wasn't the first time that a beautiful girl had looked at him. In the past, he had many other concerts where there were also beautiful girls looking at him, but this time everything was different. This girl kept looking at him without blinking, and she herself realized that he got her attention, so she kept looking and looking at him. She was not excited. She didn't even look like a girl who was enjoying the show, but more like she was captivated by him. He tried not to look at her eyes in order to keep performing. He didn't know if he wanted time to pass by faster or slower. He was simply happy. Unfortunately, however, after that concert he never saw her again. He kept playing, doing concerts and expecting to see that lovely face, but nothing happened. As the time went by, he got old waiting for that beautiful lady, but she never came.

The moral of this story is: if you love someone or fall in love with someone, stop what you are doing, and go to that person, and let her/him know what you feel. Don't wait until it's too late!

Love
Seuth Sue Saly, Minneapolis

Love is a grateful thing.
Love is with a pure heart.
Love is with a charity heart.
Love the person that loves you.
Love the person that hates you.
Love your friends.
Love your enemies.
Love your family.
Love your neighbor.
Love your teacher.
Love one another.
Love the world.
Love will never end.
I love you with all my heart.
Love God.

Seuth Sue Saly is originally from Laos.

My Father
Mai Yang Chang, Saint Paul

I admire my loving father the most. He was a great father, and he brought me up carefully. My father's name is Xai Law Chang and he was a friend of mine in every aspect of my life. He brought me up with all his gentle heart and strength.

My father was a tall man, caring, hard-working, and intelligent. He always made me happy and taught me good manners. Like how to respect others. He also taught me how to behave in a good way and to never talk down to people. My father was a very kind-hearted man. He never said anything to hurt others' feelings. I wish I could have my father's character. I love him a lot. I miss him in every inch of my life. He used to take care of me so much that nobody could compare to him. My dad was a great father, and I am very proud to be his daughter. He meant the world to me. He was a very important person, and I will remember him for all of my life. I will not see him any more in this world, but he is always in my heart forever.

Mai Yang Chang is originally from Thailand.

Stand By Me
MingHai Zheng and MingYing Zheng, Minnetonka

A long time ago, there was a little frog that lived in a well by himself. The most delectable time of his day was watching shining stars as he looked up from the well. He would always sit in the middle of the well when the sun was going down. He thought that watching the stars at night was the most wonderful thing ever.

One day, the little frog sat in the middle of the well as usual, quietly, waiting for the dark, even though it was a rainy night. Suddenly, the rain stopped. He raised his head with hope. One hour passed and the stars were still hiding. He felt sad, and right at that moment a glimmer appeared behind the cloud, then disappeared, then showed up again. He looked at that particular spot without a blink. "I saw it, I saw it," little frog said to himself. Clouds faded gradually. It was a very little star with a

unique purple violet light. His heart sped up, like a fire burning inside of him, but he couldn't figure out with his little brain why this was happening. Where upon all the day, the little frog would sit in the left corner of the well looking toward the place where he had seen the star the other day and gone into a sweet dream.

Until there was a night when the little frog noticed that the little star was gone. He felt anxious, and jumped around in the well, and tried to find his favorite star. "Where are you?" he shouted, but there was no one answering him except the echo of his own voice. "I should jump out and go find it!" he said to himself. Therefore, jumping out of the well became his daily routine.

Finally, the little frog jumped out of the well. It was a cloudless midnight, the sky studded with twinkling stars. The frog was pleasantly surprised. He had never seen so many stars before. "Hey! There you are!" little frog yelled to the sky. He found the star and felt so happy and satisfied. Then he turned back to his well. The frog believed that the little star would always be there and stand by him, even if he couldn't see it. After that day, people could always hear a frog singing under the well, no matter if it was a sunny day or a rainy day.

MingHai Zheng and MingYing Zheng are 24 and 22 years old and are originally from China.

The Thought of You Keeps Me Strong
Jesus Malave Arroyo, West Saint Paul

I am grateful for all the happy moments she has brought to me. I must admit, her love and friendship has made her the one. She touches my heart and soul. I love her. These are not just some words I say. In my mind and deep in my heart is where she will stay. Her love makes me glow. That's something few have seen and only she will know. Reminiscing of good times, looking at her brown eyes, her smile, her hugs and kisses; her loving.

Conversations keep me facing toward a better future, leaving the hurt behind. She and I are intertwined. I am in her mind and she in mine forever. Together there is no such place as time. With all my love I promise, as witnessed from above to be completely honest. She completes me. No other woman can come close to competing. The thought of her keeps me strong in moments of weakness, full of life always. My gift of speech honors her. It is a way to hold out my hand and reach to hers. Preach to her maybe, but only for a minute. I speak my vows, promise to love her inside out. As these words surround us a lovely storm of bliss, I feel an electric charge upon my lips when we kiss. My sweetheart, my soul, I will make it home soon, complete. I love you Tani.

Jesus Malave Arroyo is 40 years old and is originally from Puerto Rico.

From Inside
Ricky Villarreal, Sacred Heart

Molded by the hands of an artistic kind, are words of mine, written through the poet's eyes. Words unspoken, words long kept, hidden deep in this heart, the truth, the lies, the trust. All the love I possess, locked inside for a baby I'll never forget.

Her first everything was special for me. Her first birthday—still a fresh memory. Her smile, her eyes, her size. Her laughs, her hands, her cries. Memories I'll cherish for my life time.

God knows I tried to do right. I tried so hard to compromise, so I could be by your side. But things happen, like times change. People grow to face their mistakes, then reap what they sow without turning back.

If I'm to blame for the way our lives turned out, I apologize for leaving us all without. Hope you know, I loved, never hated, you. Although it hurt at first, I had to accept the truth of you, eventually continuing with a life you were meant to live. All I ask is that you keep me in her mind. Don't let her forget about the love coming from inside my heart.

My Brother Had a Bad Accident
Anonymous, Roseville

In 2007, my brother had a bad accident. A guy hit my brother. My brother broke his legs. The doctor said he had to cut one leg off. I was crying. Another doctor came and saved his leg. The other guy is in jail.

When I heard about the accident, I went to Buffalo, New York in January 2008 to help my brother. He is older than I am. He is a funny guy and he is single. My brother was in the hospital for three months.

I am so happy when I see my brother walking, driving, and running. He is a lucky boy.

The Birth of My First Child
Aide A. Hernandez, Elk River

When my first child was born, it had a great impact in my life that changed my whole life. She was born in Minnesota on October 27, 2004 at 1:30 AM. My husband and my parents were there with me expecting my first child. She is a blessing that God give me. When I saw her face and her wide open eyes, the only thing I can think and feel is the joy of having my first child in my arms. I will never forget that miracle happened, and three years later God gave me the same experience.

My Daughter
Mohamoud Haji Mohamed, Minneapolis

My name is Haji. I have ten children, six boys and four girls. I love all of them, but one of my kids, she is the best. Her name is Noura. She is in Somalia. Last time I saw her she was five years old. Now she is ten years old. She still remembers me when I talk to her. She asks me when I will come home. I do not know what to say to her because I do not know when I can go back home. We miss each other.

Emotions of the Heart
Breanna Mz Rokke, Otsego

Water falling on the edge of overflow,
Her eyes blinking away, there's passion that's to grow.
What is thought to be a sadness of tears,
Really is a happiness; a want to keep feeling this for years.
This emotion of the heart can be as rocky as the ocean,
One striking beat after another, filling up with an undying potion.
Her lips slowly start to smile, spreading from ear to ear.
Still a desperate wish inside that he was very near.
This electrifying spark of a newfound love,
May have finally come, after old prayers sent to the Power above.
She never thought to feel this way,
And now never wants to say. . .
Goodbye.

You're My Friend, Sweetheart and Wife
Nico M Allen, Virginia

You're my Friend
The one I turn to when I need somebody
There to laugh with and to talk with,
To understand and care

You're my Sweetheart
You're the one I need to kiss and to hold me tight
To say the words, "I love you"
Every morning and every night

You're my Wife
The one I need to have forever by my side
The one I can depend upon
In whom I can confide

You're all I'll ever need to have a full and happy life
My special friend, my sweetheart,
my dear and loving wife
I love you very much,
and can't wait until I come home
To marry you, my love
Forever yours,
Nico M Allen.

Nico M Allen, Virginia

An Angel In The Sky To Me–To My Sister Diane Johnson
Omega Johnson, Minneapolis

When I look up in the sky I feel you
Looking down on me. An Angel in the
Sky you are to me.

When I feel the sun shining down on
Me I know you are smiling upon
Me. An Angel in the Sky you are to me.

When I feel the wind blow I know you
Are saying hi to me. An Angel in the
Sky you are to me.

When I'm walking on the beach I see
Your footprint in the sand. I know you
Are walking beside me. An Angel in the
Sky you are to me.

When I look up in the sky
I see a star.
I know you are looking down on me. An Angel in the
Sky you are to me.

When I lay down at night I see a star in the
Sky, you twinkle twice to say goodnight.
An Angel in the
Sky you are to me.

In My Real Dream
Anonymous, Brooklyn Park

"Brown eyes…what?"
"Brown hair…what?"
"Blue short-sleeve shirt…what?"
"Carry his Bible. What?"
Then I met a man from Kansas City, Missouri.
That is him.
He is now my husband.
I happened to dream about him four years before I
met him.

Love Hurts
Larry Flowers, Minneapolis

I am now over something I thought would be.
I was blinded by love that ended up hurting me.
Hypnotized in a thought of us being eternally.
Infatuated with a woman that only loved me physically.

Love Hurts…
I can accept responsibility and take some of the blame.
I don't think I've done enough to be left in so much pain.
She was different; she tricked me when I thought I was hip to the game.
Because of her, I don't think I could ever love again.

Love Hurts…
I tried to make it work but she never told me what it would take.
It's not like I was cheating, I spent time with her every day.
Even though she hurt me, no one could ever take her place.
I was young and dumb at the time and I've learned from my mistake.

Love Hurts…
I remember when I trusted no one and showed no emotions.
That was until she came in the picture and had my feelings open.
The day she left, I felt really heartbroken.
Igniting cigarettes back to back so stressed I was chain smoking

Love Hurts…
I just knew she was the one; she was in college and obtained
A good occupation, she made me smile in difficult situations,

Then she just up and left with no explanation. Was it because of me?
Catching cases or because I haven't achieved in pursuing higher
Education? The question is still unanswered but I'm still waiting.
Love Hurts…
As the days go on every now and then, she's on my mind,
But I'm moving on because my vertebrae is gone and I am
Left without a spine. Now I'm focused and back on my grind.
I will always remember Love Hurts so I'm gonna take it slow next time.
Love Hurts

Sisterly Love
Tereca Burnett, Saint Paul

A sister is someone who loves you with all her heart,
No matter how much you two go through you cannot be apart.
She is a joy that cannot be taken away,
Once she enters your life, she is there to stay.

What she means to me is more that I can express.
It's a wonderful thing having an older sister to call on when in distress.
You can tell her your story, and she will help you with a smile, not a frown.
God had a plan throughout the years,
How we would be perfect for each other,
To share life's smiles and tears.

When she is by my side, the world is filled with life;
When she is not around, my days are full of strife.
A big sister is a blessing, who fills your heart with love,
She flies with me in life with the beauty of a dove.

Work Hard to Love
Julie Vang, Minneapolis

I am a mom who works hard to love my children.
When I became a mom I knew how to love my children.
Loving my children is very important.
The ways I love my children are by cooking for them and by learning English to be able to talk to them in America.
I have to be a good example to my children in the USA because I want them to continue their education.
I want them to go to college and even be a doctor like my uncle.
I have big dreams for them and myself. I bow to God to give my children a blessing to have a good life.
I also bow to God to help all the teachers in the past and now. I also bow to God for helping all the people in my family in the past when we first came to the USA.
I also bow to God to please help all people in the USA to have more jobs and for all people and my family to have a good life.

My Mom
Play Htoo, Saint Paul

Everybody in the world has a mom. Without a mom we cannot become a person and we cannot know about the world. So, for that I love my mom so much. Because of her, I'm alive. I grew up with happiness. My mom is very generous, kind, lovely and honest. She always gave me strength, happiness, advice and a hold on my life. She taught me to be a good person and how to solve the problem. I love you, mom. I won't forget you. I promise you that I will be a good daughter for you and in front of everyone. I also want to thank every mom in the world because every mom is the pathfinder for us.

Play Htoo is 21 years old and is originally from Burma/Thailand.

How Lonely When You Are Married
Pang Thao, Minneapolis

When you are married the first month, you and your husband feel very good and excited, but the time is short to be in love. Who knows how long the love will stay with you? Even today no one knows if you feel lonely, sad, hurt, or upset. You can't let someone know how lonely you are. No one knows and you can't explain it. It is more than you can explain to someone. If you talk to someone, will your love come back and be the same? No! You are hurt and upset, no one can know about it. Only you know yourself. You feel very hurt when your partner does something bad to you and good to someone else. You must feel sad for yourself. When you feel very bad, no one can take care of you. No one likes to talk to you and do something for you. You feel no independence for yourself. No one likes you and they look at you like something you said or did was balderdash. If your husband loves you and sees you like an impressive person, that means his family likes you too. But, if your husband doesn't see you like that, his family doesn't care about you. You feel lonely when you stay home with his family. They pretend they can't see you and they don't ask you for help or tell you how to do anything at home. You just stay home and have nothing to do and it is wearisome.

If you and your husband don't come together and have more time together, you feel very lonely or sad for yourself. You might feel like your husband will betray you. You feel like people around you try to pull you down. You feel very irritated, frustrated, and bored for everything in your life. When you think about the past life, your heart feels very hurt. You feel your heart might come outside.

If you have a child, remember to tell your child "Don't marry when you are a very young child."

This story is true for many people's life in the past or right now.

Enjoy your marriage when you are in the life today!

I Was a Teen Bride
Lori Smith, Saint Paul

I met my husband in 1980, and we dated from 1980 to 1987 before we got married. I was in the 10th grade and my husband was in the 11th grade when we met at Central High School. He was tall and dark. He was the cutest boy in the school and captain of the football team. I was captain of the cheerleader squad.

He was very outgoing and popular. I was shy and quiet. We met in the lunchroom when he walked up to me and asked me to go to the movies with him. I said yes, and he said he would pick me up on Saturday. We started dating from there. We had our ups and downs, but we stayed together.

The years went by and we started to get serious. One day he came to my house. I asked why he was there so early, and he said he had something he wanted to ask me but he wanted the family there. We waited for my mother and his mother. He took us all out to Benihana.

At the restaurant, he grabbed my hand and I got down on one knee before he could. We both said it at the same time. "Will you marry me?" I was so happy. I said yes and he said yes. We got married two months later.

My Story
Francis Santos-Perdomo, Saint Louis Park

I am from Honduras. I have ten years of being in the USA.

I have three kids; one boy and two girls. My son is ten years old. His favorite food is BBQ. He likes school and his favorite class is math. He likes to draw and is very funny. He is special to me. My older daughter is Milca. She is five years old. My younger daughter is Cesia, and she is three years old. Milca is in a.m. kindergarten. She doesn't like school. Her favorite food is pizza. Milca is very, very shy. Cesia is in preschool. Her favorite food is Chinese food. She is very funny, too. My daughters like to buy makeup and they like to play in snow in the winter. In the summer, they like to visit the Como Zoo and Valley Fair. My kids are very important for me. I love my kids.

1987 in Bulgaria, Europe
Vladimir Zubovich, Minneapolis

In 1987 in the spring season, I moved to Bulgaria for my professional interest. I enjoyed this time there. After business hours, I took time to visit historical places. I made an excursion to the mountain Shipka and saw a battle cannon memorial from the Russia-Turkey War on the top of Shipka. On the bottom of Shipka; Bulgarians built a nice memorial church to Russian Soldiers who died during the war and protected Bulgaria from the Turkish army and from slavery.

Next on my excursion, I went to the city of Plovdiv. Before WWII, this city had seven hills. From old legends, these hills were said to give the city happiness and success. Hitler ordered these seven hills destroyed during WWII, but they destroyed just one hill. On top of the biggest hill are two memorials made from granite. One memorial is to the Russian Tsar Alexander I, and the second memorial is for simple soldiers from the Soviet Union's Red Army. The memorials are on opposite sides of the mountain. The Russian Tsar memorial shows just the bust. The memorial for the Russian soldiers has a composition of a soldier and a little girl on the hands of the soldier.

Bulgaria is the most beautiful, green, and friendly country. I love Bulgaria.

Vladimir Zubovich is 51 years old and is originally from Ukraine.

My Story
Delfina Cruz, Saint Louis Park

My name is Delfina Cruz. I'm from Axochiapan, Morelos, Mexico. I came to Minnesota eight years ago. I like Minnesota. I love my family. I have a sister, brothers, and mom. Every time we share food, we talk about our feelings so we can help with problems. I love my children, but my little girl is very energetic. I need to watch so much because she does not know the consequence when she runs or falls, because three months ago she fell and broke her tooth. She cried for 15 minutes. I was worried when I saw blood draining from her mouth. I told her to open her mouth so I can see what her teeth looked like. Oh no! I saw a hole in her gums where her tooth had been. I thought she looked funny when she smiled with her missing tooth.

Delfina Cruz is 40 years old and is originally from Axochiapan, Morelos, Mexico.

Times
Jeremy Zimmerman, Saint Cloud

Times change and people change with the times
Times are tough and times are hard
Sometimes simply doing your best is not quite good enough
It is critical to form a pact with someone who will have your back no matter what
I know with me I want a friend to stand beside me instead of behind me so I can use their
Shoulder to lean on because in times of trouble everyone needs a shoulder to lean on
I want that shoulder to be my best friend
I want that shoulder to be my companion
I want that shoulder to be my lover and my ultimate other
During trying times I ponder what my future has in store out there on the horizon
There is a place for me like the sun has its place rising on the horizon
I too can be on top of the world but it will not mean anything unless I am on top with you
I do not know where I fit in but I can promise you that I will
Do my best to impress you with my dress attire and show you the fire which you admire
I do not know where my destiny will lead me but only time will tell….
Throughout these times of adversity there is no help
Only hate
But wait it does not have to be too late
The both of us can dominate this life together like birds of a feather who flock together
Even in times of poor weather
I know that your back is against the wall but please know that when you need me I will

Be there to catch you when you fall
My hand will never lose its grip
I will continue to fight the war of 1816 establishing my land and securing my freedom
Ticket
Let liberty ring…
It takes a real woman to keep it real
That is why I fight for you
That is why I fight for your love
We must hang together as a team or else we will for surely hang separately
It is said that it takes team play in order to win the game
Individual play produces stats but it does not win the game
Times change and people change with the times…
Embrace them changes and be a team player

Ricky Villarreal, Sacred Heart

My Testimony

Juan Carlos Galan, Bloomington

Hey, I'm Juan. If you knew me you probably think I'm weird. In my childhood I always was a quiet boy, until my teen years when I entered the world. I was full of anger and hatred, mainly angry at myself. I dropped out of school because my parents didn't have money to pay for college semesters. I did everything I wanted wrong. I drank alcohol every weekend in nightclubs, playing with people's emotions. I was depressed, lonely and in darkness.

But there's a bigger reason here, in late October of 2011, something amazing happened. I met a young Galilean guy who is simple yet powerful at the same time. He showed me his love. He was always there when I cried alone, even when I was born. The shepherd goes to the lost lamb just to save it. I was that lost lamb. Jesus Christ is the man who changed my life forever.

After I did my retreat, one day I stood in my room and asked God what he really wanted of me. You see, when you ask He speaks! I decided to serve my Lord, but it's not easy to follow him. I opened my holy Bible to Ecclesiastes 2:1: "My son if you decided to serve the Lord be ready for the trials. Keep your heart right. Be sincere and determined. Keep calm when trouble comes. Stay with the Lord; accept whatever happens to you. Even if you suffer humiliation, be patient. Gold is tested by fire, and human character is tested in the furnace of humiliation. Trust the Lord, and he will help you. Walk straight in his ways, and put your hope in him."

The Lord has blessed me. He is great. There is no love in this world like the love of the Creator. You can try to find it in drugs and material things, but these things last for a while and you will never really be filled, because God is love and author of the holy Bible. Why get a cheap fake copy of love, when you can get the real signature of the love from God? I want God to be my number one.

Juan Carlos Galan is originally from Mexico.

This Angel and I

Michael S. Thompson, Saint Cloud

As I sit in my four cornered room day by day
My mind searches my heart for the right words to say
Oh, Heavenly Father I give thanks once again,
For life, good health to me, my family and friends.
But most of all Father I give praise to thee
For sending from heaven this angel to me
All the angels must miss her, I'm sure you do too
If I were to loose, her Lord what would I do
She has been like a light in my darkest hour
From a field full of thorns shone this bright and sweet flower
Though I am not thief I plotted to steal
Begged your forgiveness, prayed it be your will
For my journey was for riches, fortune, and fame
Worldwide recognition was in store for my name
Who would have thought I'd push all that aside
And desire only this sweet flower to have as my bride
I will give her my strength and hers will be mine
I'll celebrate each year the day I made such a find
I will love her and honor her and the world will be told
That I shall never trade her for a large sum of gold
Oh, Heavenly Father let her know my love is true
Let her know she was sent here for me, from you
We will love one another until the day that we die
And you shall have no greater servants than this angel and I

My First Pregnancy

Esmeralda Solis-Miranda, Minneapolis

I missed my period. My body was feeling different symptoms than usually. I had a feeling I knew what that meant. I went to the pharmacy store and bought me a pregnancy test, got home, went to the bathroom for a couple of minutes, waited for the results, wishing that it would say no. But I looked at the results. It said yes, that I was pregnant.

I felt like the whole world fell on top of me, that there was no way out, that everybody was going to look at me a bad way because I was going to be a teenage mom. I just wasn't ready to be a young mom.

I went to the clinic really upset and talked to my nurse. She told me "don't worry" everything was going to be OK, "There are a lot of girls your age that go through this and do their best." I went home after the clinic to go talk to my mom about my pregnancy.

I was really scared what her reaction was going to be. I got home, sat her down and told her, "Mom, I'm pregnant." She's like confused at first. Then she said, "Don't worry; I'm going to help you and be with you."

Two months passed, and I realized that I had to accept it. My stomach started to get bigger and bigger. I started feeling my baby move; it was something incredible to me. I started feeling something really special that I had never felt.

I got to nine months and I was in labor. I was really scared and nervous; I had never been through this. Once the baby came out, the doctor said, "It's a boy!" I was so emotional and excited. My life changed completely, and this is why I get up every day to do the best I can do to be the best mom for him.

Esmeralda Solis-Miranda is 23 years old and is originally from Mexico.

Expression Without a Father
Nou Thao, Saint Paul

I always live now without you and your generous heart, a heart like the love of fresh water and white cloud
I never heard a voice the same as yours that would teach me about the good experience to share with the world
It is dark and blue inside of my eyes and you still shine into my heart
It sad as dark blue as the dark night without the light of the moon
It's raining as my tears drop from my eyes as the water falls from the sky
Sun shines into my eyes and it makes my tears bright on my face—an expression of my heart
I can't pull my hope and my smile back
My heart is as crushed as the rapids, as the sound of the ocean
When I hear that I don't have someone like you, it hurts so much inside of my heart

The sadness of my eyes and the hurt of my heart is like the thunder and lightning striking the earth
I am so upset because I never have your embrace around me, but I will always love you forever
Love you so much, Dad!

Nou Thao is originally from Thailand.

My First Job in America
Safiya Hussein, Minnetonka

I am writing about the first time I got a job in America. It was a beautiful day. I was a looking for a job every day. I asked my friends and I looked in the newspaper. Finally I found a job. It started at 7:00 in the morning. That night I couldn't sleep because I was worried about my new job. It was exciting! But I had to stand all day. I couldn't stand and felt very tired all over my body. My feet hurt because I didn't have comfortable shoes. I cried. I remembered my mom. She worked hard for my whole family. Still, I never forgot my mom because she is a hard worker.

My Daughter
Pauline N., Minneapolis

I have a two-year-old daughter by the name of Munachi, but everybody calls her Muna. She is a loving child, who took after her father in everything. She is fair in complexion, has a round face, long bones, thick dark hair and a gap in her upper teeth. Anyone that sees Munachi will hurriedly carry her, and she will not cry but rather be smiling.

Munachi is my God-given baby girl. When I was coming to America, I couldn't come with her because I didn't plan to stay more than two weeks, but here I am almost seven months without her. I am missing her terribly. I must go home to take her along. Each time she hears my voice on the phone, she will cry until she goes to sleep, and I will also be here crying. But whenever she speaks on the phone with her father, she will smile and sing all through that day. Maybe she loves him more than me.

Muna, I love you, but daddy loves you most, so stop crying. "You will see me very soon" have always been my consoling words to her. Some months ago, Muna took ill with measles and a rash all over her body. When I heard the news I was depressed, but I started praying to God to heal my baby, and God answered my prayers and now she has recovered very well.

Opportunities
Maria Soler, Austin

My name is Maria Soler. I am from Cuba. I have been living in the USA for five years. It is a beautiful and wonderful country. We have many opportunities, as individuals. I have dreams and goals to obtain. This is the reason that I like to be here. It is marvelous to feel free and live in a great country and so on, but at the same time, it is very hard because one part of my family is not here. Therefore, seeing my family is a priority.

Really, I do not have a big family in Cuba. I only have there my oldest sister, her three children, and my brother-in-law. My parents and my grandparents died. I have here my husband and my wonderful children, and each day I say to my Lord, Thank you very much for them. But I wish my other loved ones were here.

I like remembering how well our life was with my family, my sister, and me. We have had a very close and good relationship. We always were together; we spent all the time together. I wish my children could enjoy having my sister around them because she is a great blessing.

I hope God helps me, because he is always with me, he always comforts me. My feelings about my family are stronger and stronger. It is very important to me to see my family again.

In the last five years, I have understood how really important the family is. For me, it is like jewelry, like a marvelous treasure. The life is nothing if you do not have all people that you love around. I say one more time that I need to see my family again.

My Tears
Mai Lee, Saint Paul

Tears are for love
    When I love you
Tears are for happiness
    When I have you
Tears are for sadness
    When you are away
Tears are for something
    Good and bad in our love
Tears are for missing
    When I miss you
Tears are for many different feelings

Struggles

Escape From Burma
Roll Na, Saint Paul

My name is Roll and I was born in Burma. I have one sister. My parents were farmers. There was not enough food for us and we tried hard by ourselves. One time when I was two years old the enemies attacked my family and brought me to the town. After two months my grandfather gave money to the Burmese army and my mom received me back. For the next three years my dad would go into the town to buy food. Once, while he was gone for two days, we didn't have food and we ate only bamboo shoots. My father died when I was six years old and then my mother took care of us. In my village there was no school, so I couldn't study. There was never enough rice for us. At that time I faced many problems because the Burmese military continued to attack our Karen people. They burned our villages and damaged our places. The villagers ran to other places. I fell and broke my hand before I got to a new village. After five months my hand was better. I then immigrated to the Thailand border. I stayed there for two years, but I faced many problems because my family and I were sick for two months. But I persisted and kept trying.

Then the army came to our place, so we immigrated to another refugee camp in Thailand, located by the mountain. When I was there I went to school with my sister for grades one through nine. In September 2004, the river flooded and damaged our place so we couldn't stay there and we went to another camp. It was near the river side. I lived there for seven years and then graduated from high school. Then I continued to study in the post-ten school first year. I began teaching in high school, grade nine. I taught English and social studies. I got money and then my wife and I had a son. In 2011, my family immigrated to Saint Paul, Minnesota. We arrived in July and I started English language school in September. In the first months I didn't know the situation here and it was very difficult. I thank God because he took care of me and helped me all the time.

Roll Na was born in Burma at a time when life was unbearable for many Karen people. At age seven, he walked to a refugee camp in Thailand with his mother and sister. Eventually he would live in 3 different camps. Life in the camps was hard, but his family was safe and the children could go to school. Later he married Kee Lah Paw and they had a son, Hay Doh. In 2011 they came to Saint Paul where they attend MORE Multicultural School. They are a happy family looking forward to a promising future.

Thai's Jail

Joua Yang, Minneapolis

When I was in Thailand, it was the first time of my life that police took me to the jail with more than a hundred Hmong people.

Early in the morning, about five o'clock, we're still getting up, some people still sleeping, and some people still cooking breakfast but didn't eat yet. That time we felt happy, because we have United Nations papers to prove we're refugees, but we didn't have passports any more. That morning a lot police came over the building, and took everyone in to the jail. The reason is because we didn't have passports, we gave United Nations paper to prove, but Thai police didn't care, and took us to the jail.

When I was in the jail, I saw a lot of scary things, and terrible life for people in the jail. Some people got hit by police, blood out, very, very scared, but polices didn't hit us because some people from UN came to stop police. That time police put us with about 500 different people in to the same room. That means we didn't have place to sleep, we just sat down and stood 22 days. After that UN came to talk to police, and move us to another place, but another jail.

Poor Family

Vang Kai Thao, Minneapolis

My father married too many women, he can't support my family. Because I have too many brothers and sisters living together, we don't have a lot of clothes to wear. I have no shoes to wear. That was not good for our family. When I got married, I thought I had enough education. I continued to go to school to get my high school diploma. When I finished, I came back home. My father and third mother already moved to another house.

That time was difficult for me, life on my own. But my mother still lived with me. I continued to think, I needed to live a different life. One day, many people left the country, and I followed them. The decision was very difficult, life and death. But we pray and pray for God. When we saw the soldiers' footprints in the dirt, people were scared to die.

The Gift of Children

Carolina, Shakopee

When I was 15 years old I had a dream about how I would help people with special needs. I saw poor people who needed help but didn't have money, and I thought I could help them. In my country I couldn't study about special needs, because my parents didn't have enough money. My sister helped me to finish my studies as she was able to provide money for me. I studied accounting, and soon after I finished school, I got married, and then I got pregnant. My sister told me that it was a good idea for my baby to be born in the U.S. because it could have better opportunities.

My husband came first and later he sent me money so I could come, too. I remember that I arrived on January 20, 2003, and it was just two weeks before my baby was born. Little did I know that my life would change when my son was born. When my older boy was 1 ½ years old I noticed that he was different from other children of the same age. I started to worry and I talked with my husband about my concerns. We decided to talk to our boy's pediatrician. We went to a specialist and he did many tests on my boy and he told us to return for the results. Two weeks later we went again, but during the trip I felt scared and worried. Finally we saw the doctor and he told us that our boy had Autism and he explained what Autism means and how we could help him. It was hard to realize, but we could get therapy so he could have a better life.

I waited one year and decided to have another child but I was scared because I didn't know if he would be the same as my first son. When my second boy was born he had the same symptoms. The doctor gave me the same diagnosis. It was hard for me to understand it. Both of my kids had Autism. With time, I now understand and I work together with my husband to help our boys.

Now I understand what it is to have two children who are special and I give thanks to God for having two wonderful boys and a family.

Carolina is 37 years old and is originally from Veracruz, Mexico.

Time

Demetrius Bowen, Detroit

Time is precious, time is something you cherish
Something so important it's bad when it perishes
You can't get it back, you can only move forward
Sometimes you find yourself asking for more
Being locked up…that's something you can't get back
Just plan for the future as you sit back
And think about the things you can change
Because when you hit the streets things will have rear-
ranged
The time you spent is in the past, you can't get that
Don't dwell on it because time moves so fast
Have things planned out in your mind
Because there's no sense in wasting time

Help! I'm Falling

Marsha Schroeder, Stewartville

All I know is pain and sorrow.
I wish I knew happiness and love.
I hope that I can smile again,

But I feel no laughter in my mind.
I've lost all that made me happy.
All I have is fear and pain.
The evil that goes through my mind won't go away.

I wish they could see inside my head.
Then they would know just what I see and fear.
I find myself screaming and no one hears me,
So I must face my demons by myself.

No one is ever there to hear me,
So I fall and fall into a hole.
I never stop, I just fall.
All I see is black cloaks that float in the air,
And when I try to see their faces,
There is nothing, just a black hood.

Why do demons fly and float but I fall and scream,
And there is no one to catch me or save me?
Why do I feel this way?
Can't they just go away?
Please help me!

Ode to a Great Warrior

V. Hays, Rochester

Here, all alone, I sit
In the deep, dark pit
One of my own making
Instead of leaving my soul for taking

To say I died by the sword, a glorious death
Would be both truth and lie in one breath
A blade was my end indeed
My own weapon saw my spirit freed

Not many can say they fell themselves
With a cut so small and barely felt

I was sharpening my lovely weapon with care
When suddenly it was as if my hand wasn't there
And down the blade slipped
The back of my ankle it clipped

It did not take long for the wound to fester
And meat with bone alike became lesser
First the ankle, then the leg and soon everything
Was rotting away and in constant pain

The gods, oh so cruel and just
The ones who placed upon me the battle lust
Shall not have my soul, this I pledge
But even I can only barely keep away from the edge

Let it be known, that by some random fate's sneeze
Death and doom came to the mighty Achilles

Vietnam War

Sia Vue, Minneapolis

I lived in Laos and there was a Vietnam War. Some Hmong people died. I am really sad. The Vietnam people shot me in my leg and it really hurt. There was a lot of blood, but I got better. There was no house and it was raining really hard. We just go live in the jungle. I lived in the jungle for three years.

Sia Vue is originally from Laos.

Prisons and Projects
Donny "Steady Hustlin" Helps, Fergus Falls

They're cagin' us in prisons and projects
Confining us on Indian reservations
Delaying our progress
Entrapping us in concentration camps
Keepin' us uneducated, poor, and jobless
Silencing us by confining us
To prisons and projects

They're planning our demise through platinum and diamonds
Filling our imagery with visions mindless
Enticing us to spend on the clothes in which we dress
Yet the time we spend with our children is becoming less and less
They're manipulating us like pawns in chess
Once a powerful nation we've somehow digressed
Into inmates and residents
In prisons and projects

They're killin' us with lethal injections
Poisoning our minds with ill-given directions
Coaching our daughters to accept disrespect
Training us to depend on food stamps and WIC checks
They're distributing propaganda, distorting the truth
Blatantly stunting the growth of our youth
Misinforming us with lies blinding us with ignorance
Deafening us with the noise of our own belligerence
They are teaching our children to follow the same path
Teaching them violence and hatred instead of science and math
Not equipping them to do battle with the authorities
Teaching them that all they can be are minorities
They are infiltrating our homes, taking over our neighborhoods
They're hunting us down like deer in the woods
Depriving our people of substantial opportunities
They're pumping AIDS and plagues into our communities

Protecting themselves with diplomatic immunity
One may ask what exactly do we do with these
Institutions of unspoken indignities

That are often referred to as prisons and projects
Whose idea was it to create
These identical complexes surrounded by gates?
Affordable housing is the wolf in disguise
Which they use to mask their plans for our demise
Ever notice that we are raising generations
In these institutions that hold back the Native Nation?
Have you figured out yet that it's all part of the plan
That was masterminded and carried out by the man
To ensure that we would never escape our shackles
Every step forward is conquered and tackled
They're limiting our choices, diminishing our prospects
By keeping us caged in prisons and projects

Evil
Alexander LaFave, Cloquet

Evil is a dark place inside me
Evil wants to jump out
Evil lurks in the back of my mind
I won't let it out 'cause it'll be the end of my time
It gets me locked up; it takes my freedom
Darkness all around me
Evil inside me

Life's Storm
Dev Martin, Duluth

Life in jail, a dry drought
Waste of time, mists not out
The hail of nothingness
Drops of soft pain
Heat is a wasted, jail-time rain
A cry of thunder announces a storm
The weather is welcome where family is torn
Only seeing flashes of lightning
And feelings of scorn
From lightning and thunder
Understanding is born

About My Country
Alexis Daguste, Roseville

My name is Alexis Daguste. I'm from Haiti, and I came to the USA in January 2011. To explain about life in Haiti is not a good sensation for me because a big part of the Haitian population is poor.

Every Haitian parent wants to lead a good life, and would like to see their children go to school, give them food, and have health care for them. But it's different in Haiti. Only the rich people have these opportunities. It has too many problems, for example: discrimination and economic problems, security, health and education problems. My goodness, with those problems if somebody doesn't have work there they can't live peacefully. However, Haiti is a good tropical country where everyone would like to visit or to live. The government never took their responsibility to change Haiti, but they wanted to become rich and also their families and their friends. Then the poor population perishes in their misery.

Alexis Daguste is originally from Haiti.

How to Reach My Goals
Lu Lee, Minneapolis

In the future I want to be a phlebotomist. But right now it is difficult for me because I don't know how to pronounce the biggest words. The big words are difficult for me. I think about myself, if I can do something I am interested in. I don't even know why I am very interested in the position. I always watch YouTube online about how they prepare about phlebotomy.

I tell myself that I have to speak and learn more English and study hard. But I am not moving up. I'm feeling bad about myself because I have never learned English before. I am very sad about myself for everything. What I learn I do not remember in my brain. Please can you help me to resolve that situation? How do I reach my dream?

Am I Better Than This?
Terrence Wren, Fergus Falls

Am I Better than this? Better than all the criminal activities I've joined in? I'm 26 but can age really make a man? And with all my foolishness and rowdiness I wonder am I just an adult kid? Right now am I an infant. Am I not making sense? When I was young I had a dream. It never came true. Does that mean I should never dream? Not addicted to drugs but seem to be trouble. Does that make me a fiend?

Am I Better than this? Better than the hearts I've broken? I wasn't raised with a mother and a father. I was brought up in many foster homes. Like an animal in the wild, was my only option to roam? I've messed up opportunities then looked for someone to blame for my mess up. I'm never wrong. Now isn't that messed up? Afraid of attachments, I always run from happiness and leave a streak of emptiness. With the nerve to ask God will I ever find happiness? Ha. I'm just laughing at myself because now I feel the pain others felt. No more cheating my way in life but am I really man enough to play the hand I am dealt?

Am I better than this? Better than seeking revenge against the world thinking everybody's against me? Knowing I should focus on raising my son and baby girl? Sitting in my cell the devil tempts me. He wants me in hell. Saved by God many times, but this time will he pay my bail? Afraid I don't know why. Maybe I'm scared of success. I try to give it my best and push it to 1,000 percent only to find out the scale goes to 10 grand. I'm sweating bullets out here. Am I really only giving it 10 percent?

I'm better than this. My heart says never quit. Head screams you can do it. I feel the power in my tongue and like a language I'm speaking it fluent. My hands clench into fists, legs ready to kick, anything the devil pushes at me—I can overpower it.

A Hero is what I need. Someone to push me, guide me, never leave me and walk beside me, someone who loves me. The answer to my question: Yes, I Am Better than This, As Long As I Keep God with Me.

Life Change
Rachel DeFoe, Brookston

Life can change in a blink of an eye
And we question ourselves why?
We all want to cry because we told a lie
But this isn't good bye, we are all locked in cages
Wishing we could fly

Our smiles may be fake, but we've got to give it a try
This is not a place to stay and we all know why
Being locked in a cell is nothing but hell
Eating their food makes our stomachs swell
We're all dressed in jump suits, oh boy, can't you tell
Well, do you want to come to hell?

My Life So Far
Grae Kpaw, Saint Paul

I was born on June 9, 1990, in a small village. My village was beautiful and peaceful. I enjoyed fishing with my father and swimming in a big river that was nearby.

In December 1994, my village was burned and destroyed by the Burmese Army and D.K.B.A. Many of the villagers including my family moved to Thailand to be safe. In 1995, I became a refugee, which meant I had a chance to go to school and be more secure. I also got rice and other food from the U.N. (United Nations.)

Unfortunately, two years later the D.K.B.A. came to our camp, burned many houses, and hurt many people. Every night, my family and I slept in the forest outside the camp to be safe.

In November 2000, the U.N. provided us a new camp that was far from the border so we'd be safer. The new camp was better, and the weather was not too cold or too hot. There was a school, hospital, library, playground, and many other things.

In June 2001, I went to school in another camp to learn English and lived on campus. I was sad and upset because I was far away from my family. However, I tried my best in my studies to make my parents proud and happy.

In February 2006, I graduated high school. My family came to my graduation, and they were proud of me. We took many pictures together, and I moved back to my camp for trade school.

On September 2, 2009, I immigrated to Saint Paul by myself. I really missed my family and wanted to go back. My life isn't stable, and I'm far from my family. But I have been blessed by God. My life is better than in the past. I hope one day to reach my goal and become a United States citizen.

Grae Kpaw is originally from Burma.

A Good Son
Na Xiong, Saint Paul

I was born in a poor family with two brothers and two sisters. I am the middle child. When I was a little boy, I had an accident that damaged my head. I fell from a tall tree, and my head hit the ground. Since the accident, I have not been normal. I couldn't learn as well as other students in school, but I didn't give up. I hoped to be a good son for my parents.

Today, I am the only child that my parents have here. My sisters got married and live far away with their husbands. My brothers didn't come to the United States with us, so that's why I say I'm the only child that stays with them today. The best thing that I can do for them is to get a good education. For thirty years of my life, I haven't done anything that I am proud of. I went to school for a few years when I was still living in Thailand, but I didn't learn anything from school. I knew my parents might not have enough money to pay for school either.

Since I came to the United States, I knew this was the best time for me to get my education. I registered for school right away after I arrived, but after six years of studying English, I still feel that I'm not able to speak, write, and understand English well enough. However, I am happy that I am close to graduation and hope to be one of the students who are going to graduate in 2012. Therefore, I am studying hard and hope to have a good job with good pay someday.

Matthew

Betelehem Weldekidan, Rochester

I am from Ethiopia. Marriage was my reason to come to the United States in November of 2009. My visa process had finished two months after my wedding day and I flew out with excitement to see my husband with a nine week baby.

In June 2010, our son Matthew was born, and we were so happy about the little addition to the family. Moreover, we were able to bring my mom from Ethiopia. She is a mother of six and a grandmother of two, and her presence made it easier in taking care of our baby.

When baby Matthew was five months old, my mom went back home, and it became our sole responsibility to take care of our son. Matt was a happy, healthy and well growing baby until six months old, but after that his development became delayed, and he couldn't reach the developmental milestones for his age. He was unable to sit or crawl until age one. He frequently avoids eye contact, doesn't respond to his name or have any meaningful body language. He can stay for hours without crying in his room, and doesn't show any excitement and interest when he's held up.

Doctors checked everything and couldn't find anything that explains his developmental delay. At the age of 15 months, the developmental specialist called us into her office and told us our son has Autism Spectrum Disorder. It was heartbreaking news for us. As new parents, we didn't know what to do.

Matt is now 19 months old and able to sit and crawl, but still not walking or saying a word.

Although our hearts are broken with this devastating news in our life, we are praying all the time for God to give us the strength, understanding, and a much needed healing to Matthew, for nothing is impossible to God.

Betelehem Weldekidan is 26 years old and is originally from Ethiopia.

Tornado

Stuart "Chewy" Abramowski, Cloquet

Tornados come as the army coming across the land
It comes down and rips through houses just like troops in Iran
Somewhere in the land of the free
It will come with no warning
And it leaves with a mass destruction
Like an atomic bomb
And scares the land as well as the people's minds

Stuart Abramowski, Cloquet

My First Problem
Murio Khayre, Minneapolis

I came to the United States in 1996 in Lansing, Michigan. When we stayed in the States only two weeks, my son called the police because my daughter was sick. When police arrived at my house, I could not speak English. When the police saw that my daughter was very sick, they called the ambulance and took her to the hospital. The police officer told me to go with them in body language by flicking his finger back and forth. That is taboo in my culture, and I thought, "Now they took my daughter and are insulting me!"

When we reached the hospital, no one could understand me. The hospital employees and the police called many different nationalities, but no one could understand me, and worse, they did not know my nationality or where I came from. Body language was my hope of communicating to America.

Murio Khayre is originally from Somalia.

The Cancer in Our Family
Sarai C., Minneapolis

My name is Sarai. I am from Guerrero, Mexico. My family includes six sisters, one brother, and my mom and my dad. When I was eleven years old my mom was diagnosed with terminal leukemia. She needed to have a transplant of bone marrow before beginning chemotherapy.

It was very difficult for us because at the time my dad died. My grandmother came to take care of my sister and me while my mom was in the hospital. For many months we could not see her. She recovered fantastically. She is magnificent and strong. After two years of this struggle her doctor says she is healthy.

We were back to normal until my brother was diagnosed with leukemia. He was only ten years old. He is innocent and little to have to be a fighter. So I decided to come here to the United States to help. It was worth the trouble. Now he is healthy and strong.

Sarai C. is 28 years old and is originally from Mexico.

My Journey
Khadra Abdille, Minneapolis

I'm from Somalia in East Africa but I grew up in North Somalia. I was born able to hear and throughout most of my life I could hear. When I was 14 years old I began to have hearing loss and I don't know what caused it. I have an Auditory Neuropathy kind of hearing loss. I went to many doctors and I didn't get any help. I dropped all my education because I couldn't hear anything. I didn't know any sign language and my whole family can hear and don't know sign language. I felt isolated and alone everywhere I went. I loved my education and when I became deaf I dropped out. Every few months I would go back to school and pay much money without learning anything because I couldn't hear and there were no sign languages.

For five years I had no communication. I was communicating with gestures and universal sign language. I tried to hear what people were saying but I couldn't hear. I also tried to lip read but people wouldn't look at me while they talked so their faces were looking the other way. It was too difficult to live in there. I even went to doctors without communication with no writing and using sign language just to talk only. After being depressed for so many years I came to the United States in 2008. I went to a deaf school and I started learning sign language and English but my family still didn't learn except for my second oldest sister, who is ten years old. She can spell A-Z and knows a little ASL but my mom communicates with me by writing my native language. I'm happy in here and love my education; soon I'll go to college. Thanks to everyone who has supported me to change my life.

A Hard Change
Miguel Torres, Rice

I had worked at Stearns, Inc. in Sauk Rapids for 17 years. I started working in 1991. My job title was Lay-up Bundling. I worked for seven years on the first shift. In 1997 they said that there was not enough work for third shift. There were 17 people and the supervisor. They moved us all to the second shift.

During those years I was happy working and I had about eight supervisors, during those 17 years. They were good for me because I learned a little bit from my supervisors. I learned something different from each one of my supervisors. In my first year I did work in different departments and after one year I started as a Lay-up Bundler.

During the 17 years that I worked there, I was glad because I did like my job very much. Every time that I had an interview, my supervisor said that my job was excellent. I always had good communication with my supervisors and my co-workers. During those years I made many friends. But in 2008 the economy went bad, hundreds of people lost their jobs. And I was one of them. Even to this day, two and a half years later, I am still without a job. I feel a terrible destructive change in my life.

Miguel Torres is 64 years old and is originally from Mexico.

Refugee Life
Oretha Flah-Coward, Brooklyn Center

Refugee life is tough, difficult and very complicated. You find yourself in situations that you never thought you would ever find yourself in. You find yourself in a land you have not seen before. You cannot relate to anyone because you don't know them and you can't even speak their language. You don't know what to do and you start to freak out about everything around you. Looking back, you realize that there's nothing left in your country to go back to. Your house has been looted and burned down. Most of your beloved family members were killed and if any are still alive you don't know where they are. You then tell yourself "Well, I still do have life so I must move on." You have courage and try to make things work but the thing is, no one cares about you, what education you have or what your family values are.

World Food Programs brings food each month which we have to stand in the hot sun for three to four days before you can receive your ration. The food doesn't even take you to the end of the month because these people, who are supposed to make sure we have food, steal half of it for themselves and gave us just a little bit that only lasts for a few days. Then you have to go and do hard labor on someone's farm to get you through until the end of the month. The people with large families suffered the most. When you or your family members get sick it's a long process to get to the hospital. Sometimes it takes so long the person dies before getting there. They don't give you enough materials to build your own house to live in; you have to go in to the bushes to get stuff to complete the house. All I'm trying to say is that refugee life is not fun; a person can look to God and shouldn't give up on their hopes for a better life. I was lucky to be resettled in the United States 11 years ago, and I'm happily married with three wonderful kids.

Trying
Rosa Herrera, Saint Cloud

My name is Rosa Herrera. I am 23 years old and I have three kids named Joseluis, Jaquelin, and Sergio. Joseluis is eight, Jaquelin is five, and Sergio is three years old.

Life hasn't been very good for me because since I was nine years old me and my brother and sisters were taken away from my Mom for almost two years. When she got us back we went to live with her in Austin, Minnesota. Then we came to live in Saint Cloud, Minnesota in 1998.

In 2000, we had to move to Avon, Minnesota into a new place because my mom lost her job and our home. We moved to Fresno, California for nine months.

We moved back because my kids' dad got a job in Saint Cloud in a factory. We were staying with some friends, but then we had to move out because they were moving away. We didn't have anywhere to go so we had to stay with my kids' dad's uncle. We could only stay there for two weeks.

We were homeless for about two weeks until we found a trailer in Saint Cloud with my kids' dad's cousin. We lived there for three years with them. In 2006 I had my daughter, Jaquelin, then in 2008 I had my son, Sergio, but before I had him I was having problems with their dad.

So when my son Sergio was five months old I left their dad because he was doing some bad stuff. When I left him, I lost my trailer. I had no place to live and no money, no food. My sisters helped me out when they could. I was so stressed out I didn't know what to do. Sometimes I wanted to give up, but my kids gave me the strength to keep going.

I was homeless for about a year and a half, until I found this nice guy named Juan. He helped me out. I had a place to live, food, and he helped me with my kids to get them in school, take them to their doctor's appointments, etc. I am so thankful that I met him. Now I have a stable place and I am very happy. Sometimes I still have some problems, but I keep trying to be happy.

Difficult Times
Imelda Gutierrez, Shakopee

I remember when my parents divorced it was very difficult for me. They argued all the time and my father even hit my mother a few times. My brother told my father to leave my mother alone because he was very mean. My little sister was scared by everything my father did. My father fought for the house, but my mother wanted the house to belong to her sons. When my mother and father went to court, the judge agreed that the house was for my mother and her sons. My father was so angry.

My father didn't understand why the judge decided not to sell the house and give them the money. My father was very angry with my mother. She went to live with my grandparents for a month because my father remained angry. My father continued to frighten my mother so she went to the court and got a restraining order because he was displeased a lot with her. She continued to be afraid of my father. Now my father leaves my mother alone and she has a quiet life and is happy. My father lives by himself.

Sometimes life can be difficult for many families, but everything worked out for the best for me and my family.

Imelda Gutierrez is originally from Guadalajara, Jalisco, Mexico.

First I Fled From Civil War
Halimo, Minneapolis

In 1991, my country started a Civil War. My baby and I ran away to Kenya. From that time until today I have not been back to Mogadishu because that place was not happy. That's why I came to America.

The Civil War started on a Sunday. After two days, I moved to another place out of Mogadishu. I fled from the Civil War. I took a boat but the boat sank in the ocean. All the people were in the water after the boat lost control. Many people died. The Kenyan police came to the place where the accident was.

I had no food, water, or house. I had a small baby, too. I didn't know the Kenyan language. My husband did not come to that place. I was a younger woman at that time. What could I do? Only cry like a baby.

Halimo is originally from Somalia.

A Day in Iraq
Wisam Ibrahim, Mounds View

It was March 15, 1990. The people in my country didn't want the Saddam Hussein regime. Many people protested. They wanted a new government. The Saddam Hussein regime had lost control of all of the cities except Baghdad. But on March 23, 1990, everyone in my family was fasting because it was the month of Ramadan. In the morning, we heard the army coming to kill the people.

At ten o' clock a.m. we heard a big boom. Then everyone in my family went outside to see what had happened. We saw people running away from the army. My father said, "Let's run away!" But my mother didn't want to because her two older sons weren't there. Then my father said, "Let's go! We don't have time to stay." We ran away. We walked five hours and my mother cried because my brothers weren't with us and then we found a safe place. Then my father said, "Stay here. I will go back to look for your brothers." We stayed with many other people in the school. We had no food, no water. Everyone cried and my mom was very worried about my father and my brothers.

We stayed all night and no one slept. The next

day, my father came to the school. He brought food and water. We asked him about our brothers. He said, "They are good. They are at home. Don't worry, everything is okay." But his face said something different. When we went back home my father told us, "My two sons are in jail. The army took them to jail for no reason." After a week, the army freed my brothers. They told them to go home. When they came back home, we saw the army had hurt my brothers, but day by day they got better.

Settler on the Great Plains: New Life!
Najat, Brooklyn Park

Even though we moved to the Great Plains, our life is still not easy. We are going to start a new life again. We have to build houses and grow farms, so we could have food to eat and a house to live in. We will do whatever it takes to settle.

At first, we thought we were going to have a lot of rain, but the rain stopped after a while. So now we are left with nothing, my family and I don't have water, food or a big comfortable house to live in and keep us warm. Our home is really small, uncomfortable, and so cold. We have no bathroom, and also when the tornados come, they blow our house down very easily. Because the house is made out of mud and wood, it's very weak and not strong enough. Our land is dry because we don't have rain at all, so now it's very hard to grow corn and wheat because it is dry and dying from no water.

Life is so difficult for us without all of these things. To get water we have to dig a hole or walk a long distance. We chose to live like this so we can get freedom, have our own land, and a house. No one has control over us, so we can just live like this until we get a better life for the future, with God willing.

Najat is originally from Ethiopia.

Dušan
Andja, Blaine

I remember my brother, Dušan. He was captured away. I don't know why. He was a very, very special person to me, because he was always giving me a gift. If something was wrong with me, he knew right away. A big problem is that we kept looking for him on the computer and in the newspapers. When somebody asked me about him, I would cry every day, because I missed him. I love my brother a lot. I have many happy memories of him. He is my favorite person in the world. I went to Croatia to look for him. He is always in my heart. I will never forget him.

Andja is originally from Croatia.

From My Home Country to My New Country
Fauzia Shawich, Andover

I was born in Sudan. My husband was forced to leave Sudan because he did not want to fight anymore in the army. So he left for Eritrea. After he left, I was beaten. I was two months pregnant at the time. They also took my two sons, ages seven and nine. I had to look for them, so I walked for three days to find them. Then we all left for Eritrea. We were hungry and I had no milk for my baby. I couldn't speak the language. Some people helped us and took us to a camp. After four years, we came to the United States. After we came to the U.S., I could go to school and my children could go to school. I am thankful I can live here.

Fauzia Shawich is originally from Sudan.

God Had a Special Plan for My Life
Valentina Boutko, Elk River

I was born in a big family. My mother and father had five children. I was the second to the oldest child. We lived in the small village in Belarus near the big forest and small lake.

It was a very difficult time in my country. Most people were poor. My mother worked as a nurse at the hospital four nights a week. During the day, she worked on the collective farm. We helped her pull out weeds on the huge fields. We had field jobs working with our hands, like digging potatoes, beets, and carrots. We walked a long distance to reach the field and didn't have a car or even bicycle. I remember that it was very hard.

In the summer every day, we gathered berries in the woods. In the forests of Belarus are a lot of blueberries and cranberries. We walked into the woods with the neighborhood kids. It was difficult to walk long distances. But we tried to gather the berries to get the money for them. It was a small amount but we could buy something for school, like pens, notebooks, and pencils.

Prior to 1991, Belarus was ruled by the communist regime for 70 years. People did not have freedom. Many of them were in prison. Many of the better people were killed. The Government did not allow children to go to church. My father was a communist. My mother believed in God. We wanted to go to church, but the authorities persecuted believers. We had a secret church and went there at night. The communists forced my father to divorce my family. We had a very difficult time then. My father took a large part of the house and we slept for some time in the barn.

In 2011 I got the chance to come to the United States with my family. God had a special plan for my life. Now we all live in Minnesota where we are safe and happy. I have five children and nine grandchildren. I am very glad that my children and grandchildren can enjoy freedom of speech, freedom of religion and have good food. Praise the Lord.

My Story
Prince Wylie, Bayport

I was born in Liberia. Liberia is a small country on the west coast of Africa. When I was a little boy, my country had a bad war. My mother and father came to America and left me with my grandmother and grandfather. I had to go out to find food for my grandparents and myself. I went to Freeport to look for food. I went to a warehouse and found thousands of hungry people looting food. I took some powered milk, rice, and coffee. My grandparents were happy. The coffee was important because we needed to stay awake at night because the war always came after the sun went down.

Every day when the sun came up, I went to look for more food. Sometimes it was hard to get into Freeport. Some days the peace-keeping forces stopped me. Some days the rebels stopped me. Some days my grandparents stopped me because they were afraid that I might be shot.

Two weeks before Christmas, when I was 12 years old, I was very happy because my father had sent us money for Christmas. My grandparents took us shopping at the mall on Broad Street in downtown Monrovia. We bought some beautiful new clothes.

A week later bad news came that war had started in the countryside and that the rebels were coming toward the city. We started to panic. We gathered food into the house. We thought that the trouble would be short like it was in 1985. We thought that we could hide in the house until it was all over. We were wrong. The war would last for ten years. We hid in the house and listened to the news on the radio and television. We heard that the rebels were shooting people and looting their houses. This frightened us even more.

For six months, we waited and waited. Each day the rebels came closer and closer. It took two and half years before the rebels approached the capital city. We were surprised that some of the rebels were people we knew. When the rebels filled the city some of the people joined them.

I left Liberia in 1998 and went to a refugee camp in Ghana. Then I flew from Ghana to New York City and then I came to Minnesota.

Destiny
Bankole, Fridley

Philosophically, destiny is a predetermined course of events considered as something beyond human power or control. Similarly, it is the inevitable or necessary fate to which a particular person or thing is destined. In summary, it is the will of God that will not be altered by human efforts or Jupiter but by God Himself.

This is not the issue that I wanted to discuss at length per se, but correlate with the topic of my article. It was a long time ago that a man of God prophesied into my life that I have been destined to go overseas in my life but the enemies had blocked the way. On hearing this pronouncement, I started to struggle here and there with fasting and prayer with a view to overcoming the enemies to open the way closed by them. However all efforts proved abortive.

I got married and began to have children. The children grew up and started to go to school. Along the way, I met a powerful politician (senator) who decided to assist me to come with him overseas. In the process, he met his untimely death. Then everything went back to "square one."

My two sons attained adulthood and attended high school and University respectively. Fortunately, they got a sponsor who brought them to this great country but they came at different times. They got married and settled down. After some years, one of them became a United States citizen.

Sometime in the year 2010, my son called and informed us that he had applied for an immigrant visa for both of us and we should be expecting the forms.

We were invited for an interview at the consular office. Unfortunately, the interview was postponed two times. Satan was at work again.

At long last, we were granted the immigrant visa. The will of God was fulfilled. Our feet touched down on the soil of this country about six months ago.

However, the main reason that writing this is to proclaim the greatness of God in my life, and to encourage you to learn from my experience and to continue to struggle, pray and live a holy life in spite of all odds until the will of God is fulfilled in your life. God is on his throne watching over his beautiful kingdom.

It's Not Easy To Be A Mother
Isabel Suazo, Shakopee

Today I feel sad. I don't want to stay in my house all day because I feel bad. My eyes can't stay open. My forehead is in pain. I want to lie down for a moment. To be a mother is not easy. If I stay with my children all day in my house it is very difficult and tiring. Sometimes I want to cry, scream, and run far away because I feel frustrated. I need help. Please, somebody help me. I want to be free for some hours. I want to go far away, to a place that is calm and fresh with beautiful nature. I want to do something that I enjoy, like playing volleyball, running or dancing. Then, I want to return to see my wonderful children.

When I finished writing what I felt, my husband saw my writing and he asked me if I wanted to lie down for a moment, to go and relax. He said that he would take care of our children. I went to lie down and tried to relax. Minutes later, my husband came to our bedroom. He layed down with me, He hugged me and talked sweetly to me. He asked me how I felt and where I wanted to go. I said to him that I wanted to talk with him and tell him all that I felt inside. When I said all that I had inside, I felt much better and happy. My husband helps me all the time when I feel like that. That day when I felt better, all the family went happily outside.

I'm a mother like others. Sometimes we all have a difficult day. I write how I feel in my journal because writing makes me feel better.

My Dream Broken
M.T. Barrera, Osseo

I am from El Salvador. I came to the U.S. in 1988 with my husband and three children. I thought we were going to be a happy family, but in 1991 my husband died and everything came down. My children grew up with no daddy, and for me was it was very hard to be a single mother. But I keep working for my kids to get a better life.

What I Never Expected
Victoria Rios Aldama, Shakopee

My name is Victoria. I have a big family. I have six children, Ana, Fernando, Jhony, Julian, Alondra, and Juanito. When Alondra was 18 months old, she was very sick. I was very upset about that. I called the doctor and made an appointment for her. The doctor told me she needed a biopsy and blood tests. He thought something was wrong. Maybe she had cancer. I felt very sad. I thought my world was ending the day my daughter had the tests. The doctor told me to return in two weeks for the results of the tests.

During these two weeks I had a hard time. I only thought about what would happen to my little baby. I prayed to God to help me. Two weeks later the doctor called me. Before I responded, I knew he had bad news. He told me to come quickly because he needed to talk with me. The next day I went to the hospital. I felt cold. I was very scared and I was crying. I felt dizzy. The doctor started to explain to me about the situation. My daughter had cancer. The results were positive but the worst was that he told me my baby only had two months to live and he could not do anything to save her because her body was injured with the cancer. He told me she didn't have enough time for chemotherapy. The only chance could be a medula transplant but that was not a guaranteed. It had a 50% failure rate. The problem was she had only two months to live and sometimes the waiting list for donors is very long. They worked quickly to find a donor. I stayed all day in the hospital. After two weeks, the doctor called and told me I had seven donors. That was good and hopeful news for me and my family. Six weeks later my daughter had transplant surgery. It was successful! We stayed for six weeks in the hospital. Every day she gained strength. When we returned home, the doctors were surprised with Alondra's improvement.

Now my beautiful girl is seven. She is a wonderful daughter and in the future she wants to be a doctor and help people with cancer. This was a sad time in my life, but now I give thanks to God every day for blessing my daughter and all my family.

Victoria Rios Aldama is 39 years old and is originally from Axochiapan, Morelos, Mexico.

Best Friend
Andrea, Monticello

On October 23, 2005, I met my best friend when I was alone with my son, Jason.

Jason was two years old and I was in a lot of bad situations. I thought that there wasn't any reason to live or even for my own son to keep going forward. I had a lot of hate in my heart for my parents, husband, and all the men in the world. My best friend taught me how to forgive and how to love myself first, and then others. The only way to learn this is by humoring yourself first and recognizing that no one is perfect in this life. But there is one who is perfect, who has given everything, even his life, for me and everyone. One who is always there when you need Him, no matter where you are. One who always is telling me, "you can do it, keep going, I am with you." His name is Jesus Christ.

Andrea is 26 years old and is originally from Ecuador.

Newly Discovered Disease
Allen Neubeck, Brooklyn Park

Right now I'm struggling with certain foods due to my newly diagnose of diabetes. I am especially struggling with hot, fresh baked breads. Do you remember how bread smells while being baked in the oven? It smells so good that you want to gobble it all up? Well with me, I can only have one slice. But if you think you can eat it all up, loaf and all, go ahead and knock yourself out. You can have one or two slices for me, too. When you get your hot slice of bread, don't forget to put the homemade jelly or jam on it. Go ahead and indulge yourself. I know I like it, but it doesn't like me! When you smell that nice hot slice of bread, make your decision. With me, I have to struggle with my decision! Should I have pleasure now and suffering later, or no pleasure now, but no pain later... hmmm?

The Trials of Being a Young Mother
Lucero Rodriguez, Shakopee

I am a very young mother. When my first baby was born, it was very difficult for me because I was only 16 years old. When I was 16, I was scared about how to be a good mother.

I really had a difficult time. I didn't know how to confront my new life with my baby and I had to work very hard. Sometimes I needed family and friends to help. They gave some advice and I appreciated that because I had to learn how to live with new responsibilities. Sometimes my baby cried and cried and would not stop. The best advice someone gave me was how to calm my baby. The man who was the father was mean and not good for me and my baby. I had to leave him. Later, I met a good man and we share a wonderful life together. We have two beautiful girls, Aimee who is three years old and Valeria who is eight months old.

Now, I am 23 years old and with the passage of years I am still learning to be a good mother for my children. I want to help them as much as I can. My children are happier. They enjoy time together and they take care of each other. My older children are very happy with a little baby sister. Now I have a wonderful family but I must continue to work at being a good mother. While it is difficult, I know it is best for me and my family.

Parenting a Child with ADHD
Amy Stevens, Minneapolis

My son was diagnosed with ADHD (Attention deficit hyperactivity disorder) and OCD (Obsessive-compulsive disorder) at the age of five years old. I started to notice that he could not sit still and could not stay with one thing for a long time. At this time, I talked to our family doctor and she suggested seeing a psychologist to start treatment. She put him on daytime and bedtime meds to help him calm down and sleep better. The psychologist also suggested seeing a therapist once a week. When he started school, we had talked about putting him on an I.E.P. (Individualized Education Program) to help him with school. We have gone through a lot of meds over five years to get the right one that works. He still has his ups and downs. I have learned that as a parent I have to be patient with kids that have ADHD and OCD and be more open-minded about this. Today my son is better and I know he has the right skills to manage his life as a stronger male.

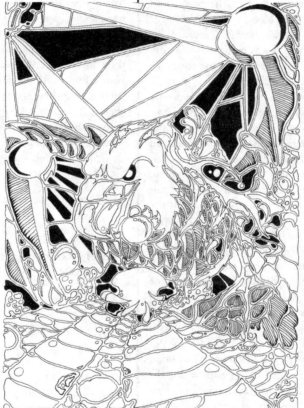

Raymond Muckuk, Minneapolis

Money is Powerful
Nengyang, Maplewood

Money is powerful and affects people in many ways.

The first reason is everyone needs money to buy basic needs for the whole family such as foods, medicines, clothes, house, and car.

Second, money can help a member of a family to get an education in college or university. My native country has many good students from poor families who do not continue their education after high school because tuition cost is very expensive and they lack financial aid. Unfortunately, the family cannot afford that cost and support their child in college or university for four to five years to finish their education.

Finally, money can save people's lives by buying medical insurance, medicine, and to pay for doctor costs. In fact, sometimes a big amount of money is needed for special treatment or a big operation. I still remember today, a sad story that happened to a young boy 21 years old who was touched by a nail that contained the germ of tetanus in his left foot. He could have prevented infection by a shot of Tetavac vaccine and SAT (Serum Anti-Tetanus) which cost less than five dollars. However he didn't have enough money to get this vaccination. Several days later, he has a scary severe symptom. And after thirteen days, he arrived in the district health center but it was too late for him. At the last minute he was dead on the same day he came to the hospital.

All these things show how money is powerful.

I Talk About History
Roda Ali, Minneapolis

I was born in Mogadishu, Somalia. I study first class until high school. I like Somalia because they have nice weather and the Indian Ocean is beautiful. I gave God Somalia peace. I remember my family lived in Mogadishu, then some my family died, some people were OK. Somalia have bad war because the war start in 1991. Right now they have war. A lot peoples died, a lot peoples handicapped, a lot peoples they don't have eyes. A lot peoples don't have their legs. I notice world. Please, you help Somalia.

Where I Am From?
Dabrian, Minneapolis

Hello, my name is David, and this is my story. I was born in the south of Texas, really close to México. When I was a baby, my parents took me to México and my dad left me with my stepmother. Living with her was very difficult because she doesn't like me as her son and my dad never was there. I was alone with another people and without parents. The funny thing is when I turned 19 years old, my dad told me the truth about my real mother and we traveled to find her.

We traveled across the country of México and finally…I met her for first time. That was hard and it was weird just to call her "Mom." She told me about where I had really been born and how my parents separated. That is how I know I am an American citizen, but I don't have the knowledge of it. I was thinking just to come here to the U.S.A. would be the hardest thing, but I was wrong. The real fight starts now, because I have a lot to learn about my country.

A Scary Night
Maria E. Del Valle, Elk River

One day in 1991 in Los Angeles, California at 3:00 a.m., my husband was out working. He walked the street and fifteen minutes before he got home, five men assaulted him. The people beat him up.

Later he came to the house. When we opened the door we were so scared of how much blood was on his face and his eyes closed. We couldn't recognize him. We rushed him to the hospital. We thought he was going to die. He ended up with a lot of stitches. All his teeth were broken.

He now has loss of memory. It's hard for him to eat. Ever since that incident, his sense of direction is lost. But he does try very hard to not let that get to him. We managed to overcome that incident, but until this date, he's still working through it. Thank God he wasn't killed at that place in Los Angeles, California.

Maria E. Del Valle is 56 years old and is originally from Santa Lucia Cotz, Guatemala.

My Life
Chansophy Van Smitham, Brooklyn Center

I was born in Phnom Penh, Cambodia on October 10th, 1965. I was engaged to a United States citizen on Tuesday, June 28, 2005 in Cambodia at the Compassion of Christ Church. During that time, I worked at Hotel Sofitel Cambodiana and my position was Human Resources Secretary. I enjoyed working there very much. Approximately nine months later, my paperwork for fiancé sponsorship was accepted and I then went to Thailand for a visa interview. I passed the interview and had to get my shots before I could get my visa.

When I returned to Cambodia, I had to put in my two week notice and prepared documents in order to train my staff and new staff of my position's responsibilities. April 24, 2006 was my last working day. It was very sad for me to think about leaving. I had a church wedding on May 20, 2006 at the Cambodian Church of the Nazarene in Crystal, MN. I was very excited, nervous, happy, sad and scared. I have such an opportunity of so much freedom, clean environment to live and the safety of family. But one sad point for me was finding a job in the United States. I was told that I could get a job as a Nursing Assistant if I finished schooling and if I am certified in the United States. However, when I finished my schooling and received my certificate I could not get a job still. The reason they gave was that I was not experienced in the United States. Employers were looking for experienced workers not inexperienced. I am very sad still to this day because I enjoy working with people and helping them a lot.

One day I applied at a hotel call Northland Inn as a room attendant. I was hired and I worked very hard. I quit my job because I had to go to Cambodia. My younger brother was very ill and wanted to see me before he died. I went to Cambodia and helped to take care of my younger brother and he was better. I believe that I helped him to survive.

When I returned back to the United States, I studied for my naturalization test and passed the test. I then applied everywhere for jobs the best that I could. I still did not get hired. Before I came to the United States, my expectations were very high. I expected to work hard, work two jobs, save a lots of money to help my family, but in the end, I still do not have a job.

Chansophy Van Smitham is originally from Cambodia.

When I Arrived In Minnesota
Roxana Paz, Minneapolis

When I arrived in Minnesota, I was a little nervous because I didn't know how I went to work, how to take the bus.

When I was looking for a job, I remember that first time I got lost in downtown. I wanted to ask to someone but I didn't speak English. I felt very bad because I didn't know how to get to my house, I called my husband and he said me that I take the #5 bus and get off on the Lake Street. Next, I waited for the #21 bus, but I take the #5 bus that go other side not the one that went to Lake Street. I felt very bad because all people that I looked were American. I looked around to see a Mexican person, and I asked him. He told me how to go and I arrived to my house.

I learned very much this experience because I knew how to come back to my house, and that it is important to speak English.

No Way Out
Lucero Solis Miranda, Minneapolis

My mind wonders, a storm of crazy thoughts circle my brain like a tornado that spins and spins and never stops. Then suddenly it loses its power. And my mind is at ease again, breathing out the mess left behind by the storm, that takes over me when I feel like there is no way out.

Lucero Solis Miranda is 24 years old and is originally from Mexico City.

My Sweetheart
Ubah Hashi, Saint Paul

I am sorry Somalia sorry
I am sorry Mogadishu sorry
My sweetheart sorry
Sorry you have been in pain for a long time
You haven't done anything that harms us
It's your citizens, the ones who harm you
Who have been self-consumed, self-hating, self-interested, self-murdering, self-neglecting
I know you have been in pain
Pain caused by your citizens
The pain that wrenched your heart
Also, I feel that pain from my heart
Even my heart is wrenched, but nobody else feels that pain
The reason that I feel pain with you is because I love you from the bottom of my heart
Because you are my heart
You are my shadow
Shadow that protects me from hot sun
You are my blanket, blanket that I wear when I feel cold
Now I am a little child, but when I grow up I'll be stronger and I'll take care of you as a newborn child
If God is willing

Ubah Hashi was born in 1976 and is originally from Mogadishu, Somalia.

Struggle and Decision
Somphet Manivong, Brooklyn Park

When I was in my early 20s, I was really struggling in my life. I was hanging out with the wrong crowd and making bad decisions during this time. I was abusing drugs. I was using heavily until the day my baby boy was born. I decided to change my ways and become a good father. Now I have been clean for a while and back in school trying to earn my GED.

Somphet Manivong is 38 years old and is originally from Laos.

Immigration
Anonymous, Minneapolis

I remember when the ICE police arrested me. It was early in the morning, around 9:30am, when they knocked on the door. I didn't even ask who it was. I didn't think twice about opening the door. I didn't even quite open the door when the ICE police very quickly came in. They asked me if I had an SS. I told them I didn't have it. They acted very quickly. There were like ten of them, some of them were inside, others were waiting out back and out front. One of them put handcuffs on me. They asked if anybody else was at home. I said "No, not that I know." They called me a liar. Then a man started screaming in my face. The ICE men were very harsh. He told me to sit down and shut up. I was shocked and very nervous. I was shaking and crying. The hardest part of it was that I was pregnant. I told the ICE men I was pregnant, but they didn't care. One of them said, "Shut up." Later, I had a miscarriage. I lost my baby through everything in this situation. I was in jail for three days. Finally, my lawyer got me out of jail. The immigration people didn't have any compassion. They were very cruel. This was a very hard time for me.

From Mogadishu to the United States
Mohamed Warsame, Minneapolis.

I am Mohamed Warsame. I'm from Somalia and I was born in the capital, Mogadishu. In 1990, a civil war started in Somalia and I ran away outside in my country. I wanted my neighborhood for refugee, then I was stayed in Kenya twenty years, and I have faced many problems in life. For example no food, no medicine and no security.

After 20 years, I got resettlement in United States, and I came USA 2006 in October. Since I came to the United States. I have felt many pains in my body. I worry about my family and friends, because Somalia still fights and there are many people dead. I will hope one day there will be a peace.

Post Traumatic Stress Disorder
Marissa Berrio, Rochester

The fact that I fear to fall asleep
Makes me feel that I am weak.
That I am conquered, that I am controlled.

What did I do wrong? The stories unfold.
Nightmares are something I pray I could dream.
But the reality is the reality I have seen.

I cannot control my thoughts anymore.
I've lost count, I've lost score.
I'm the loser in this game.
No more to gain.

Feeling so empty, paranoid and scared,
I feel like a sideshow, stripped naked, bare.
Fingers pointed at me with covered mouths while they laugh
With their tiny whispers. How long will this last?

I've tried so hard and gotten so far.
Now look at me and all of the scars.
The scars I've left at home,
Waiting for me as I come undone.

I am the loser who never got a chance,
To smile with delight to see the last dance.

Good Life in America
Carmen Rivera, Apple Valley

Hi my name is Carmen. I am from Guanajuato, Mexico. Since I first came to this country, I have married and have had two daughters. My brothers live here too. Three years ago, I was diagnosed with breast cancer. It has been three long years of fighting this disease. I feel the care of the doctors and hospitals to help me to get rid of my cancer. I think the health care is better here. I am still happy to be living in this country. I like learning and going to school. I only wish to see my dad in Mexico. I thank God for my family and that I am able to be here.

My Life
Doris J. Smith, Minneapolis

My name is Doris. I was born and raised in Chicago, Illinois. I lived in Chicago for half of my life, but something happened to me that made me leave Chicago in 1995. I left because of my family. Things didn't work out. Don't get me wrong, I love my family. I just couldn't take it anymore. I had two kids at the time. My son was seven and my daughter was twelve. I had a very hard struggle in Chicago because I had no job, was on welfare, and didn't have enough money to support my kids. But I kept up my faith, and decided to move to Minnesota with help from my niece, who gave me a place to live for a year. I got a job at McDonald's and another job at Rainbow. I had two jobs for almost a year until my daughter finished high school. She went to college, finished college, and is now a successful physical therapist. My son is still trying to find himself, but that's okay with me. I'm glad I moved to Minnesota. I've come a long way and made a lot of progress since I left Chicago.

My Worst Job
Adan Arale, Minneapolis

My first job was not good for me because everybody hated me. I couldn't sharpen my knife because it was too hard for me. My co-workers were always yelling at me and my supervisor was mean. I would cut big meat and processed bone arms. At the time, I didn't speak any English at all, everybody spoke English, and the interpreter would change my words. It was my first time in the United States. Everything was new for me and this job was my worst job I ever had.

Adan Arale is originally from Somalia.

Reaching Out
Mai Vue, Brooklyn Center

Felt lost
Didn't know what to do
Didn't know where I stood
Sought something important in my life
Started reaching out

Grabbed one offered hand, then held onto it tightly
Glanced up at a tiny light, like a flower bud
Was drawn to it, like moth to light
Felt like sun rays breaking through dark clouds
Kept reaching out more head-on

Continued seeing the gradual positive changes
Began believing in myself once more
Embraced who and what I am with humbling smiles
Unlocked the doors one by one
Still endure, reaching out here and now!

My True Life
Phuong Nguyen, Bayport

When I look back at my life and the way I have battled adversity, I realize that I was young and stupid. Now, my perspective has changed and I can finally see the opportunities that education provides for the future.
I was born in war-torn Vietnam in 1982. Before I was born, my parents were getting a divorce. I have seven total siblings. Not long after my birth, my parents were officially divorced and she won custody of us. When I reached the age of five, my mother left me and my brother Phong to my Grandma and she came to America.

Meanwhile, in Vietnam, my brother and I struggled to live on the streets. My grandma cared for us until she died unexpectedly. After my grandma's death, my brother and I went to live with our aunt. Because she was a hardworking businessperson, she did not have the time to care for us, so we were again forced to move in with another family member.

We moved in with my mother's uncle. My Great Uncle's house was full of kids, not enough space, and since we were distant relatives, we didn't all get along. We would go stay with friends to get away. Living house-to-house and day-to-day and not knowing where we would sleep was difficult. Eventually, we got jobs. We worked for a taxi, hoping to get people to ride. Sometimes, the driver would give us tips for our hard work.

And just when I thought nothing could get worse, another tragedy struck. My brother died from a car accident while working. At eleven years old, I was alone. My mother later received the news of my brother's death. After that, she pushed the Immigration and Naturalization Service (INS) so I could come to America to be with her. Three years later, I was allowed to come and stay with her.

Life in America was hard for me. It was hard reuniting with my brothers and sisters, at first we didn't get along. School was hard for me as well, so I joined a gang and started skipping. Not long after that, my luck ran out. In 2004, I was put in prison. In prison, I learned to read and to write and see the opportunities that an education would provide for the future.

When I Came to the United States
Mary Nyang, Coon Rapids

I came on June 30, 2007. I came to United States because my country was at war. There was no food and no medicine. When I came here, I wanted to go back to Africa because my family was in Africa. I came here because my husband was here in the United States. When I came here, I saw snow and cold weather. I saw many trees and different people speaking different languages. When I came here, I didn't know how to speak English. I didn't understand people and what they were talking about. I came to school to learn English; to speak English, read, write, to understand people and to get a job.

Life Changes
Shelly Lenoir, Rochester

I am so grateful that the Lord has turned my life around. And now I am helping others. I can relate to some people who have used drugs and alcohol because it took a toll on my health, my eating habits, loss of my apartment. Using drugs costs a lot of money, and once you get addicted to them, it makes you feel small, like you want to give up on life itself. Drugs can destroy your health, your respect for yourself and for others as well. Drugs can make you feel like you are on top of the world, but in reality you are useless.

When I first used drugs, they did not have any effect on me—I was able to function like everyone else. But when I started smoking, my world came tumbling down. I had to have more and more of the stuff to maintain myself. So I lost my children, my job, my car, they locked me up. They evicted me from my apartment.

When all of this stuff started to happen, this lady came to me and asked me how to help me get out of the mess that I was in. So I told her what was going on, and that I needed help. She told me about Jesus Christ, and ever since I tried him, my life has been put back on track. Jesus is the one that made all of this happen. The first thing that happened was they let me out of jail. I went with this lady and she showed me how to get my kids back, helped me get a place to live, and also helped me make meetings and find a job.

I believe this woman was an angel from God because he used her to help me and a few more of us to stay clean and sober. I know that I truly do a have a personal relationship with Jesus Christ. Now I have a purpose to live, my children have forgiven me for the things I have done to them. Now I spend time with my grandkids. I regularly tell people my testimony about how drugs and alcohol almost killed me.

A Humanitarian Case
Ulises Ramirez, Lino Lakes

Approximately 10 years ago, I saw a case in a general hospital where a couple went for a problem of their daughter's. She had a lot of pain and she looked very sick. They told me that the doctor should do a surgery very fast because she had a big problem with her stomach and no doctor had the capacity for one surgery. A woman doctor in the hospital was very worried because not everyone would help with this difficult case. She told her family, "I don't have very much experience, but I can do it." The very worried family said, "Please, it is okay, but solve it." The next day the woman doctor did the surgery and all went well. Now their daughter is running and playing with her girlfriends. She is very healthy. This woman doctor is a hero to me.

Ulises Ramirez is originally from Acapulco, Gro, Mexico.

Alexander Denning, Rochester

My Teacher's Accident
Khadra Ali, Saint Cloud

I know one person who has serious diabetes. That person is my English teacher. Her name is Asia. She was my teacher when I lived in the United Arab Emirates. She was a very nice teacher and very beautiful, but her problem was with diabetes. She was overweight and could not control herself. She ate everything such as sweets, rice and pasta. She took medication, and as her last chance she took injections. She started exercising, every morning she walked.

One day I was waiting for the bus at school. She said, "Come on, walk with me to Miss Hamda's house and we will get on the bus." I said, "OK, deal." We started to walk. When we were on the highway, she fell down. She couldn't get up. She said, "Please help me." I just screamed, "Come on, get up!" We were on the highway. The cars stopped because there was a red light. I said, "If the red light changes I will run away from you." She said to me, "Please give me your hand." I said, "Oh my God, you are very heavy. Why did you eat a lot of food? I can't help you and I want to run away from here. Then I will call an ambulance for you to take you to the hospital." The cars were beep beeping! Finally she got up. We ran away together. When we crossed the street she hugged me and said to me, "Thank you for the help."

Home
Brad Barney Jr., Cloquet

Home is where I belong
It makes me happy
It feels like it's been so long
Soon enough I'll be out
but for the meantime
I'll have to deal with this doubt
It's painful sometimes
but I did it to myself
So it's up to me to deal with it
No one else
Home is where I belong

Thank You for My Joy
Zechariah Clarence Campbell, Brooklyn Park

I'm from Minnesota. I've always lived near highway twelve. My family always had less money than anybody around us. Rust cars and late bills are a way of life.

I graduated from Orono High School. When I grew up I had good jobs, but I was still poor. I did lots of drugs, but I thought I was poor for some other reason. When I stopped using drugs I was still poor, so I started smoking pot again. I was always getting the job that would pay the most whether I liked it or not. I spent money to make myself happy and it was never enough. Jealousy clouded my heart until it nearly killed me.

I realize how I can't look for work anymore; I must look for joy within myself, and I will be taken care of because I'm worth it. I may have had less money than people who had the latest gear and told fantastic stories of wonderful vacations, but I forgot to appreciate the fact that I never went hungry. I was really just poor in spirit. I believe I have Jesus to thank for my peace, and my wife to thank for my joy, instead of thanking myself for succeeding in misery.

Change of Life
Juan Carlos Berrezueta, Minneapolis

My name is Juan Carlos. I came to the United States last year. My first days in this country were very ugly and hard because my favorite brother and my family were still in Ecuador.

The next days in this country, I remembered everything that I lived with my family, with my friends, with my girlfriends, with my brother and I just wanted to return to my country. I felt very alone and sometimes cried. Each day that passed, the memories came to my mind more and more and the solitude became much greater.

There were actually many difficult days for me. It was a change—my language, my food, my customs, and of people. It was a different story.

With every passing day I realized that life continues, that it has many stages and we human beings have to get accustomed to it. From the beginning of mankind we were created to be able to adapt to all circumstances of life.

A year after having arrived here, I have been able to improve myself a little and have continued with my self-help. I am coming to school to learn English and continue my studies, working to help myself with my expenses, and especially enjoying the family that lives with me in this country, by showing them my respect and affection.

Something I can say to the people that are not from here is that we should not forget that we came to this country to surpass ourselves and help this country overcome day to day, and to be able to help our loved ones. Do not let ourselves be swayed by the temptations or by the bad acts of people, and be strong, because there are people behind us that suffer if we are being subjected to crying or if we mourn. We are strong and happy if we are strong and happy.

Juan Carlos Berrezueta is 22 years old and is originally from Ecuador.

Shame
Aaron DeGuire, Richfield

Shame for me has been a huge black rain cloud that seems to have been constantly hovering above me. It has persistently followed me to and from wherever I have gone, constantly pouring down on me its overwhelming pain and heartache. I have been drenched in its grief for the better, or should I say "the worst," part of my life. Although the cloud of shame may, at times, for the most part recede, I still remain cold and wet from its downfall.

Being cold, I sought constant warmth. Already being wet, my mentality thought it no more harm to soak myself further. Alcohol was the cure and my relief. Alcoholism was the result and an alcoholic was born. So began the downward spiral of insanity. The more I drank to temporarily numb the pain of shame, the more problems I incurred. And so that cold black cloud re-accumulates and even more alcohol will be required to sustain the coming storm. Though, in time, that cloud may recede as did the last. I will always be left with its aftermath.

A time comes when I must exchange my wet clothes for clean, dry, warm ones. I must change in order to change the vicious cycle. I must humbly accept all the mistakes I have made and honestly admit all my wrongs. I must realize that my life is, from here on out, of my own making. I must constantly acknowledge this. I must have faith and come to terms with my life as well as life in general. A day will come when I am comfortable in my own skin. Therefore, I will break out from the fog I have been enveloped in as I search for the promise of clear, bright, sunny days.

GOD Almighty created me, and has continually loved me unconditionally. Therefore, I know there is nothing to be ashamed of.

Keith Rossberg, Annandale

Journeys

Many Great Experiences
Lina Hondel, Medford

I was born in 1960 in the Philippines. I have six siblings and my mother is still living. In 1984, I met an Airman at Clark Air Base, and in 1986, we got married. I had many great experiences living in three different countries and three states.

He took me to the United States in 1988, and it was a big dream that came true. Owatonna, Minnesota was the first place in the United States I set my footprint in, and was where I met my in-laws.

While living at Chanute AFB Illinois, I first laid my hands on tools to shovel snow, rake leaves, and mow lawns. It also was when I first wore hats, mittens, scarves, thick boots, and triple layers of clothing to keep me warm in winter.

In 1993, we moved to Anchorage, Alaska. This is where I gave birth to my son in 1996. Alaska had very short daylight in the winter and long daylight in the summer. I would go outside and look up at the sky and see the sun at twelve midnight. I would place aluminum foil on the windows to darken them in my bedroom to get a good night's rest.

Then in 1997, we transferred to Panama, which has the same climate as the Philippines. We had many fruit trees in our yard, such as bananas, coconuts, mangoes and tree nuts. The summer was hot, humid and rainy. The winter was cooler with the trade winds blowing across the isthmus.

Our last destination was to Japan at Yokota Air base in 2002. My family and I experienced many adventures together, such as mountain climbing and garden walks. I met and made new friends and worked with the Japanese people. They were very nice to me because they taught me to speak their language and eat their foods.

The time had come for my husband to be deployed to Iraq. My kids and I continued our lives without him. Several months later, my husband returned home and retired from the Air Force in June 2007. I was very sad when we left Japan because I miss my friends. They might not be with me now, but the memories of our time and laughter together will always remain in my heart.

Marcelina (Lina) Hondel was born in Makati Manila, Philippines. She has been married to Floyd Hondel for 26 years. She is the mother of two, a 16 year old daughter, Robelene, and a 15 year old son, Donald. She has lived with her family in Medford since 2007. She attends classes at Roosevelt Community School in Owatonna. She is also currently employed at Wal-Mart Supercenter in Owatonna.

Summer Vacation
Mai Lee Yang, Minneapolis

In the summertime, I had a great time with my husband. We spent time with each other and went on a vacation; we went to Montana and Yellowstone. It was so beautiful. The park had many animals, like buffalo, moose and bear. I took a lot of pictures at the park and waterfall and geyser. It was so beautiful and very interesting. I had never seen a place as beautiful as this before. Every morning, when the sun rose, I felt like I lived in the sky. I had a great time with my husband. If someday I had a job, I would want to take him on my vacations with me, and I'd like to go all over the United States. I have great memories of my summertime.

Problem When I First Came to the United States
Tue Vang, Brooklyn Park

When I first came to the United States, it was very difficult for me to understand any other English words except for yes and no. I didn't even know how to use general electronics. Every time that I needed to buy something at the store, my husband had to go with me even though he didn't want to go. It took me a couple of months to learn how to use a stove and microwave, and took me two years to know how to communicate with my teachers.

For the first couple months I wanted to go back home so bad, but my father called me and told me: "This is your new life, new home, so it will not be easy, but you need to go to school and learn. Don't give up, because you're young and so lucky to have the opportunity, so just grab it and hold on tight— don't let go. Some day in the future you will be happy to be there." After I heard that from my dad, I started to realize that this was my new home. I had no other choice, and that's why I decided to go to school. It took me five years to graduate from high school, and those five years were the most incredible experiences for me.

Now I am very happy to be in the United States because I have a job. I don't make a lot of money, just enough to support my family, and the most important thing is that I live in a country that has good hospitals, good technology, good education, and safety for my children.

Happy Journey
Abdi Ige, Saint Cloud

My name is Abdi Omar. I came from the Somali Regional State in Ethiopia. I arrived in the U.S.A. on July 11th, 2008 in Washington, D.C. After a few hours I came to the airport in Minneapolis. I stayed one hour and then I came to Saint Cloud. Here was where my family stayed. My first goal was to find a job. After three months, I got a job.

My second goal was to go to schood to learn to speak, write, and read English. I started my first class at McKinley Adult Basic Education in Waite Park, Minnesota. Now, I am better than before because the economy is strong in the United State. and I work hard. I am more tired because I have to work a lot. In my country it is more difficult to find a job.

I got used to America and I am happy to be with my family.

My Life
Malyun Gedi, Minneapolis

I am an immigrant. I was born in Somalia. I lived there until I was 15 years old. I didn't go to school. When I was young, I didn't play sports. My family was middle class. We lived in Mogadishu. My father had a job. He fixed machines. My mother stayed home and took care of the children. I helped my family. I worked at home.

When I was 12 years old I was short and heavy. My hair was black and straight. I had many friends. I still remember them. I had six brothers and five sisters. I left Somalia when I was 15 years old. I went to Kenya. I came to Minnesota in 2004.

Now I live in Minneapolis. I am a student at Learning in Style School. I study English, math, and computer. I go to class five days a week. I'm married. I have three children. Mohamed is five years old, Fowsiya is nine years old, and Ayan is eight years old. Sometimes I help my children with their homework. I'm a busy mother. I also do home care for my father every day. I like my new country, but I miss my old country. I studied Citizenship very hard. I passed my test and became a U.S. citizen in May 2010. Now I'm helping my husband study the 100 questions because he wants to be a citizen, too.

Coming to America
Fatumo Abdi, Minneapolis

I came from a big family and they have 100 camels in the bush. My family also has a farm in the suburbs of the capital in my country. When I was young, I never had a chance to go to school because my mother told me to cook and care for my brother and sisters. When I came to the U. S. at the Washington D.C. airport, it was the first time I traveled outside my home country. I was surprised at what I saw in the Washington D.C. airport. I got lost in the airport and it was my first time seeing an elevator. It was scary. My daughter was with me, she is my first child. It took me four hours to find out where my flight was to get my boarding pass. I was very scared. I didn't speak English, not even a word. The people I saw in the airport were a different color than my country. Most of them were white people. My clothes were even different then clothes they had on at the airport. I didn't see one person wearing clothes like me. Finally I found my flight, now I am happy and I study in school. I like my teacher and my class.

Fatumo Abdi is originally from Ethiopia.

My Life to the United States
Thao Xiong, Minneapolis

In 1989 I came with my family to the United States. I packed the clothes, winter clothes, shoes, boots and jewelry in a big bag. Someone or some things I left behind were my book that I wrote about the country and the people's lives. I left my mom, my brothers and sister and cousin and all of my friends back home. I just brought my passport, many clothes, and shoes because I need to change every day. I wanted to learn English and help people, or develop my dream and help my people to make a great nation.

Thao Xiong is 47 years old and is originally from Xieng Khoua (Laos).

My Trip to Nigeria
Florence Iketalu, Brooklyn Park

My name is Florence Iketalu. I am from Nigeria in the West part of Africa. I am married and blessed with two kids. My happiest day in my life was visiting my two adult children in Nigeria. I have not had contact with them for 15 years in my life.

I went to Nigeria last October 2011 and saw them in good health. I traveled with them to different parts of my country. The places I visited were Akure (in Ondo States of Nigeria), my village (Akwu-ukwu) in Idemili local government, Enugu State, and Lagos States of Nigeria. In fact, it was a wonderful trip with lots of fun.

I went to my Catholic church in Lagos, Nigeria, and found out that everything had changed. In the church, you are not allowed to wear pants or leave your hair open. You are allowed to wear dress, skirts, cover your hair and so on. Another thing that interested me with my journey back home was "Corpus Christi" procession. A lot of people turned up in this wonderful procession. We were singing and dancing on that day to our final procession. After we reached our final procession, all the priests that were accompanying us celebrated Benediction to everybody, and they blessed everybody.

In fact, it was a wonderful trip to Nigeria. I will love to visit it again, because I had fun. More grease to your elbow! Long life and God's guidance. I end so far.

Florence Iketalu is originally from Nigeria.

My Life
Luis Fernandez, Minneapolis

When I came to the United States I was just 12 years old. I didn't know where we going. The only thing I knew was that I came with my dad. He was already here for a long time. He didn't see me for so long, I just decided to come to this country. I left all my family back in my country, like my grandpa and grandma. They stayed there but I came here to live with my dad.

Luis Fernandez is 21 years old and is originally from Mexico.

When I First Came to the U.S.A.
Manivone Syphokham, Luverne

The first day I came to America, when my family saw me, they were all happy and I was so happy too and I can't speak English either. Next day, my parents go to work, my brother and sister go to school. I stayed home by myself. I am little bit bored and when everyone comes back home I am so proud. Later on I go back to school so I am not bored again.

After that we decide to move to Kansas City and I cannot go school no more and I find some job to work on. I think I like to work better than study so I decided to get work at that time. I turned 18 years old one day my friend want me go to party with her. I said yes I'll go for it. And then I met someone his name is Sountha. We talked and played together and later on we decided to get married. He likes me and I like him, too. So we got married in the church and at our house we invited people to come and enjoy the party.

After that I started having babies. The first baby is a boy; his name is Billy. Second one is Matthew and the third one is Merphy. The fourth one is Christopher. Now I am a mother of four children. My husband goes to work and I stay home to take good care of the kids. I love my family so much.

Later on we decided to move to Luverne. My kids love the school and we decided to stay. My husband likes to work hard at the company. So that's the story I have.

Manivone Syphokham is 43 years old and is originally from Laos.

Surviving the Path
Fermin Chavez Nieves, Minneapolis

I came from Mexico. I only brought my wallet, a picture ID, money, some pictures and my good luck. When I left Mexico, my mother wished me good luck.

Fermin Chavez Nieves is originally from Mexico.

My Journey
Mohamad Alkabbani, Minneapolis

When I was working in the Embassy I went to journey for a vacation. I went to Turkey. I stayed there some days. Turkey has very nice places for tourism. The second vacation I went to Cypress. Cypress is an island on the Mediterranean. It has many nice views. The first time I travel by airplane. I was afraid but there is no way to get there except airline or a ship on the sea. But the ship will take a long time to arrive.

I spent six days in Larnaka, the city in Cypress. I enjoyed there, and I'd like to go again with a friend.

Mohamad Alkabbani is originally from Syria.

My Life
Stephanie Smith, Minneapolis

I was born on November 7, 1956 and my name is Stephanie Diane Smith. I have had somewhat of hard life because of the choices I made when I was younger. I dropped out of school in the 11th grade thinking I was grown. If I had stayed in school, I would not be here writing this essay. I made a bad choice and I'm thankful that I have survived for the most part. I am 55 years and my life is a lot better now because I'm making better choices. I just finished outpatient treatment and am now in aftercare. It's really good to know that I am trying very hard to move on and set my goals. I'm going to get my GED this June and who knows, I might even go to college. I have two daughters, Tiffany and Makeda, who are doing very well in school. One is in college and the other will graduate high school in May.

When I was their age I would always babysit for everyone, family and close friends. I have worked in daycare, too, so I had a lot of experience taking care of children. I never wanted kids until I was older. I had my oldest daughter at 36. So much for working with other people's kids! I moved on from that to work in various jobs from housekeeping to collections to cashiering and dry cleaning. I think now I'm going to put all my experiences that I have and start my own catering business with my daughters because I also love to cook. The future is bright!

Life's Difficult Decisions
Argelia Garcia-Varo, Shakopee

Sometimes life is hard, but we can always find a good way to have a better life. When I was little, my parents decided to divorce. My mother took my sister with her, and went back to Veracruz. I stayed with my father in Puebla. When I turned six years old and finished kindergarten, we went to visit my mother in Veracruz. This was the first time I saw her in many years. I was excited to know her. We went to my mother's house. I was nervous and scared when my mother told my father she wanted me by myself with her to talk and to know her better. Later my father would pick me up. When my father left, I started to cry. My mother told me that we were going to take a bus to buy new shoes. In that moment I was very scared because I was wearing new shoes. I felt like something bad was happening. She took me out of Veracruz to hide at one place my father did not know. She kept me there for three months. I cried every day. Then she took me back to her mother's house and left me there with my little sister and she left. I was not happy living there because my grandmother was very strict.

The years passed and I still missed my dad. After some years, my dad got married again, and my mother, too. They left us with my grandmother. My life was unhappy. When I almost turned 18 years old, I decided to come to the United States with my uncle to find a better life. I took my sister with me and we came to California. My life had a big change because I started to work and have my own money to spend the way I wanted. I could buy clothes and shoes that I liked.

After one year, I moved to Minnesota to get married to my husband. This was my first party in all my life. My marriage made my life better. I have two sons. I enjoy giving them things I never had, like birthday parties. My marriage and my kids help me to understand the difficult lives of my parents and grandmother and their decisions. This understanding helps me to make my life better, and the lives of my kids.

Argelia Garcia-Varo is 30 years old and is originally from Veracruz, Mexico.

I Like Snow
Huda Kareem, Saint Cloud

My name is Huda Kareem, I am from Iraq. I arrived in the U.S. on September 14th, 2011. I am married and I have two children. In Iraq, I lived in the southern region where the weather was hot. I dreamed that I would someday live in a cold area so I could see the snow falling on the ground and see how white it is. When I decided to immigrate to America, I wished to God to live in the northern region of the United States. On July 27th, 2011 The Organization for Immigration called me and told me the place they were choosing for us, which was the state of Minnesota, in the city of Saint Cloud. I was very happy because I would go to America and to the region that I wished to live in. The region would be in the north. When we came to Saint Cloud the people who lived there told me that it is very cold here and that there is a lot of snow. I felt happy because I would see the snow falling down and how the ground would be covered by the snow.

I am not able to describe to you my happiness when I saw snow for the very first time. I had dreamed for a long time to see the snow on the ground.

My Life
Carolina Esquivel, Saint Cloud

Hello, my name is Carolina Esquivel and I am from Honduras. I was born in El Progreso Yoro where I lived until I was 16 years old. My country is very beautiful and we also have a lot of bananas!

I came to live in the United States with my parents in 2001. My family and I lived in Sumter, South Carolina. I liked living in Sumter, because the weather was always nice. We lived very close to Myrtle Beach where my family and I would often take vacations. I met my husband at the place I was working at in Sumter. We dated for several years before we got married.

I now live in Saint Cloud, Minnesota, where I like it very much because it is a nice place to live. I take classes at Hands Across the World, so that I can better my English. They are very good people and I enjoy my time there.

How the Spider and Monkey Became Friends
Anonymous, Brooklyn Center

It all started a long time ago in a kingdom called Buduburam. This is a place where the animals would gather to celebrate events such as birthdays in honor of one of their fellow animals. All the animals seemed fond of the idea of merry making with others; except for the Monkey and Spider, that has been totally against one another since their last encounter over food. One day Spider decided to throw a party honoring himself and asks all his fellow animals to come dressed in white. The following day all the animals arrive at the party. While entering the party hall, the animals notice two guards standing vertically at the door asking to inspect everyone's hands before entering the party hall. Concerns grew among the animals and they began asking what the purpose was of them being inspected. As Spider made his dramatic entrance, welcoming everybody to the party, he explained why it was important for everyone at the party to have their hands inspected. Spider said the reason behind his great idea was to make sure everyone had a fair hand color like him. Therefore anyone that didn't have the same color as him would have to go home and clean his hand before entering the party hall.

Even though the animals could not fully comprehend the main reason behind Spider's great idea, one by one they all went through with the inspection until it was Monkey's turn. Monkey gave his hand and immediately realized that Spider was trying to get at him for having a darker hand color. He anxiously left the party to go home and have his hands wash. But what Monkey did not know was that, his hand color was permanent. Monkey went home and decided to wash his hands. But when he went back to the party, the inspector told him that his hands were still dark. Monkey went back home to try and get his hands washed for the second time. Upon his arrival to the party for the second time, the party was over. Monkey became furious and decided to host a party of his own. He had inspectors placed at the entrance of the party hall. Monkey instructed the inspectors to only allowed animals with four legs into the party hall. Upon Spiders arrival to the party, he was told only animals with four legs could enter the party hall. Spider had no choice, but to go home. From that time onward, Spider and Monkey became friends and hosted parties with no rules attached.

If I Was a Settler on the Great Plains: My New Life in the West
Lisa Liu, Minneapolis

I just moved to the Great Plains because I felt very tired in Boston. I couldn't find a good job there. I like the Great Plains, it's fresh for me, it's hopeful for me. There are many cute animals and beautiful plants that I'm interested in.

But there is a new land and there are many problems to solve. There is no river and there is very little rain, so I have to dig a hole to get water. The land is flat and there are few trees. So I have to grow many plants. For example: trees, wheat, corn, and grass. When the windstorms come the trees will stop some wind. There are terrible snowstorms in winter and it is very cold, so I have to build a strong house to live. Sometimes we need to eat meat, so I kill some cows and pigs…There are no police, so it's not safe for me and our animals. I think I have to get several big dogs. There are no machines, so I have to do farm work with my body. I must do some sports every day. Then I can become stronger and have much energy for work.

I need to buy some books and papers and pens. When I have a rest I can do some interesting things. If I have much more grain and animals I can sell some of them. I will get more money to buy something I need, like a machine. I think my new life in the West will be happier. I will like it here more and more.

Lisa Liu is 27 years old and is originally from China.

A Journey
Zhou Qun Sherry, Minneapolis

We like to have a happy family. I believe it is very enjoyable to travel with my family. I especially remember traveling to Washington D.C. with my son and my husband. In 2008, my husband's company had a convention there.

On our way, we had a plan to visit our friends. It was a pleasant morning in the summer. We drove towards the southeast. We stopped by my friend's home, which was located in Cleveland, Ohio. They were happy to meet my family and we had a few beers to celebrate us being in America.

The next morning, we drove from their home to Boston. It took us almost 12 hours to reach my best friend's house. She and her husband gave us a warm welcome. We had delicious Chinese dishes for dinner. We also shared our happiness with each other. Early the next morning, we were reluctant to part and continue our trip to Washington D.C.

We drove nine hours to our destination, Washington D.C. It was a beautiful city. The green grass looked spread out on the ground and the aroma of flowers filled the air as we passed the gardens. My son was especially interested in the exhibitions such as the historical, aircraft, and the tropical museum exhibits.

My husband's friend invited us to his home and we had many joyful hours with his family. His wife was very happy to guide us around Washington D.C. We saw the Lincoln Statue and the Washington National Monument. We all visited Washington's home and his museum as well. We wandered around the White House for a while. Then his friend drove us to the air force PX to get some drink and food because we can get discount purchases as veterans. My husband and his friend talked of their success in their careers and families.

On our last day, my husband went to a rally for Obama's election. He seemed very content with his choice that Obama could win the election. My son and I went to an aquarium and China town when my husband attended his meeting.

The last day of the convention, my husband's company had a big banquet for workers and their families and we celebrated our wonderful journey.

I photographed many things on our journey, and they always brought back vivid memories of happier days.

Zhou Qun Sherry is originally from Chongqing, China.

I Moved to Yemen
Fadumo, Minneapolis

In 1992, I moved to Yemen. I came from Somalia by ship with my sister and three children. I was on the ship for 4 days. It was difficult to leave my family and my country. Also, I got seasick and couldn't eat anything. After I went to another city, everything was hard for me because I didn't know the language and couldn't understand people when they were talking. If I wanted to buy something, I used sign language so they could understand me. Most of the time, I stayed home and watched TV. After a couple of years, I learned Arabic.

Fadumo is originally from Somalia.

Coming to the United States
Michael Maltsev, Coon Rapids

I came to the United States in January 2011 from Russia. I came here because my wife's family is here. I came here with my wife and two children. My trip here was 2 days long. First I went to Moscow, after that to New York, and then finally to Minneapolis. I brought clothes, shoes and documents with me. I planned to come to the United States and had thought about it for a long time. On my first day in the United States, I saw the airport, my family and snow. On my first day in the United States, I felt tired, so I slept and called my family. The best thing about living here is the cars, houses and roads. The worst thing about living here is that people speak English all the time. I'm homesick for my family in my native country. I don't miss the criminals in my native country. I like my new life in the United States.

Michael Maltsev is 35 years old and is originally from Russia.

My Trip to Madrid
Maria Ochoa, Minneapolis

I went to Madrid, Spain for two weeks. My favorite moment was when I saw the Pope. I was at least 15 feet away from the Pope. I was very excited when the Pope passed. I saw many people from different countries. I was very happy to see people from my country, Guatemala. One day I went to a church that had 408 steps in total. Six days later, we walked for four and a half hours until we reached the camp, Cuatro Vientos. One night we slept in Cuatro Vientos. The place is very big. There were millions of people in this place. In the day, it was very hot, 115 degrees. In the night, there was a hurricane that came very hard for four hours. I was asleep for four hours. I enjoyed it very much. I will never forget this trip. I then came back to Madrid. I took the metro. I also went to different places, especially churches in Avila and Valencia. I went to Paris in the night and saw beautiful places. I walked for two and a half hours to get to the beach. I was happy. The people sang while we walked. I saw anise growing on the path. I was very thankful to God for letting me be in Madrid with many people and my two daughters.

Coming to the United States
Hagere Demissie, Coon Rapids

I came to the United States in 2007 from Ethiopia. The reason I came here is my husband lives here. I came here with my daughter too. My trip was 17 hours. First, I went to Washington D. C. I brought enjara, spices, gold, clothes and pictures. I had planned to come to the United States. On my first day in the United States, I saw wood lying on the ground here and nobody took it. Wood in my country is used for cooking food. I felt bad. The best thing about living here is that there are laws and rules, and if you work, you can have a good life. The worst thing about living here is that the weather is sometimes bad. I am homesick for my mom and sister in my native country. I would like to go back to my country and live there, but I like my new life in the United States!

Hagere Demissie is originally from Ethiopia.

Albert Lea
Priscila Sanchez, Albert Lea

Albert Lea is a city in southern Minnesota where you can have a peaceful life and enjoy the nature that is around there.

Albert Lea in the summer time has many advantages. You can go for a walk or bike around one of the beautiful and quiet lakes. Or you can go to one of the parks to find a good friend because people from Albert Lea are nice and friendly. Its neighborhoods are cozy and safe. There are schools near everyone in town and it has an interesting downtown with a lot of businesses.

However, Albert Lea also has disadvantages, especially in wintertime, because it is so cold and you have to shovel a lot of snow. Also, in summer you always have to stay alert for tornados, and sometimes it gets very hot.

Albert Lea is a good place to move; you can find the peace and tranquility that you are looking for, come and see.

Priscila Sanchez is 25 years old and is originally from Mexico.

Coming to the United States
Jean Claude Ntambwe, Coon Rapids

I came to the United States in 2011 from Congo. The reason I came here is I won a United States visa lottery. I came here with my wife and four children. My trip was two days. First I went to Brussels and then to Chicago. I brought clothes, shoes and many documents with me. On my first day in the United States, I saw tall buildings and highways. I felt very happy and I called my parents and brothers in Congo. The best thing about living here is I can have a good job and my children will have a good education because they study here in good schools. The worst thing about living here is the children are bad to their teachers. I am homesick for my parents and family in my native country. I don't miss the politics in my native country. I wouldn't like to go back to my country and live there. I like my new life in the United States.

Jean Claude Ntambwe is 48 years old and is originally from Congo.

One Box
Guadalupe Meza Ibaniez, Minneapolis

I came from Mexico. I only brought one box. I put my boots, pants and sweater in my box. I took my purse and my passport. I took money. I came with my sister and my husband.

Guadalupe Meza Ibaniez is originally from Mexico.

Long Travel
Fadumo Osman, Minneapolis

My name is Fadumo Osman. When I moved to the United States, it was very long travel. When I came here, I saw different tradition and language, however it was very interesting to know about other countries and their cultures. When I lived in Nairobi, Kenya, I really could understand why people moved to the United States because my country was at war. However, now that I have had the opportunity to stay here I can see that the lifestyle is very different, which makes things easier and more comfortable for us. I am glad to stay in the United States because I get a lot of opportunities. I am learning the language and I love the United States for many reasons, because this is my country and I am a United States citizen.

Looking for Job
Anonymous, Minneapolis

When I moved to Minnesota a lot of things changed my life. Things changed, like I have to take care of myself, look for job and a new apartment. I lived with my family before I got to the United States. I have to look for a job and get a resume. I never worked in the United States so it was so hard for me to find a job. It took me one year to get a job.

The Best Experience of My Life
Riyadh Al Abboodi, Blaine

I think my best experience was my travel to America because it changed my life and my family's life too. I spent a difficult time in my country. I was born in Iraq on August 6, 1955. I am married and I have five children. My job was being an assistant pharmacist for 34 years. But when the government changed and a new government came in, life was changed. There were no laws and there was killing everywhere. My older brother was killed in Iraq, so I decided to leave my country and come to America to protect my family from the killings. I am very happy in my new life and for my family. I think this has been a good experience in my life.

Coming to the United States
Mai, Coon Rapids

I came to the United States in July 2007 from Laos. The reason I came here is because my husband lives in the United States and I married him. I came here with nobody. My trip was 24 hours long because I went from China to New York. I brought pictures of my family and clothes with me because I didn't have any clothes like in America, so I thought the first day here I could wear my clothes. I was too tired to go shopping for clothes. I brought my family pictures because sometimes when I miss my family, I look at their pictures often. I saw McDonald's and a nice house on the first day in the United States.

On my first day in the United States, I felt nervous and tired because I didn't know what to do in the United States and I felt different from other people. My first day in the United States, I slept for 8 hours. When I woke up, my mother-in-law and my husband took me shopping for clothes, shoes, and shampoo at Kohl's.

The best thing about living here is that when I met my husband, he helped me come to the United States. The worst thing about living here is the snow because I feel cold. The thing I don't miss is farming a lot in my native country. I wouldn't like to go back to my country and live there. I like my new life in the United States.

Day by Day
Hong Nguyen, Edina

Have you ever lived in a country that has no government, no jobs, and no activity? This question is part of my journey. It took me a long time to reflect on the very sad ending of war in Vietnam, and what happened to me, my family and my country. Now, 32 years after coming to the U.S., I am ready.

I clearly remember April 30, 1975, when the Vietnamese Communists suddenly won over South Vietnam. It created chaos in Saigon, the capital where I lived. I was 35. It was the first time in my life that I faced a great loss of freedom, which our people had been fighting to get for many years. Now it was gone. Since we knew the Communist regime did not accept us, our hearts were broken when we heard the news. Our tears poured down and we were shocked. Now that the war was ending and the Communists had won, what could happen next?

No jobs, no money, and a whole city as quiet as a cemetery because everything was shut down. No one showed up for work. Everyone lived in fear. Garbage piled up in the marketplace, a mountain of smelly trash.

With two small children, we had to figure out how to survive day-to-day. I knew that with little money left, I should cook rice soup for breakfast and, in the evening, bake sweet bread to sell. We didn't mind working hard every day, but then my son got sick. He had to stay at the hospital for four days. But he didn't survive: he died because of the shortage of doctors and medication. That was a heart-breaking moment for us. On top of that, a year after, I had a miscarriage with our baby. What a sad experience! In spite of this sadness, I was still alive and healthy, so I praised the Lord for helping us to live.

My nightmare has been over for decades, but it is clear to me that I didn't get through this sadness alone.

My faith led me through those past day-to-day challenges – and has also helped my belief in Jesus Christ grow stronger, day by day.

Hong Nguyen is originally from Vietnam.

Education Opens Doors
Anna Moon, Minneapolis

My name is Anna Moon. I came to the U.S. from Seoul, South Korea. I was only a teenager in high school when my mother died. My father died in the Korean War. I had one older brother, one older sister and one younger brother I helped care for.

Life was very difficult because at the time, South Korea's many education systems were not good. I went to nursing school because I wanted to be a registered nurse. Finally, I graduated and become an R.N. It was like a dream come true and was the happiest day of my life.

I was 23 when I worked in the operating room and the recovery room. After I got married to my husband, I only worked for two years because I was pregnant with my first baby. At the time, the tradition was that a woman stayed at home to take care of the children. I had three sons and one daughter.

I really like the U.S. education system because it opened doors for me and my children. My oldest son is a information technology (IT) director of a company, my second son has an MBA, my youngest son is a psychologist and my daughter is a family physician. Thanks to the U.S., now I am studying advanced English speaking, listening, reading and writing every morning. I have worked hard to reach this level at my school. Education has opened doors for me.

Anna Moon is 76 years old and is originally from Korea.

Mall Of America
Arturo G., Circle Pines

When I went to Mall of America, my nephew came with me. The day was Black Friday. We were looking for clothes but after a few minutes, I lost my nephew. He was lost for 30 minutes. I was very scared because my sister has only one boy. So I was running all over the building. I saw my nephew and I felt good, and I cried. One woman found my nephew and then the women found me. We were happy because finally I had found my nephew.

Hijacking
Ahmed, Minneapolis

In 1984, my family and I were residing in a village near the capital of Somalia. It is about 30 km away. It is a farming village, called Afgooye. A river, Shabelle, runs through it. It is a nice place and I had a farm there.

One day, one of my sons became sick and the doctor advised me to take him overseas where he could get treatment. His mother, the boy, and I flew to Saudi Arabia. Unfortunately, some Somali men, who called themselves secessionists, hijacked the plane. They shot a man in the airplane and they wounded the pilot and co-pilot. After long negotiation with them, they agreed to save the plane and the passengers. After many long struggles, we arrived in Ethiopia where we were under the protection of the hijackers. The United Nations staff negotiated with them. They demanded that the Somali government release high officials who were in prison, but the government refused their request. The UN promised to give them political asylum and then they agreed to release us. It was a horrible situation that I will always remember.

Mexican Adventure
Mulki Mohamud, Minneapolis

When I left Africa, I went to Mexico before I came to the United States. I was in Cancun, Mexico City, and Tijuana. It was not an easy time. When first I went to the Greyhound bus station, I didn't know how to buy a ticket. The people looked at me because they hadn't seen someone my color. I was scared and I cried. When I had to take a taxi to the hotel, I also didn't know how to do it at first. When I wanted to buy food, I pointed with my finger. I said, "I want chicken." The clerk laughed and said, "that's pollo." It helped that I spoke Italian, because some people could understand it. I was in Mexico for one month, and then I went to the United States and lived in many different states.

Mulki Mohamud is originally from Somalia.

My Life
Carolina D., Minneapolis

My name is Carolina. I'm a native of El Salvador. I lived there until I was 14 years old with my stepmother, two brothers and three sisters. My three sisters moved to the United States when I was little, so I don't remember their faces. I was a student in my country for seven years.

Then one of my sisters came back to El Salvador to stay with us for a few months. She tried to take me to the U.S. My stepmother disagreed with my sister about me. My sister talked with my stepmother about it. She wanted to take me to study in the United States because she wanted a better life for me. Then my stepmother understood and let me go with my sister to the U.S. My stepmother gave me permission to come to study in the U.S. She made a notary letter and my sister took me to the capital city of El Salvador, San Salvador, to get the passport to came to the U.S.

I arrived in October of 1999 in California. I was living with my sister in her apartment. On December 24 we celebrated Christmas, but for me it was difficult to celebrate Christmas far away from my family. I became sad to be very, very far away from my family.

In a few months I started to study English in Bell Gardens High School in California. I studied there for only two years, 9th and 10th grade. Then I moved to Minnesota in 2002 and lived in Saint Paul. I started to study English in Leap English Academy in downtown Saint Paul.

I was in 11th grade. On the school bus, I met a student from Leap English Academy. He became my friend. He was from Ecuador, but when he saw me he was in love with me and I didn't know it. But in a few months he told me that he was in love with me and I told him I didn't want a boyfriend because I wanted to study. My sister, too, said she didn't want me having a boyfriend when I was in school. But in a few months I was in love with him too. So I accepted him. We moved to New York and had two children.

Carolina D. is 33 years old and is originally from Ecuador.

My Life
Chamroeun Se, Brooklyn Park

One night on New Year's Eve, people around the world were very happy with their parties. They were waiting for the countdown with their families and friends. Some people kept playing games or having conversations until morning.

My parents didn't sleep at all that night. However, they were not waiting for the countdown or playing games; they were waiting for my arrival. I was born on the early morning of January 1st. My parents were so happy because I was the only son and the youngest child in my family.

My parents were farmers. We lived in a small village in Cambodia. They worked on the farm every day. After school, I usually went to the farm to help them. I helped them to grow the plants. I still remember that we had many kinds of plants like corn, chili, sugar cane, potatoes, and so on. I really loved being a farmer.

However, at the age of 15, my life was changed after my parents came to the United States. I had to move to Phnom Penh, the capital of Cambodia, and livd with my aunt. Everything was new for me – new house, new friends, new school, new neighbors, and so on. It was so complicated for me to adapt to that new environmen, because I had never separated from my family before. First, I really missed my family. Then, day by day, I started feeling better with my new place.

Now I have the same situation again, I just moved to the United States two months ago. However, this time I feel it's more difficult for me to overcome this situation. Even though now I'm living with my whole family, I still have some problems like school, travel, and language. Whenever I want to go somewhere, I cannot go because I don't have a car yet. Another important thing is language. Sometimes I can't understand what people are talking about or telling me to do something. Even though I can speak English, it's not as comfortable like when I speak my own language.

Finally, people always have obstacles in their lives. Sometimes it's hard to overcome or easy to overcome. My advice is: Do not give up. Just remember that all problems always have solutions. I hope I will be able to overcome my situation soon.

My Life Trip
D. Ali, Minneapolis

I am deaf and I'm from Somalia and I came to America in 2005. I lived in Somalia as a war refugee, then left to go to Kenya for almost nine years. The UN (United Nations) supported us. Thanks, USA.

I left Somalia to Kenya, and was very lucky because it's a dangerous place. I grew up, never going to school and never being taught education of the world. I went to the hospital, and the doctor checked my body. After I asked the doctor about wanting to go to school and also why my family all went to school, and only left me at home; the doctor said don't worry, I will call a social worker for you, okay. I waited for the doctor's reply a long six months, and I was not patient. I had another appointment, and again I asked the doctor. He said a social worker will come to my house and discuss signing papers to start school in September. I was excited to sign American language but did not learn enough of full school. In 2008 I was on trip to Ohio, to stay six month in Virginia, Washington D.C., and Maryland. There were many deaf people there and I was going to move to D.C. for a school called Gallaudet. After trying, I had no success. America is better than my country because America supports opportunities for the deaf.

Thank you, America. I wish to go to Gallaudet.

About Myself
Fadumo Omar, Saint Cloud

This is my story; I would like to talk about myself. My name is Fadumo Omar. I was born in the capital city of Mogadishu. In 1991, civil war started in our country. My family and I fled from the capital city to a small village. We lived in that village for around ten years and did not have school. In 1999, I came to Kenya. Then I started in the Islamic school there. At the end of 2005, I came to the United States of America. Then I started working for the first three years. In 2009, I joined ABE/ESL school. I want to continue my studies until I reach my goal. I hope my dream will come true. Thank you.

Why I Left My Country
Glory Si, Saint Paul

In this story, I would like to tell you about why I left my country. In my life before, I left Burma. My parents and my brothers and sisters stayed together in my village. I remember something when I was nine years old; my parents were very rich in my village because at that time my father was a business supervisor. When my father was rich, he also helped the villagers who were poor. In 1988, I didn't have any opportunity in my village because the Burmese soldiers attacked my village, and my parents hid in the jungle for five years.

At that time, we didn't have enough food, clothes, and always were in fear in the jungle. Then my parents left for a place where there was no fighting. When I was staying in that place my parents didn't have enough money to send me to school. So, my parents asked one of my brothers to send me to the refugee camp. At that time when I left my parents, tears came down because I never was far away from them before, but I stayed strong and went to the refugee camp in Thailand. When I was 19 years old, I graduated from high school with a diploma. When I was 20, I heard a sad message that my mother had died of cancer. I still miss her very much.

I was a teacher in the refugee camp for one year. At that time, I got married and had one daughter. I came to the United States in October 2011. We are very happy to be here, but everything is new for my family.

Glory Si is 23 years old and is originally from Burma.

Wanting to Come to America
Sahardid Ahmed, Minneapolis

My name is Sahardid. I was born in Hargaysa, Somalia. I will never forget how badly I wanted to come to the United States. I arrived on March 28, 2006, and at that time I didn't know anything about America. I was scared to go anywhere because I didn't have any idea.

Two Worlds
Fredy Solis, Crystal

It is very difficult for illegal immigrants to be deported when they have a life in the United States. The absence of family members is a great difficulty for all involved. Also, there are immense financial repercussions in the deportation of a person. Finally, since the person has become accustomed to living in the United States, it is very difficult to return to the customs in their country.

When I came here, I did not intend to start a family, but I ended up getting married to a United States citizen and having two children, a girl and a boy. When I got taken by immigration my life changed instantly, bringing pain and sadness to my wife, children, and close friends. I had to go back to Ecuador, losing my children and wife for a period of time.

When I was taken in by immigration in 2009, it affected us financially. We had to pay a lawyer to fight my case to get me back here and to start the legal process for permanent residency. In time, we lost our house and cars due to the lack of my income during my absence. Since I had lived in the United States for nine years, I had become accustomed to having a well-paying job and the convenience of a car. Our local grocery store and Target were only five minutes away, and a large mall only ten. Hot water, electricity, and phone are always available. When I went back to Gualleturo, Ecuador, my vehicle was a bus which left my home town only once a day. My store became a local farmer's market which I visited once a week, leaving us to raise the rest of the food on our own. Bare necessities were sold at a tiny store in my little town. The hospital was a two hour bus ride and there were no ambulances. Most houses in my town are not equipped with hot water and the government decides when they need to shut off the electricity.

It was very difficult for me to leave this country when I was deported. I had to leave behind my family and life, as I knew it. It was costly, not only in the area of finances, but also in the way it touched people's lives. After being gone until 2010, I came back here legally this time. It was like heaven.

Fredy Solis is 32 years old and is originally from Ecuador.

The Journey of an American
Jo Anna Thomas, Minneapolis

Being born an American is not always what it seems. I was born in Mississippi and raised in North Minneapolis. I lost my father when I was ten years old. Consequently, all my dreams had come to an end knowing my mother had to raise three kids on her own. I wanted to finish high school, but dropped out in my junior year. I wasted enough time in my life when I only had one year left.

I had this fantasy of graduating and going to college, also owning my own business. I thought I was being ungrateful taking advantage of a free education. Many people in other countries would love to have this opportunity. The thought of people who lack proper schooling and unequal rights for an education, yet some people don't have resources like Americans. Someone asked me why I didn't finish high school. I was thinking of people who lack proper schooling and unequal opportunities for education.

I have worked since I was 14 years old taking care of my family; I just turned 27 in January. There was a topic in high school where they ask, "Where do you see yourself in five years?" I never really answered, but would have wanted to be the first in my family to receive a certificate or diploma. Some days I've sat and reflected on my life and what will be my next step in life. I am an American; there's nothing that I can't do. I do have dreams and goals. I have talked to my peers and we have talked about graduating to better ourselves. Being born an American is not always great. What I'm trying to say is I want to better myself.

Up and down like a roller coaster, in the back of my mind saying and I quote, "I have a Dream." So now there's nothing or no one who will get in my way and keep me from learning. I am currently studying to get my GED; I want to go to college. I say, the Journey of an American is to get your education first. Never settle for less, strive for the best. So the lesson is that education is the most important thing in my life—never take anything for granted. The sky is the limit.

My Life
Wah Man, Saint Paul

My name is Wah Man. I was born on January 9, 1972 in Burma. I have three brothers and two sisters. My village is near the forest with hills. My country is very beautiful. My country has waterfalls. The waterfall sound is like music.

I am so sad about leaving Burma, but I cannot live there because the army attacks the Karen people. I went to Thailand in 1994. First I lived in Maw Ker Refugee Camp. When I lived in the refugee camp I had many problems. We were not free to walk. We were afraid and not safe.

In 1999, all the people in the Maw Ker Camp moved to the Umpien Refugee Camp. All the people were happy to move to a new camp, but in the new camp many people had problems. There was too much rain, not enough food, the houses were not good—there was no clean water, it was very cold and very windy.

In 2010, my family moved to the USA, to the state of Massachusetts. We lived in Massachusetts for one year. We moved to Minnesota on April 16, 2011. I have lived in Minnesota for 10 months. I am studying in English class. I remember all the people in the refugee camp. Thank you.

Wah Man is 40 years old and is originally from Karen State, Burma.

Peace
Kao Yer, Saint Paul

Peace is a light to brighten the world
Peace is a heaven for people to enjoy together
Peace is when everything is silent and comfortable
Peace is when there is no fighting and no violence
Peace is a place where there is a bright life of happiness
Peace is a love of freedom
Peace is a new world to invite family and friends
Peace is a wonderful life for everyone to wish for freedom and hope
Peace is a way for people to find their happiness
Peace is a sign of freedom

Kao Yer is originally from Thailand.

Life Is Different from My Country to the United States

Neng Thao, Saint Paul

My name is Neng Thao and I was born in Laos. I came to the U.S. in 2002. When I see my family's lives in the U.S. I think about our lives in my country. I think about my parents, brothers, sisters and other relatives.

Then I compare the U.S. to my country. I really feel bad about our lives in my country, because I still remember when I was a child.

At that time, I didn't know about anything in life. Every day I just went to the farm with my mother and father. I just knew that I needed to help them to take care of my younger brothers and sisters. My parents needed to take care of the rice and vegetables, and we also raised animals like chickens and pigs.

At that time, I was little. I couldn't help them a lot, but I saw them work very hard at the farm every day.

When I first came to the U. S. I saw a lot of different kinds of things and many different lives. When I saw some people having a good life, it made me feel sad about our lives in our country. I started to learn a lot about how to live in this country and how to learn a lot of new things in this country, too.

When I went to start school on the first day, it was very hard for me because I didn't know any English at all. My teacher asked me about my address. I didn't know what that meant. So she drew me a picture of a house, so then I thought that she might mean the address, and I wrote my address for her. Then she asked me if I was married or single, but I didn't know that either. Then she drew me a picture with people and she asked me if I was like one person or two persons. I pointed my finger to the two persons. Then she understood that I was married. I told my husband that it was too hard for me to live in the U. S. He told me that I needed to do my best and work hard for it and that things would get better in the next couple of years.

Traveling to the U.S. with my "Albir-roja"

Natalia, Minneapolis

I first came to this country during the summer of 2010. I was visiting a guy who at that time was my boyfriend. Today he is my husband and we are living in Minnesota. That visit was a special time. I was very excited to travel to the United States, but I have to confess that I was also very scared for such a big trip—by myself and without the language. At the same time, something special was going on in another continent—the soccer World Cup. For people like my husband and me, it is a little difficult to ignore when the soccer World Cup is happening. Whoever likes soccer, I'm sure you can understand me!

When I was traveling here, I was wearing the official soccer t-shirt of my country, "the albirroja" as we call it in Paraguay. I wore it because Paraguay was participating in this event and I was very proud of it; and of course, I was supporting the team. As I went through different airports, before arriving here, the fact that people recognized the colors of the flag on the t-shirt was a good conversation subject, especially during long waiting hours for connections, and even in the boarding lines. I had a lot of fun receiving compliments like: "Paraguay is going to do well this time," or "Your country's team has a very strong defense." In fact, that was a very good World Cup for us; for the first time we passed to the quarter finals and we just lost against the team that, after all, became the world champion: Spain.

Now, remembering everything, I think that the most amazing thing, besides the fact that our Paraguay team ended up in the 8th position, was the face of my husband who was waiting for me at the Minneapolis International Airport with a BIG, BIG smile when he saw me with my "albirroja."

Natalia is originally from Paraguay.

Something About Me
Anonymous, Minneapolis

Maybe this is not the best story you will read but it is real. I grew up in a small town in Mexico. Every morning was nice to wake up and see beautiful sunshine. It was a very nice place where everybody knew and helped each other.

We are seven members in my family: myself, my parents, grandmother, two sisters and a brother. I remember all the times when all of us ate breakfast together. I still remember my favorite place in the dining room.

When I was 19 years old I made one of the most important decisions I've ever made: I came to the United States of America and started a new life, but I never thought about the language. When I just came and tried to find a job, the applications were written in English. It made me sad and I thought about going back to Mexico. Instead, after some time, I started my own business in construction and I'm learning the language

My Story
Chee Mya, Saint Paul

My name is Chee Mya. I am from Burma. My birthday is September 3, 1967. I have five brothers and two sisters. When I lived in Burma, I worked on the farm. We had many animals: pigs, dogs, cats.

Before I came to America I lived in Mae La Oo refugee Camp. I came to the U.S. on July 23, 2010. Now I live on Westminster Street in Saint Paul.

I have four people in my family. I have two children, one son and one daughter. My son's name is Law Lay Say. My daughter's name is Your Hay Blu Paw. My husband's name is Saw Nae. My son's birthday is December 13, 1983. My daughter's birthday is January 19, 2000. My husband's birthday is March 9, 1976.

My husband goes to a job at Marshall Company. My son goes to a job. My daughter goes to college prep elementary school. Sometimes I am busy.

I love my children very much because they are very cute. They are clever, too. They have different hobbies. I hope they will be good people. Every day I go to school. I like it. I'm happy.

Chee Mya is 44 years old and is originally from Karen State, Burma.

Luwell Carter, Minneapolis

My Story
Dee Wah, Saint Paul

My name is Dee Wah. I was born in Burma. I lived in a small village near the river in a beautiful house. We made our house of bamboo, small trees, leaves and nails. We planted many flowers. We had some animals; chickens, dogs, goats and other animals. There were many mountains and green forests.

I am homesick. Therefore, I miss my parents every day. They are living in a Thai refugee camp. They have nine children. Right now they have three single children. In my country, my father was a hunter. My mother is a teacher. I feel she is a good woman.

I got married on March 19, 1993. I had my first child on December 28, 1993. Burmese soldiers came to my village many times and killed many people and animals. On March 17, 1997 they came to live in my village. We moved to another village. We were still very afraid of them, so we moved to Thailand in 2000. My family lived in Thailand almost eleven years. I was a teacher there.

On May 3, 2011 we left Mae La Oon refugee camp at 8:00 a.m. At 4:00 p.m. we arrived in the city of Mae Sot. My family stayed there seven days. On May 10, 2011 we left Mae Sot to go to the U.S.A. On May 11, 2011 we arrived in New York. The next day we left New York and moved to Minnesota. In the afternoon, we arrived at the airport. There I met my case worker, who picked us up.

The next week my case worker took my husband and me to Ramsey County. My financial worker's name is Andrew A. Sisson. My job counselor's name is Glaw Dee. She works at Hmong America Partnership.

Now I am a Karen Community of Minnesota member and a student at VSS. I like my school. I learn about computers in ESL class.

I love my children and my husband. They love me too. We like our home. It has three bedrooms and one bathroom. I have five children: four sons and one daughter. Three are students and two are in daycare because they are small children. My husband has a job in Austin. He is a meat packer. I have no job right now. I want to be a good woman.

Dee Wah is 39 years old and is originally from Karen State, Burma.

My Humanitarian
Kinnari Shah, Blaine

Let me start my story by talking about India. There are many people in India. They can't afford medicine and doctor's fees. Some people were even living in our apartment complex's open space.

One day my father-in-law was thinking about poor people. He loved to help. He was thinking about how to help people. After a few days, he decided he wanted to help people with getting medical supplies. Then he contacted the hospital's doctors and he talked to them about his thoughts. They then decided to act on his thoughts and started building a check-up center. The check-up center ran very well.

A year later, with the help of several other doctors, he rented a new space in another location for the check-up center. He put some money down on medical supplies too. Then they decided to give a specific name to the check-up center. The name is Jansuvidha Medical Services. The medical service helps many people who can't afford the money for their treatments, which includes cancer and kidney replacements. Now Jansuvidha Medical Services has connected with the cancer hospital in Ahmadabad, Gujarat, India. This is why I feel my father-in-law is a humanitarian. He has helped many people get medical care that could not get it before.

Kinnari Shah is originally from India.

My History
Ronal Zambrano, Minneapolis

When I lived with my parents, I enjoyed my days with them. I also enjoyed the beautiful weather with them. Every morning during the week, we all had to be ready to work. On the weekends we played soccer and had picnics but we usually went to the river to swim and catch fish. That was my favorite. At the end of every month, we had to go to town to buy clothes, some sweet caramels, sodas, and every little thing that we liked we bought. That was an amazing time with my family.

Ronal Zambrano is originally from Ecuador.

Dreams

Looking for Success
Daniel McDowell, Brooklyn Center

When I left Chicago I didn't really know where I wanted to go, but my thought was to go to Baltimore. So when I got to the bus station, I walked up to the counter and said to the ticket agent, "I want a one way ticket to Baltimore." She said to me, "Brother, no, you want to go to Minneapolis, Minnesota. There are lots of jobs, programs, and most of all, there is basic education." So I told her, "Let me get something to eat and I'll be back before the bus departs." So when I came back I said to her, "Alright, I want a ticket to Minneapolis, Minnesota." When I got my ticket, I said thank you.

Now I am on my journey to Minnesota. When I arrived, I didn't know where I was going, but thank God I was across the street from the Salvation Army, known as the Harbor Light. When I got settled down and in a warm bed I was ready to meet Minneapolis. I got up the next day to meet new friends and to find out where there was work and I got lots of good information. One piece of information I got was to Western Staff Service, a temporary job service. The agency sent me to a company called Batch Bakers where I began making cookies, pastries, and pretzels. I worked for Western Staff Service for quite some time; they sent me to a lot of different companies. Over the years, Western Staff placed me on a lot of other jobs. Some were long term. It's been a good journey since I came here and now my journey has taken me to a new level. I am going to GED classes now and taking that for the better.

I would like very much to thank the Lady Agent in Chicago for encouraging me to come to Minneapolis, Minnesota for my success. Now I am on my way to getting my GED and I will be successful in getting it. I would like to get a good paying job that requires my skills and experience.

Thanks for reading this one.

Daniel Eugene McDowell grew up in Canton, Ohio, where he loved to explore the woods near his home. He attended Allen Elementary and Hartford Jr. High, where he played football. At age 10, Daniel was given a drum set for Christmas. After high school, he played with the band Zambeez (or The Flowing River of Africa), which became one of the top bands in Canton. He enjoyed writing his story about success and wants to thank all the great teachers at Northside ABE.

How Would I Change The World?
Obssa, Minneapolis

If I could do it, I would like to help everyone in this world to get better access to health care, education, and clean drinking water. Especially in Africa, where there are too many people who don't have any access to clean drinking water, health care, and education. I know too many children who don't go to school; they just grow up without any government enforcement to educate them, not even high schools. Ninety percent of my people live in a countryside where there is no primary school. Those are very basic necessities for human beings to survive. I hope one day everyone will have access to all of these and be happy. Even their children might be educated better than their parents. I know a lot of my people who don't have any access to health care, education, and clean drinking water. These are what I would like to do, and hope to whenever I get the chance—Insha Allahs (God willing).

If I Could Change the World
Yia Xiong, Minneapolis

If I could change the world, there are many things that I would do. Firstly, I would stop cigarette and chemical producing companies from making cigarettes or chemicals anymore, so people could have a longer life, and there would be less pollution on Earth.

Secondly, people would have to walk instead of driving cars in downtown because it's too crowded for people to get to and from places on time. Lastly, I would change the world back to ancient times, when we cut wood to make fire, instead of using electricity. People worked in the fields, they exchanged crops with each other, and they didn't have to buy food from the store. They enjoyed their lives more than people do today, and they didn't have as much debt.

I believe people had greater delight in life in the past. I would seek to change the world by going back to older ways of living life. This would be a great change.

My Dream
Ofelia Cortes, Fridley

My name is Ofelia. I am from Southern Mexico. I have two children, one boy and one girl, and I have a good boyfriend.

I came to the US on June 29, 2006, looking for a better life for my son, but also for me, too. I have been living here for almost six years; that is the same amount of time that I haven't seen my family. They are in my country waiting every single day for my return. They don't know my children, and I know they love them, even when they have never met them. Every time that I talk to my mom, she asks me the same question, "When am I going to see you again?" And I always say the same answer, "Soon."

I wish to see my mom, my brother, all of my family that now have new members that I don't know, and also my friends and their kids. But I know I have to wait because I can't travel at this time. My mom is always sick. She has many health problems, and I am worried for her. This is something that makes me sad, but I believe in God, and one day I am going to visit my mom with my family and I am going to enjoy every moment with them because that is my dream.

Ofelia Cortes is originally from Tabasco, Mexico.

A Huge Wish
Joseph Saul Hernandez, Minneapolis

I am a person who has a wish, who believes in a better life and an improved future for the next generations. However, we need to do something to make that happen. The key to improving our lives and our relationships with others is education, because we will have an opened mind to resolve or understand the many problems of our world. The main objective is to be more human with humanity. People think more about money than before and don't care how to get it or the consequences. We have completely forgotten this: "We live on the same planet and we are part of it." I want to help remember.

From Childhood to Adult

Hibo, Blaine

I was born in Mogadishu, Somalia, and when I was four years old, the fighting started. My family ran away to a safe place but fighting came there too. So then, we left Somalia for Kenya. We were in a refugee camp where we didn't have much food and clothes. We had some classes where we learned Swahili and a little English. After three years in Kenya, the Kenyans told us that we had to go back to Somalia. We went back, but the fighting forced us to go to Balad Xawo near the Kenya border. I was 14 years old and we stayed there about two years while family members sent some money to help us. One day my aunt's daughter sponsored her mother, sister, brother, and me to go to Kenya so we could come to the U.S. I have been here five years. Since I have been in the U.S., I have been going to school; now I can speak, write and read English much better. I am also working in a hotel and I send money back home to my family. I hope one day they can also join me in America. One thing I am proud of is that in 2011, I became a citizen of the United States.

Hibo is originally from Somalia.

Hopes and Dreams

Miski, Brooklyn Park

My dream is to have my own business because I want to help my country of Ethiopia. My other dream is to earn my GED. I want to go to college to get my nursing degree. After I finish my nursing degree, I will work hard and make a lot of money by owning my own business. After that I will go to my country of Ethiopia and help the less fortunate. I would build schools for them so they can go to school and live a better life. In my country the lifestyle of the people is very difficult. For example, they don't have clean water and more importantly they don't have a good place to sleep. When I return to Ethiopia, I want to do many things to help the people in my country.

Miski is originally from Ethiopia.

Struggles and Goals

Sudi Mohamed, Minneapolis

Every day I focus on my goal even though every day I struggle. In my lifetime, I have lived in England, Kenya, and now the U.S. I was born in May 1982, married at age 18 and had my first child at 19. Now, at 29, I have four kids. I am the youngest in a family with three brothers and seven sisters, whom I haven't seen for 12 years. I miss them very much every day and one-day hope to see them all. I struggle in everyday life because I have two jobs, four children and I go to school. Some days I feel like I'm dying, but I tell myself if I stop, I will never achieve my goal. My goal is to become a doctor someday. I would like to be a physician because I have four kids to raise and I want to give them the life I never had. To reach my goal, I recently started a pre-certified nursing assistant (CNA) class. Every morning when I wake up, I look at my kids' faces and I see what I can do for them. I think about that when I struggle, too.

Sudi Mohamed is 29 years old and is originally from Somalia.

Shining Armor

Carrie, Maple Grove

She looks at him from a far, high tower above thinking, "He's my knight in shining armor, I hope one day he will save me." One day he sees her from afar, locked away in the tower, with the townspeople looking at her as they walked by. He thinks to himself, "What a pretty princess, how will I save her and be her knight in shining armor?" He tried to save her one day, but didn't get far before falling off the tower. She looks down as he's trying and thinks, "That's my knight in shining armor trying to save me, I feel so honored." Her knight in shining armor tried again the next day and made it all the way up the tower. He reaches the window, climbs in and says, "Princess, I'm your knight in shining armor from afar to save you from the life you don't like."

Jungle is Dangerous at Night
Ojulu Omot, Bayport

Jungle is dangerous at night time.
In Jungle you cannot see anything at night,
Because there is no flashlight, no light from moon and stars.
The open fire for safety will not allow you to see around the camp at night,
But if Rhinoceros see the fire, you are in big trouble.
Hungry Cheetahs, Lions, and Hyenas,
Will come to take your meat away.
Not only to take your meat away alone,
Also they will attack you to be their dinner.

Jungle is dangerous at night.
Jungle is home for different dangerous and peaceful animals,
But Jungle is not safe for peaceful animals at night.
Jungle is not safe for human beings at night.
In Jungle it is easy for anybody to get killed by the dangerous animals at night.
At night it is easy to get lost in the Jungle,
Because there is no regular paths to follow.

Jungle is dangerous at night.
In the deep Jungle you will not hear people's voices,
You will not hear any car and airplane sounds,
You will not hear animal and bird noises,
You will not hear any living things making noises at night for their own safety.

Jungle is dangerous at night.
In Jungle you will not see peaceful men,
But strangers.
You will not see farmers but dangerous hunters,
You will not see children and women but crazy men.
You will not see fearful people but courageous ones.
You will not see lazy people but strong ones.
Jungle is dangerous at night.

See You Soon
Kendra Oros, Minneapolis

My family is small but means everything to me. This is especially true because they are back in Mexico, and I am here. I have just one brother and an older sister. My brother has two little boys and my sister has three little princesses, including my spoiled little niece, Michelle. She is almost 12 and she is very pretty. When I call Michelle, she tells me that she misses me a lot and then she asks, "When will you come back to Mexico?" I lie to her, answering, "Very soon, Michelle…maybe next month." And when I talk to my mother, too, it is the same. "I will see you soon," I tell her. It's very difficult for me to stay in another country without my family. However, I hope to achieve all that I want in this country. I hope, too, my family will be proud of me, like I am about them. And hopefully I really will be with my family soon. They always are in my thoughts and in my heart.

Kendra Oros is originally from Mexico.

Changing the World
Anonymous, Minneapolis

If I could change the world, I would do the following all over the world: help every country strive for peace and find ways to not make wars anymore. If I had global influence, I wouldn't allow any weapons to be made. Instead I'd spend that money on poor people and give them jobs. So they could have a decent life and support themselves. When people are independent, free and safe, things are that much better in every aspect of our world. The best change I could imagine would be this. My other thought would be to keep our environment clean, because human beings depend on breathing pure air. And I wouldn't let people destroy the forests. Instead, I would encourage more tree-planting. These are the best changes I can think of and would like to see.

If I Could Change the World
Soua Thao, Minneapolis

If I could change the world I would do the following:
I would work to become more knowledgeable about more things, to become more intelligent. I would plant more trees to decrease or get rid of pollution completely, and preserve and provide clean water for people, as well as find ways to reduce tsunamis, and prevent or lessen natural disasters, conserve natural resources and help make the environment cleaner in the future. I would also help resettle and establish people who are refugees. In addition, I would like to create sustainable farming for people who don't have farms; where everyone would have a place to plant crops, fruits and vegetables, without poison, and they would have healthy food to eat, and no one would go hungry. I would open orphanages, provide homes and food for the deformed and disabled, and open clinics for everyone so they could get medical care. Another thing I would do is build schools in the countryside for everyone, so they would have a chance to get an education. I would also build a lot of factories to make more jobs.

These are my deepest wishes in life, and the things I would like to see changed. If all of these things could be changed, everyone would have the chance to be happy, and the world or everything in it could be so much better.

If I Could Change the World
Asli Abdi, Minneapolis

If I could change the world, I would do the following: make the world a better place by bringing people together and showing them how to make peace with each other. People must stop fighting and learn to love each other. All people deserve to live in safety, prosperity, and peace. Also, I would make jobs available to people, provide affordable health care, and abolish guns, except for the police. Make certain everyone has enough to eat, a good home to live in, and the ability to pay their bills. Finally, I would give teachers the salaries of athletes or executives, because the work of really educating people in order for them to become independent and help themselves is so important in the world.

Asli Abdi is originally from Somalia.

Stanger at the Door
Angeria, Brooklyn Park

Knock
Knock
Knock
Someone at the door
Who is at the door?
Stranger at the door
Peek through the hole
You don't know who that is
Knock
Knock
Again
Stranger at the door
Hands start to sweat
Hearts began to beat
Minds began to wonder what should I do
Stranger at the door
Stranger at the door
Think fast before you're the next to go
Kick
Kick
Kick
Stranger coming in
Oh too late
Stranger in the house
Run
Run
Run
Stranger behind you
Scream
Scream
Scream
As loud as you can
Calm silent
Stranger got you.

Angeria is originally from Liberia.

My Exciting Life
Houa Yang, Minneapolis

My wife and I came from Thailand in 2004 to live with my brother. We lived in his house for about one year. Many things changed in my life because we had to learn how to spend our life in the U.S. Before I came to the U.S., I didn't know how to write, how to read, or how to speak English. I started in first level at Northside ABE. So now I felt better than before.

I have a dream: someday I'll have my own house. In September 2011, my wife and I tried to buy a house from Habitat for Humanity. It has a very good program to help families with low income. My family qualified for that program. Before we moved to our house we must dispatch first our sweat equity hours. I went to many houses for my sweat equity hours. I learned a lot of skills from that. Before I didn't know how they build houses, but now I know how they built it. When I went to work in my new house and another house, I saw a lot of volunteers who came to help us to build our house. We worked together and taught each other. We had a lot of things to do and we had a lot of fun, I felt eight hours were not enough for me. I learned two things from them. They always said safety first and don't kill yourself.

After that, I received a note from Habitat. They made an appointment for us to close our house on December 20, 2011. My family was very excited when we heard this! When it was close to the close of our house, my wife and I could not sleep at night. I felt my heart dance very fast. When I went to sleep at night, I turned my body around and around more than a thousand times. I saw my wife do the same. After we closed on our house, moving around didn't happen again. Now my family and I moved to our house, and my dream came true. I found the right house for my children. Next spring I'm going to volunteer to help other people to build their house. That is my goal.

Houa Yang is originally from Thailand.

My Future Life Dream
P'saw Paw, Saint Paul

I want to tell you about my future life dream. When I become an old woman I will stay alone. I will build a small house at the base of a mountain. In my new small house the surroundings will have a waterfall and a stream. The stream will flow everyday all the time. I will build a small beautiful bamboo bridge. This stream's flowing sounds I will hear for a long time. Every night I will sleep by the stream's flowing sounds. In front of my house I will plant many kinds of flowers and behind I will plant many kinds of vegetable and fruit plants. I think many small birds will come singing and a lot of butterflies will fly by, from place to place. In this time I will see in the stream small fish swimming from place to place. When this time will arrive I will be busy every day and all the time, but one thing will be a surprise: I never will be tired.

P'saw Paw is originally from Burma.

If
Debra Chatman, Saint Paul

If life was like my dreams,
I would be living like a queen,
Elegant gown,
Ball room dancing.
If life was like my dreams,
Money would never mean a thing,
Because I'll have more than I need.
If life was just right,
He'll be here tonight,
But that would be too much like right,
And you know he likes drama in his life.
Why, you think he lives a double life?
If life was like my dreams,
He would know what romancing means,
More Unique than most men pretend to be,
He'll have eyes only for his queen,
If life was like my dreams.

Untitled
Anonymous, Columbia Heights

I want to write about the most important and appreciated thing in my life: my daughters. They are Alejandra, age 9, and Valeria, age 6. They are like each other, although they are different in character. Alejandra is very responsible and intelligent at school. She is also considerate of others. Valeria is smart, even though she is a lazy girl. She likes to go to school only to play with the other kids, not for study. Some of her good qualities are she is happy and lovely all the time.

My husband and I are very content and proud with our children. They make us laugh and mad. For example, Valeria is in kindergarten, and when I had the first conference, I guessed that she wasn't good academically because she didn't like to study, but I never guessed the teacher told me she doesn't speak too much and she is a shy girl in class. I was surprised because at home she is all the opposite. She talks and plays and dances around the house all the time. So, for this reason, she got a lower score in school. Then I encouraged her to participate more in class.

Alejandra, she is amazing. I am so proud of her.

The American Dream
Anonymous, Minneapolis

I have been dreaming about many things since I came to the United States, because I had a dream to come to this country and change my life. My American dream is that one day everything in this country will be different for everyone. There would be more opportunities at work, school, and better health access. My dream is that one day immigrant people can fix their status and be good citizens to help this country. Also, I dream that one day, I can help do something to change the situation in my country. What it is like now makes me very sad because I want peace for the people who live there.

My Dream
Abel Oduro-Afriyie, Saint Paul

My dream is to obtain my GED and go to college. If I have my GED, I could apply for a job. Then, when I fulfill my dream, I can do many things. For example, I may build a new house. I could buy a new car to drive. I might set up my own business. Moreover, if I want to fulfill my dream, I should study hard and be who I want to become. If you reach for your dream, then you can achieve your goals in life, and the dream that you wish will come true in life. In addition, when you have a dream, you may do many successful things in life. However, you should not be lazy in life, and it all depends on you. Finally, I think that if you have a dream you will go a long way. Having a dream is very important, but it is a choice, so I think people should know what their dream is, what they can do with their dreams, and also what decisions they'd like to make to help them reach their dreams.

If I Could Change Our World
Dory Puth, Minneapolis

I would focus on literacy, and establish ways for people to receive free education, especially poor people. I would also find ways to provide free or low cost health care to everyone. Also, I would seek to abolish racism because it is so destructive. In addition, I would end war and stop violence, especially by destroying weapons and defunding in war. I would also like to see improvements in caring for the environment because we need a clean Earth. The other things that bother me are drugs and gangs. I would fight them, or legalize certain drugs to stop the problems they create. Another way to stop this problem is for neighbors to get to know each other and be aware of what's happening in their area. The last thing I would really like to see is more people visiting the elderly, and creating activities for them. These are the changes I'd most like to see in the world.

Dory Puth is originally from Cambodia.

Believing in Yourself
Dawn Rozmarynowski, Columbia Heights

I dropped out of high school when I was 17 years old. I was pregnant at the time. I tried going back twice to graduate high school. I didn't know at the time that I only needed ¼ of a credit to graduate high school. I want my GED because education is very important. You can't get anywhere in life without an education. I want a better life for my children and myself. Plus, I am the only member of my immediate family who doesn't have a high school diploma.

Going back to school after 20 years is different. At first, I was very scared; I almost didn't go into the building. In fact, I walked by the building a million times before I found the courage to walk in and talk to someone about getting my GED. Then when I came in to take the tests the next day, I noticed I wasn't the only older person going back to school after all these years. That was very encouraging.

My goal is to get my GED and go to college for computer programming. When I get my GED and graduate from college, I will be the only one in my immediate family who will have a college degree. This is very important to me.

My sisters all got married out of high school and started families. They didn't need to improve themselves. My two older sisters have careers that didn't require them to have a college degree. My youngest sister has five young boys and is a housewife.

Having somebody believe in you and encourage you to keep studying and learning makes all the difference in the world. If I didn't have Lisa as my teacher, I know I wouldn't be writing this essay today. She is very nice, smart and supportive. I look forward to school on Mondays and Wednesdays. When I get my GED and degree in computer programming, I will owe Lisa many thanks.

So in ending this, the reason I am getting my GED after 20 years is to make something of myself; to make myself proud. You can learn new things after 20 years. It might be scary at first. In the end, it will all be worth it.

Hopes and Plans
Anthony Sor, Rochester

I'm a dreamer and I dream every day, no matter if I'm sleeping or awake. I always wanted to be popular in life, all through school and out in the world. I used to be an illegal street racer, and I was starting to meet and talk to other people in the race world. I got a 2001 Acura Integra GS-R shortly after receiving my learner's permit. I hoped one day I could be a star in "*The Fast and the Furious,*" and till this day, I'm still dreaming. I was known in the surrounding states as "Mr. Integra." I had my own "My Space" page, "Team Integra" page and "Club RSX" page where people joined to forum.

I registered the car for sponsorship, but got offered sponsorship under conditions I couldn't meet. I was only fifteen or sixteen years old at the time. Now I'm twenty. The car was stolen and stripped. I'm now at ground zero with a three-year-old daughter and have nothing. I had friends, money, cars, and it's all gone.

As a single father, I'm struggling in life. My daughter's mother hasn't seen her since she was five months old, and I don't have any family besides my child. Hollywood, Florida is my dream destination. I want to take my daughter there and start fresh, hopefully attend college and work for a wealthy income. I'm to the point of giving up. I'm getting older each day, and I'm being held back with no place to start. I hope, one day soon, I'll be a celebrity and living large with my child. Racing is what makes me feel better. I shall not give up without trying first. I encourage whoever reads my story to chase their dream and not let anyone stop them.

Being Strong
Kristen Remington, Minneapolis

Life is what you make of it. No matter your situation, you can make it through anything if you just set your mind to it. Being a strong person means knowing that in the end, everything is going to be okay. And if something is meant to be, you realize no matter what, it will find a way.

My Childhood and Life
Annette, Columbia Heights

I just want to start out by talking about my childhood a little bit. I had a wonderful childhood. I grew up in North Minneapolis on 14th and Morgan. It was pretty safe back then in the 60's, 70's and 80's. My mom and dad lived there up until 1997 and 1999 when they passed away. My dad owned a cabin in Grey Eagle, Minnesota. We went up there every weekend in the summer. We always had a good time. I had cousins, aunts, and uncles that would come up there too.

At the age of 17 or 18, I got pretty bored up there so I quit going up there. I ended up dropping out of high school. I started going out to clubs and partying. I got pregnant at the age of 18. It was hard raising a baby that young. I'm lucky that I had my dad and Grandma Kay. She was my kids' great-grandma. I had three more kids after that.

When my youngest was two or three, they all went to live with their grandma because I chose the party life. I do regret that to this day. I'm sure they still resent me for that. Now they're all grown up and have kids of their own.

Now I'm finally trying to get my life on track by getting my GED and going to college and getting a degree. I want to be a dietician because I do have experience with the dietary field. My kids are really proud of me right now. It has been a little rough for me because I haven't been in school since 1980. But like they always say, IT'S NEVER TOO LATE!

My Future, My Story
Fartun Kahiye, Waite Park

My name is Fartun Kahiye. I was born in Mogadishu, the capital of Somalia. I like my country because it has good weather, health and more animals.

I lived in Somalia in a medium sized house until 2000. I have many brothers and sisters. I lived in Uganda for many years before I came to America. I came to America in 2011 so that I can get a good education, peace, health, and a job. I need a good education because I want to be a doctor. I would like to go back to Somalia and help my people.

What Drives Your Life?
Jane Agnatodji, Crystal

A man without a purpose is like a ship without an anchor. Everyone's life is driven by something. Dictionaries define the verb drive as to guide, to control, or to direct something. Whether you are driving a car, a nail or a golf ball, you are guiding, controlling or directing it at that moment. What is the driving force in your life?

Right now, you may be driven by a problem or the pressure of an illness. You may be driven by a painful memory, a fear or some other belief. There are hundreds of circumstances, values, and emotions that can drive your life. Here are four of the most common ones:

Many people are driven by guilt.
Many people are driven by resentment and anger.
Many people are driven by fear and trauma.
Many people are driven by materialism.

I don't know each person's key to success, but the key to failure is trying to please everyone and being controlled by the opinion of others.

Knowing our purpose gives meaning to our lives. If you feel hopeless, hold on and never give up. Wonderful things or changes are going to happen in your life as you begin to live. God says, "I know what I am planning for you. I have good plans for you, not plans to hurt you." Have faith and keep trusting in a brighter tomorrow.

Jane Agnatodji is originally from Togo.

Dreams of Education
Farah Nur, Eagan

My dream is a high school diploma first. My second dream is a technical college diploma. My third dream is a university diploma. When will I get a university diploma?

Farah Nur is originally from Somalia.

The Happiest Day of My Life
Farhiyo Ali, Rochester

It was 2010, the day I came to the United States to meet my family because I use to hear that I have little brothers and sisters on my dad's side. My father left home back in 1991, and I was five months old. I hadn't seen him for a long time. The first day I saw him was in March 2008, and I was in Kenya at that time. Actually, I grew up in Kenya, but I am from Somalia. I couldn't believe that I saw my dad, my brothers and sisters. Now I am one of them and I am so excited to live with them. I am also happy to come here to the United States because of the opportunity for my education. Now I am in Hawthorne Education Center and I am doing my GED. My dream is to finish my schooling and to go to college to learn something that will help me and will help others. And that is to be a doctor one day if "God says."

Farhiyo Ali is 21 years old and is originally from Somalia.

To Change the World
Fredy A. Ramirez, Fridley

The first thing I would like to have is peace, and no wars. I would like the entire world to have good relations between the nations. Instead of fighting, I would try to teach people better ways to resolve conflicts through special programs; having such programs might help people change their minds. I constantly think about the suffering caused to people who have to live in areas or countries plagued by war. The pain and fear they feel must be overwhelming, and the difficulties they have in trying to support themselves, and the stress they're under.

Also, the future of the world belongs to the children. However, it is in our hands to help provide them with a good future, especially because children, or the next generation, are so important. I would focus a lot of my attention on serving them. I believe the best thing I could provide them with is education. I would also ensure that the children are never hungry. I know from experience that it is hard to learn when you are hungry. Therefore, I would set up special schools in which the children not only have their minds fed, but also their stomachs. A large portion of their education would be directed towards helping them to communicate effectively. As children learn to communicate better with words, and not their fists, we will start to experience more peace. This is the way that I would accomplish my first objective, which is to have peace, no wars, and good relations between the nations. Most of all, I'd like to see greater peace in the world for all people.

Fredy A. Ramirez is originally from Honduras.

American Eagles Freedom Joy
A.L.R., Prior Lake

Eagle goes by the name Ya L. He loves to fly with tail feathers and feet in the water, splashing as he feels good, cool, and clean on his feet and tail feathers. Ya La flies by and plays peek-a-boo, teasing the teen eagles to follow. Ya La flies cruising down rapids as his feet touch the La Da teen eagles. In turn it's time to chase another teen eagle and Ya La and the teen eagle fly up and down cruising the rapids to surprise Red teen eagle.

Red teen eagle got a good idea to fly down the rapids behind La Da teen eagle. Ya La eagle follows Red eagle down the rapids and goes to catch the red salmon fish jumping in the big, wild Canada and Minnesota rivers.

They didn't know that Red eagle wants to surprise them when he caught a red salmon and went cruising up the rapids holding it with his feet.

La Da teen eagle and Ya La eagle got there too late and didn't catch the red salmon. They lost the game, and they sat on logs and watched Red teen eagle eat the red salmon.

Bad luck for La Da teen eagle and Ya La eagle.

Dreams from Thailand
Nirandorn Lindberg, Minneapolis

My dream is to have a good job and good family. I am from Thailand and my family is in Thailand. I like Thai food; that is my favorite food. I have one son. My son is nine years old. I came to Minnesota two years ago. I want to learn more English.

I want to finish GED and have good money to take care my family. I want my son to finish college; that is my dream. I want to have a good life with my husband in the future. I want my son to have good family and be a good man.

Nirandorn Lindberg is originally from Thailand.

My Big Dream
Luis Loja, Minneapolis

Hello my name is Luis. I would like to tell you about my big dream. My big dream that I always I had from when I was a child was to come to the United States. All this started from knowing this country has many opportunities. You can make your dreams true if you follow your heart, and try to make everything right.

I was very young when I started to follow my dreams. However, I knew then that I could do it. So I thought about how I could travel to the United States. After that, I asked my mom for help. She said I will help you, if you promise me you will never forget your family, because we love you and we will miss you a lot. However, if these are your dreams, I can't do anything, she said, crying.

So after that my mom went to find all the money that I needed to travel here. Then I had to wait one week to start my adventure. I left my country on March 24 to find my dreams. I left my heart in my country because my mom and my brothers stayed there. However, I can't turn back because I was very decided to continue in my way.

Luis Loja is 27 years old and is originally from Cuenca, Ecuador.

American Dreams
L.Z., Minneapolis

When I came to America, I brought some clothes to change, a pair of shoes, and a blanket. I also brought one picture of all my family. When I came here I packed only the most important things I might need during the trip. There were two bags of my stuff, so I decided to change the clothes I was wearing for a new one and make some room for my blanket which was in the other. It was hard to carry the two packs. My brother and I were coming together. But at the airport, he returned back and he told me that we should go back to the house; that this was a bad idea. But I told him to go, and that I would get to America and help him to study, and I could also find some opportunities there. I left my brother behind.

L.Z. is 25 years old and is originally from Ecuador.

How Can I Reach My Future Goal?
Salma Said, Minneapolis

When I came to this country my life was changed in many ways. I get time to go to school and I work full time. I never had these opportunities before. The school is free, especially high school in the United States. The country I grew up in doesn't have free high school and I didn't have enough money to pay for the school. I think this is a very good opportunity to learn my career and to get a better life.

When I get my diploma I will go college and learn my favorite program. I have always dreamed to improve my knowledge and this is the right time to build my skills. I know when I get my goal my life will change right away. I want to become independent. The one thing I always tell myself is to never give up, until I get what I want to be. That is how I will achieve my plan. To learn a second language, it's not easy but I need to work hard, be patient and do more practice. Anyway, education is the power of knowledge, and you can use that whatever you are.

Living with Different Cultures Is Great
Miguel Guallpa, Minneapolis

It's incredible to see how our lives change sometimes. When I lived in Ecuador, we used to have the same style of life because we have the same culture. When I got to the United States, my life changed suddenly, because I found many different people from other countries with different culture as well. At first the weather was too cold, because I arrived here in the wintertime, but now I am accustomed to it. Also the way to prepare food was different and I had to adapt to it. But, the hardest thing for me was the language in this country, which is English. It was very complicated to learn. Everywhere I used to go to apply for work, they asked me if I spoke English. I used to say no, and then they wouldn't hire me.

So, at the beginning, living in the United States, everything was different and hard for me, but I used to think quietly by myself about what to do, go back to my country or stay and learn to improve my life. I decided to stay and learn, because I don't want to feel like a loser.

Now I'm still here and I am learning English. I do speak but not enough and I want to keep studying because I have an aim. My aim is to get the GED and go to technical college. I think I made a good decision, because some day I want to be one of those people who have a good job to support my own life and my family in the future. I want to be a good example for them. I have hope that my goal will be achieved.

Miguel Guallpa is 33 years old and is originally from Cuenca, Ecuador.

Recycling Ideas
Long Lor, Saint Paul

Nowadays trash is more and more in the world. It makes a lot of bad things for the environment. So this is a problem we should think about. If nobody cares about this trash, let's see what will happen.

If we think this is not our problem, and nobody cares, maybe someday we won't have a place for our next generation to live, or they will have to live with the trash, and much pollution in the air. Do you think this would be a good place to live? I think nobody would want to live there, so this is a problem we should think about.

It's not too late to start recycling the things we can. I think it is a good thing to do If everyone keeps doing the same, it will make our environment clean, and there will be no more global warming for this world.

In Laos, they recycle, too, but not too many people care about it. Many people just make it easy for themselves and throw the trash and recycling together. Some people separate it into two things, and save the recycled things to sell, so they can make some money.

These are some of the good things about recycling, and the bad things that will happen if we don't care about recycling. We don't want to live with trash, and I think the Earth doesn't want it too, we should teach the children to know the importance about recycling. So when they grow up, they will do the same as what we did.

Long Lor is 26 years old and is originally from Laos.

If I Could Change the World
Kimiya Aliy, Minneapolis

If I could change the world, I would do the following: I would like to do everything I could to help free all those who don't have rights. I would like to make everybody rich—so no one in the world would be poor. Also, I would like people in the world to be happier, especially the children in my country of Somalia. They don't currently get enough food to eat, clothes or shoes to wear, because they are so very poor. I would like to improve these things or change them and make the children happy. Finally, I would make education or school free for all children, because it's so important for their futures. If the children of my country of origin, Somalia, were happy, I would be so happy.

My Story
Oswald Reid, Bayport

I have proved to myself that I am not too old to learn. From my past, I remember growing up in Jamaica. My family was poor. My mother had eight kids, and had to provide for us all. Sometimes we would go weeks without having a hot meal or any suitable clothing to wear. We often lived off the land.

Here in the United States, I have my own family, and now I am able to give them what I never had growing up, like a warm meal, suitable clothing and a father. Now, my kids can go to school and get a good education and have some type of degree in something they love doing.

Lastly, in addition to providing for my family here in the United States, I have begun to help myself with my own education and future goals. Currently, I am in Stillwater and I am enrolled in school. I am trying to get my GED. Yet, both my reading and my self-confidence have improved magnificently. These are the reasons why I believe that anyone is not too old to continue to learn. Thank you for reading my story.

The Advantages of the U.S. Education System
Dorette Mefeune, Maple Grove

After one year in this county, it is still hard for me to believe how countries are different. I am always thinking of the fact that the Americans don't know how lucky they are. They have the best education system I have ever seen.

In my country, it is a big challenge to get to school because many people don't have money to pay the tuition. The tuition is very expensive, and we don't have loans. More than 75% of the population is poor and the government of my country doesn't feel very concerned about education. From where I come, many people would like to be a doctor or a teacher, but they can't afford to pay. We don't have many opportunities.

In the U.S.A., education seems to be the branch people of all ages and genders have the opportunity to go as far as they would like. There are so many things

to study, different schedules, and wonderful teachers, whose contributions are essential for enjoyment and increased knowledge. This is a blessing in this country.

I want to ask young American people to take every benefit of their age to increase their knowledge as much as they can because they are in a good place and have a real opportunity for success. I want to plead with immigrants like me to remember that we could change many lives in the future if we stay quiet, follow the laws in this county, study, and work very hard.

Many people would like or dream to have the opportunity we have today. I remember that paying the tuition for my children five years ago in my country was the biggest challenge in my life that I will by the grace of God never have again. This is an opportunity for us to study very hard and challenge ourselves. May God help us to trust ourselves to make the future better than today.

Dorette Mefeune is originally from Cameroon.

If I Could Change the World
Der Yang, Brooklyn Center

I would give equal opportunity and power to everyone, no matter who they are. I would give them the opportunity to be what they want to be, and I would give people the chance for happiness, especially in poor countries.

First of all, I would change things so that every country in the world would be free like the United States. Also, I would bring equal opportunity to everyone in poor countries because in some of the poor countries of the world the governments take and control everything.

If I could change things I would give them freedom of speech, and the ability for all to express their opinions, especially in those countries where so many are without a voice and not involved in making national decisions. In some of the poor countries, like my country, men use to have more power than women, and in the family the husband could, and often still does, make all the decisions for the family. The women just stay home and do everything at home, or on the farm. If I could change this, I would give both men and women equal rights, because I don't think things are as good as they should be.

In addition, I would help children in poor countries by providing them with affordable education, because in many poor countries they don't have any programs to help children go to school. It all depends on whether your family has enough money or not, and there are thousands of children in many poor countries who can't go to school with other children because of money, as well as the laws of those countries. These countries aren't thinking about the future, and that if these children don't get an education, they could end up as criminals or bad people.

Finally, I would like to help solve these problems because I do believe in my proposed solutions—they could make things so much better!

Der Yang is 26 years old and is originally from Laos.

The Life of an Amazing Woman
Olivia Reed, Crystal

This woman's name was Theresa, my grandmother. She was sweet, loving, kind, caring and had strong faith in God. She was not educated. The little education she obtained was from Sunday school. She was a traditional midwife, a quilter and a homemaker. She raised her eight grandchildren on her own. She used her God-given skills to feed, educate and clothe her grandchildren.

She was loved by all in the community. Everyone's problem was her problem. She was never too busy when someone called upon her. She never turned anyone away who did not have the money. She always said that God would bless her grandchildren for the favor that she renders to people.

Because my mother died when I was very young, she was the only mother I knew. May the honorable life she lived continue to shine through her grandchildren.

Written in loving memory and gratitude by her granddaughter.

Olivia Reed is originally from Liberia.

My Mother
Thea Deng, Saint Paul

I remember my mother. Her name is Seng Bao. She is important to me because she is very nice and is a strong woman. When I grew up, I remembered that she went through many problems in her life. My mother had five children and she raised her children alone. She taught all of us to be good people and always said you have to be strong in your life. She also said that life is never easy but you have to make it the way you want it to be. She is so special to me.

Thea Deng is originally from Cambodia.

My Next Vacation
Cristina Segovia, Minneapolis

I want to go to Miami for my next vacation. I went to Houston, Pennsylvania, Harlingen, California and New York, but now I would like to know about the other places, different foods, other people and go to the beach. I will travel with my best friend, Beatriz. Maybe we will take a ticket with airport, hotel, and tours too. We imagine our vacation without people next to us. We are planning to go shopping, spa, restaurants, boutique or beauty salon (probably looking for new look), know about new museums and sports (we would like to try the rock climbing). Of course we will dance and meet our friends, we will call "Ladies Night"—no men, no work, no school and for this week no families, too. I think that we need a day when we will go. I like this idea. I feel so excited that soon Miami will have new tourists! I can't wait, my vacation will be wonderful.

Cristina Segovia is originally from El Salvador.

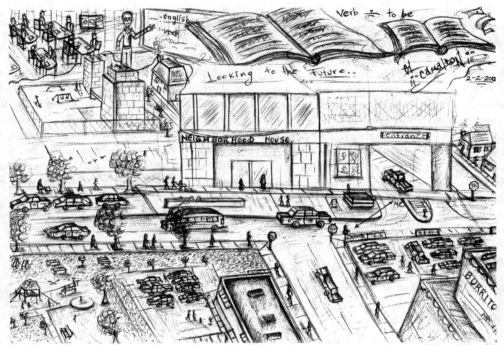

Rogelio Garcia Genis, Saint Paul

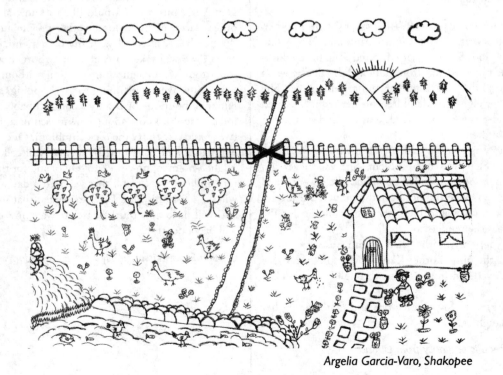

Argelia Garcia-Varo, Shakopee

Index of Authors